IPng

Internet Protocol Next Generation

Addison-Wesley IPng Series

Scott O. Bradner, Consulting Editor

The *Addison-Wesley IPng Series* provides networking and communications practitioners with vital information on the next generation technology being developed for the growth of the Internet. Technical and corporate managers, information providers, and all those with an interest in harnessing the new technology will find these comprehensive reference books invaluable. Scott O. Bradner, a leader in the field, is the Consulting Editor for the IPng Series.

IPng

Internet Protocol Next Generation

Edited by

Scott O. Bradner
Allison Mankin

Foreword by David Clark

ADDISON-WESLEY PUBLISHING COMPANY

Reading, Massachusetts   Menlo Park, California   New York
Don Mills, Ontario   Wokingham, England   Amsterdam   Bonn
Sydney   Singapore   Tokyo   Madrid   San Juan
Paris   Seoul   Milan   Mexico City   Taipei

Many of the designations used by manufacturers and sellers to distinguish their products are claimed as trademarks. Where those designations appear in this book and Addison-Wesley was aware of a trademark claim, the designations have been printed with initial capital letters.

The publisher offers discounts on this book when ordered in quantity for special sales. For more information please contact:

Corporate & Professional Publishing Group
Addison-Wesley Publishing Company
One Jacob Way
Reading, Massachusetts 01867

Library of Congress Cataloging-in-Publication Data

IPng, Internet protocol next generation / edited by Scott O. Bradner
  and Allison Mankin.
     p.   cm
  Includes bibliographical references and index.
  ISBN 0-201-63395-7 (alk. paper)
  1. Internet (computer network). 2. Computer network protocols.
I. Bradner, Scott O., 1944-   .   II. Mankin, Allison, 1955-   .
TK5105.875.I57I67   1995
004.6'2--dc20   95-20944
                                          CIP

ISBN 0-201-63395-7

Text printed on recycled paper
1 2 3 4 5 6 7 8 9 MA 98979695
First Printing, September 1995

Contents

Contents

Foreword

Dave D. Clark
M.I.T. Laboratory for Computer Science

To the casual user, the Internet is characterized by its applications: for example the World Wide Web, email, teleconferencing, or remote login. But to the builders of the Internet, it is not the applications that define it, but the foundation on which they rest. What is unique about the Internet is that it provides a basis on which a large number of applications can be built, applications with very different needs for network service qualities such as bandwidth and latency.

In contrast to the telephone network, which was initially conceived to carry exactly one application, voice communications, the Internet from the beginning was intended to provide a general infrastructure on which a wide range of applications could operate. With respect to generality, the Internet is less like a traditional network and more like a programmable computer.

In fact, the design of the Internet envisions two sorts of generality at the same time. The ability to support a range of applications is critical, but so is the ability to operate over a range of network technologies. The Internet protocols can operate over local area networks, point to point links of various speeds, other packet switched networks such as frame relay or SMDS, wireless networks, and new sorts of emerging network technology such as ATM.

To see the importance of this generality, one need only ask what engine will drive the evolution of networking. It is the creation of new applications and services, which will excite users and trigger investment in those applications. Advances in applications drive demand from users, which in turn drive innovations in network technology, to extend performance, predictability and reliability, to reduce cost and to reach into new operating regimes such as wireless networking. This drive is evidenced by the development over the last few years of ATM, 100 megabit/second Ethernet, and wireless LANs. It must be a fundamental goal of any approach to networking to allow, and indeed to stimulate, advances in applications and in technology.

The spirit of innovation and creativity that brings new applications into existence needs an environment that is open, ubiquitous, and adaptable. The importance of these characteristics in network architecture is widely recognized. A report released last year by the National Research Council, titled "Realizing the Information Future: The Internet and Beyond," articulated the power of this generality: it leads to universal connectivity for users, a foundation for innovation in services and applications, and an evolving infrastructure that can grow and change as needed. In discussions about the concept of a National Information Infrastructure, there has been considerable agreement that at least some part of such an infrastructure must be organized to meet these needs of generality and openness. This model is a compelling vision of what a network must be if it is to grow, to evolve, to stimulate new applications and be stimulated in return, and to generate both economic and technological growth.

That NRC report described an approach to achieving these objectives called the "network independent bearer service", an abstract organization of protocols and interfaces not tied to any existing protocol suite. The bearer service represented an interface within the protocol layers that cross-connects the applications to the technology without letting them become directly dependent on each other. The two can evolve independently, but the application can be assured of the behavior that it can expect from the infrastructure below.

The abstract structure of the bearer service is closely matched in practice by the Internet protocol family. In the Internet protocols, it is the Internet protocol itself, sometimes called IP, that provides on the one hand the connection, and on the other hand the isolation, between the applications above and the technology options below. It represents and captures that central core of functions that the technology must support, and the application may depend on.

To propose an interface does not mean that it can actually be realized, but the Internet protocol defines a service definition that has proven successful. While there are a number of reasons for this success, perhaps the most important one is that the Internet protocol is simple. That is, the service it defines is as minimal as possible. At its heart, it defines only two things: the addressing plan and the packet delivery service. And simplicity is key—the less there is defined, the less there is to argue about.

The addresses, the numbers that are used to identify the machines attached to the Internet, are a critical point about which there must be common agreement. In simple terms, one cannot send a message to a destination unless one can identify it. And while there are continuous debates about the need for universal addresses, and what the syntax and structure should be, the basic answer is that a common address space is at the core of the Internet.

The other aspect of IP is the delivery service. What is the expectation that the user should have when a packet is handed to the Internet service for delivery? Again, the Internet protocol makes an assumption that is simple and minimal. The delivery service of the Internet, sometimes called "best effort" delivery, is that any packet handed to the Internet layer will be delivered to the destination as soon as possible, but with no specific commitment as to bandwidth, delay, or absolute reliability. The success of the Internet is that this very simple delivery service, which can be implemented over a very wide range of technology, can in fact support a wide range of applications. The Internet protocol, while very simple, is thus at the heart of the Internet and its success.

If the Internet protocol is so successful, why does it need to change? Exactly because we can now see the limits of these two core services. The problem with addressing is very compelling; the existing Internet addresses are not large enough to provide room to address all the hosts that will be attached to the Internet in the next few years. We must either move to larger addresses, or abandon the idea of universal addressability that has worked so well up to now. The problem with the best effort delivery model is that while it has proved eminently successful for a broad range of applications, there are certain applications for which it is not adequate, in particular real time delivery of data such as audio and video. Better support for these services implies a change to the structure of the IP protocol header. Finally, of course, over the period of the last 20 years, there are a number of other issues with the IP protocol that have come to light, which should be rectified as a part of a revision.

The major issue in revising the Internet protocol is to balance two concerns. One is to respond to real needs that are beyond the current protocol. The other is to control the natural desire to add new features. This desire is universal, and if not checked can lead to the creation of a complex, overloaded, and unsatisfactory system. In fact, the tendency is so well known in computer systems circles that it was given a name, the Second System Syndrome. In the case of IP, this tendency could be particularly problematical, since one of the goals of Internet was to operate over almost any sort of network technology. If the design moves away from the very simple best effort service, it will begin to limit the range of technology it can utilize. This would represent a tremendous loss of power for the protocol. The design of the next IP has had to deal with this tension.

There is another tension in the process of evolving the Internet protocol. There are two uses for the same protocol suite. One is the building of
that global public network called the Internet. The other is building the
many private networks that are currently based on the same protocols.
These private networks, usually belonging to a corporation, are where a
majority of the Internet technology sold today is used, and these networks have a different set of requirements than the public Internet. They
are smaller, and less concerned with issues of scale, but they are more
concerned with delivering a predictable service in support of critical
applications. So there is to some extent a divergence of objectives. But the
same products, implemented to the same standards, must work in both
contexts. And this is the other major issue that the designers of a new
Internet protocol had to balance.

Replacing the Internet protocol may be the most challenging step that
the Internet Engineering Task Force has undertaken in its history. It will
eventually change every host and every router in the Internet, it requires
the balancing of a dauntingly broad set of requirements, and it will not
succeed unless it supports and sustains the current success of the Internet,
a success that, not surprisingly, is to most people more concerned with
flights of fancy than foundations. But to those of us who believe that the
future must sit on strong foundations, this effort is the key step towards
tomorrow.

Preface

The Internet is about to become a victim of its own success.

The projection in the fall of 1991 that the Internet, with the capacity to support many millions of users, was beginning to run out of available network addresses was quite a bit of a surprise. The projection was quickly followed by numerous articles in the trade press announcing the imminent demise of what had been a promising technology.

Many groups were ready with alternatives to fix the problem. Network protocols from various official standards organizations and proprietary protocols from a number of vendors were presented as solutions that could provide a foundation for a glorious future of ubiquitous networking.

This speculation caused more than a little consternation within the Internet Engineering Task Force (IETF), the organization responsible for keeping the standards of the TCP/IP protocol suite used by the Internet. In the face of all this "end of the world as we know it" talk, the IETF felt it needed to determine just what was truly happening, and, if there was in fact a problem, what should be done about it.

When the initial investigation confirmed the basic diagnosis, the IETF undertook a multi-pronged effort to devise a replacement for the current version of the Internet protocol, IPv4. This effort sought not just to solve the immediate address limitation and scaling problems, but to look into the Internet's future and develop a protocol that would serve its needs for many years to come.

This book offers an inside view of the process the IETF used in its successful effort to define the issues, and provides an overview of the resulting Internet Protocol next generation (IPng). Along the way, the book reveals the rationale behind the structure and features of IPng, presenting numerous explorations of applications and technologies IPng could potentially support.

Audience. This book has been written so that it can be easily understood by anyone with a basic understanding of networking and communications. Those who would benefit from this book include: managers of technical organizations, networking professionals, technology watchers, those with a stake in the growing on-line commerce industry, and anyone with an interest in the Internet prototype of the Information Superhighway.

Organization.

Part I provides the background on the issues and problems facing the Internet. Part II describes the process which the IETF used to develop the new protocol; and Part III examines the all-important time frame for developing IPng.

Next, the book turns to the outside perspective of the wider networking community, with contributions from numerous industry experts.

Part IV explores the potential role of IPng in the future of communications, and Part V, the innovative technologies IPng should consider embracing.

Part VI contains the technical criteria for judging IPng proposals - culled from all of the preceding discussions, issues, and contributive perspectives.

The IPng proposals are presented and evaluated against the technical criteria in Part VII.

All of the preceding sections culminate in Part VIII, the overview of the selected IPng proposal, the new IPv6 Internet protocol.

In Part IX, the critical issue of security is discussed, and in Part X, the ongoing process of developing the protocol in greater detail is outlined.

Sources. Much of the material in this book has been adapted from the Internet standard and documentation series known as Request for Comments (RFCs). The material has been reworked, with the authors' assistance, to make it more accessible to a general audience while retaining the technical detail inherent in the original work. Also included are a number of new pieces written specifically for this book.

Acknowledgements. Reaching this stage of the recommendation would not have been even vaguely possible without the efforts of many people. In particular, the work of the IPng Directorate, Frank Kastenholz and Craig Partridge (the authors of the Criteria document) along with Jon Crowcroft (who co-chaired the ngreq BOF) was critical. The work and cooperation of the chairs, members, and document authors of the three IPng proposal working groups, the ALE Working Group and the TACIT Working Group laid the groundwork upon which this recommendation sits.

We would also like to thank the many people who took the time to respond to RFC-1550 and who provided the broad understanding of the many requirements of data networking that any proposal for an IPng must address.

The members of the IESG, the IAB, and the always active participants in the various mailing lists provided us with many insights into the issues we faced. Many other individuals gave us sometimes spirited but always useful counsel during this process. They include (in no particular order) Radia Perlman, Noel Chiappa, Peter Ford, Dave Crocker, Tony Li, Dave Piscitello, Vint Cerf, and Dan Lynch.

Thanks to David Williams and Cheryl Chapman who, along with the very hard-working Addison-Wesley technical editors: Abigail Cooper and Kate Habib, took on the occasionally impossible task of ensuring that what is written here resembles English to some degree.

This book would have never happened without the perseverance and astonishingly good humor in the face of changing realities of Carol Long, our Executive Editor at Addison-Wesley.

To all of the many people mentioned above and those we have skipped in our forgetfulness, thank you for making this task doable.

Contributors' Biographies

R. Brian Adamson works at the Naval Research Laboratory (NRL) in Washington, DC. He is currently involved in NATO and DoD demonstration projects, which provide integrated communication services over mobile radio networks through the application of internetwork protocols and advanced service multiplexing techniques. To meet the goals of these projects, he has also written an experimental low data rate Internet voice communication software application.

Steven M. Bellovin works at AT&T Bell Laboratories, where he does research in networks, security, and why the two don't get along. While a graduate student at the University of North Carolina at Chapel Hill, he helped create netnews; for this, he and the other perpetrators were awarded the 1995 Usenix Lifetime Achievement Award. He is the co-author of the recent book *Firewalls and Internet Security: Repelling the Wily Hacker* and is currently focusing on how to write systems that are inherently more secure.

Jim Bound is a member of the Technical Staff in the Network Integration Software Engineering Group at Digital Equipment Corporation, and was formerly Digital's TCP/IP Engineering Program Manager in Networks Engineering. One of the members of the Internet Engineering Task Force (IETF) IPng Directorate, Mr. Bound is the IPv6 Technical Leader and one of the advanced development implementors building a prototype to test these emerging IETF specifications. In addition, he is co-author of several IETF IPv6 specifications in progress. An IEEE Computer Society Member, Mr. Bound worked on the IEEE POSIX 1003 System Services (1003.1), Test Methods (1003.3), and Real Time (1003.4) standard committees.

Scott Bradner, co-director of the Internet Engineering Task Force (IETF) IPng effort, is a senior technical consultant at the Harvard Office of Information Technology, Network Service Division, where he works on the design and development of network-based applications and manages the Network Device Test Lab. In addition, he is the co-director of the Operational Requirements Area in the IETF, a member of the IESG, and an elected trustee of the Internet Society. Mr. Bradner has been involved in the design, operation and use of data networks at Harvard University since the early days of the ARPANET. He was involved in the design of the Harvard High-Speed Data Network (HSDN), the Longwood Medical Area network (LMAnet), and NEARNET. He is currently chair of the technical committees of LMAnet, NEARNET and CoREN.

Christina Brazdziunas is currently a software engineer developing Cellular Digital Packet Data (CDPD), a wireless data technology, at Evolving Systems, Inc. She has had extensive experience as a researcher in ATM technology at Bellcore, where she was responsible for consulting with major telecommunication industry clients on IP and ATM network integration.

Edward Britton became involved in TCP/IP at the U.S. Defense Communications Agency. Since joining IBM in 1981, he has contributed to SNA architecture, OSI system design, telephony, telecommunications cross-product design, and many aspects of IBM's TCP/IP products. He has expertise in IPng, security, performance, wireless and Asynchronous Transfer Mode communications, and TCP/IP's relationships with other protocol suites.

Ross Callon is a consulting engineer at Bay Networks Incorporated in Billerica, Massachusetts, and has more than 15 years' experience in data communications. He was the original proposer of a dual stack transition scheme and of TUBA, as well as co-author of the NSAP Guidelines standard in the IETF. He is co-chair of the IETF IPng Working Group, and was a member of the IPng Directorate. He is also a regular contributor to the ATM Forum, and has been involved in the ATM PNNI routing and multi-protocol over ATM efforts.

Brian E. Carpenter has been Group Leader of the Communications Systems group at CERN since 1985. His previous experience includes ten years in software for process control systems at CERN and three years teaching undergraduate computer science at Massey University in New Zealand. Mr. Carpenter is a member of the Internet Architecture Board (IAB) and an active participant in the Internet Engineering Task Force (IETF).

J. Noel Chiappa is currently an independent researcher in the area of computer networks and system software. He has been a member of the TCP/IP technical community since 1977. While a member of the Research Staff at M.I.T., he worked on packet switching and local area networks, and was responsible for the invention of the multi-protocol router; he later worked with a number of companies to bring networking products based on work done at M.I.T. to the marketplace.

David Clark has worked at the MIT Laboratory for Computer Science since 1973, where he is currently a Senior Research Scientist. His research interests include networks, network protocols, operating systems, distributed systems and computer and communications security. Since the mid 70s, he has been involved in the development of the Internet. From 1981-1989 he acted as Chief Protocol Architect for the Internet, and chaired the Internet Activities Board. His current research includes extensions to the Internet protocols for advanced service requirements and security.

John Curran is chief technical officer for BBN Planet, where he is responsible for the company's strategic technology and business development initiatives, including establishing the overall direction for products and services. He leads design activities for BBN Planet's service infrastructure with a particular emphasis on scaling, management, and security issues, as well as providing consulting for key BBN ISC clients. Mr. Curran is an active member of the Internet Engineering Task Force (IETF) and the Internet Engineering Planning Group (IEPG), working on a wide range of topics including inter-provider coordination and IPv6.

Stephen E. Deering is currently a member of the research staff at the Xerox Palo Alto Research Center (PARC), where he works on multicast routing and such other advanced internetworking topics as mobile communications, scalable addressing, and support for multimedia applications over the Internet. He has been studying, designing and implementing computer communication protocols since 1978, including work on X.25 software for connecting to public networks, on the first implementation of the X.400 protocol suite for email, and on high-performance transport protocols for distributed systems. He has chaired numerous working groups in the Internet Engineering Task Force (IETF) and co-founded the Internet Multicast Backbone (the "MBone") group.

Deborah Estrin is an Associate Professor of Computer Science at the University of Southern California in Los Angeles. Her research has focused on the design of network and routing protocols for very large global networks. She is a co-PI on the NSF Routing Arbiter project, co-chairs the Internet Engineering Task Force's (IETF) Source Demand Routing Working Group, and is a primary participant in the Inter-Domain Multicast Routing and RSVP Working Groups.

Eric Fleischman is a Senior Principal Scientist within Boeing's Information and Support Services organization. He is the program manager for the company's Data Communications Architecture group, which establishes Boeing's tactical and strategic data communications architecture and technical standards, and oversees the many resulting projects that seek to achieve the architecture. He is also the project manager for Boeing's Virtual Collocation Project, which integrates collaborative authoring/engineering and real-time desktop video with various asynchronous collaborative problem-solving approaches. In addition, Mr. Fleischman is Boeing's representative to the Internet Engineering Task Force (IETF).

Antonia Ghiselli is a network researcher at INFN, the Italian National Institute for Nuclear Physics. She has been working since 1980 in setting up, managing, and developing software for the INFN network. She has worked at CERN as a scientific associate and is now coordinating and planning the INFN network and the Italian Research Network.

Robert E. Gilligan is a Senior Staff Engineer at Sun Microsystems, Inc., where he is responsible for developing the TCP/IP software in Solaris 2. Prior to joining Sun, he worked on Internet and Packet Radio projects at SRI International. Mr. Gilligan is also an active participant in the Internet Engineering Task Force (IETF).

Daniel Green is a staff scientist specializing in the area of tactical networking at the Naval Surface Warfare Center-Dahlgren Division. He has 37 years of experience with the Navy in various aspects of computer information technology. Currently he is technical co-chair of the U.S. Navy's High Performance Network (HPN) project, which is concerned with advanced networks for Navy aircraft, ships, and submarines.

Phill Gross is Director of Internet Engineering at MCI, where his group built the IP backbone that underlies the new internetMCI family of services. Previously, Mr. Gross was Vice President for Network Technology at Advanced Network and Services (ANS), Inc. Before that, he worked at the Corporation for National Research Initiatives (CNRI) on various Internet projects, where he organized and chaired the Federal Engineering Planning Group (FEPG) of the U.S. Federal Networking Council (FNC) and the Intercontinental Engineering Planning Group (IEPG). One of the founders of the Internet Engineering Task Force (IETF), Mr. Gross chaired the IETF from 1987 to 1994, during which time he formed the Internet Engineering Steering Group (IESG), co-chaired the IETF Routing and

Addressing (ROAD) group, formed the IPng Area, and wrote the original IPng direction statement. He is also a member of the Internet Architecture Board (IAB).

Denise Heagerty is a member of the External Networking Section at CERN, Geneva, Switzerland. In addition to her operational duties, she has been responsible for the DECnet/OSI transition and implementing CERN's electronic mail gateway strategy. Her previous experience covers telephone switching and real-time control systems.

Robert M. Hinden, Director of Software at Ipsilon Networks, a Mountain View, California startup, was formerly responsible for the Internet Engineering group at Sun Microsystems where he won the Sun Microsystems Presidents Award. He is the document editor for IP Next Generation, working in the Internet Engineering Task Force (IETF), and is a member of the IPng Directorate. He was formerly area director for routing in the Internet Engineering Steering Group (IESG) and chair of a number of IETF working groups.

Christian Huitema has conducted research in network protocols and network applications for a number of years. Currently at INRIA in Sophia-Antipolis, he leads the RODEO project, which researches and defines communication protocols for very high-speed networks, at one Gigabit or more. Mr. Huitema has been a member of the Internet Architecture Board (IAB) since 1991 and the organization's chairman since 1993.

Phil Irey is a Computer Scientist at the Naval Surface Warfare Center-Dahlgren Division. He has specialized in the application of communications protocols (particularly Transport layer protocols) to tactical applications, and recently has become involved in the instrumentation of communications subsystems. In addition, Mr. Irey has participated in the U.S. Navy's SAFENET and High Performance Network (HPN) projects.

Frank Kastenholz is currently an engineer with FTP Software, INC., the leading vendor of TCP/IP software for PCs, where he is responsible for developing advanced applications and network protocols. He is also a long-time Internet Engineering Task Force (IETF) participant and is currently on the Internet Engineering Steering Group (IESG) as Co-Area Director for the Internet Area.

Tony Li is currently a Technical Lead for Cisco Systems, Inc. where he is a bit slinger specializing in IP exterior routing protocols, high-performance switching, and fixing really nasty bugs. Mr. Li is currently co-chair of the Source Demand Routing, Mobile IP, and CIDR Deployment Working Groups of the Internet Engineering Task Force (IETF).

Allison Mankin, co-director of the Internet Engineering Task Force (IETF) IPng effort, is a Computer Scientist at the University of Southern California/Information Sciences Institute. She also leads a small ISI research office in Arlington, Virginia. Previous employers were Computer Consoles Incorporated, Unisys, MITRE, and Kaman Sciences-Naval Research Laboratory. She jumped into work on the Internet's transport performance and capabilities in 1986, and in 1991 she made the original suggestion for the MBone. Her published research includes papers on congestion control and high-speed networking. In addition to her work with the IETF on the IPng recommendation, she is the Internet Engineering Steering Group's (IESG) Area Director for Transport Services.

David Marlow is a group leader in the area of tactical networking at the Naval Surface Warfare Center-Dahlgren Division. He serves in key technical roles for the U.S. Navy's SAFENET and High Performance Network (HPN) efforts. Currently, he is technical lead for the U.S. Navy's HPN project, which is concerned with using the Internet protocols aboard the Navy's tactical platforms, as well as being responsible for several research and development projects related to high-speed networks.

Karen O'Donoghue is an electrical engineer at the Naval Surface Warfare Center-Dahlgren Division. She has specialized in the application of commercial networking technologies to Navy applications, and, in particular, has studied real-time communication architectures and time management issues. Ms. O'Donoghue has also participated in the U.S. Navy's SAFENET and High Performance Network (HPN) projects.

Craig Partridge is a senior research scientist at Bolt Beranek and Newman, Inc., where he does research on gigabit networking. One of the first members of the Internet Engineering Task Force (IETF) and a former member of the Internet Engineering Steering Group (IESG), Mr. Partridge has been actively involved with Internet protocols and research since 1983. He is a part-time professor at Stanford, an instructor for Interop,® and the author of *Gigabit Networking* (Addison-Wesley, 1994).

J. Mark Pullen is Associate Professor of Computer Science and a member of the Center for Excellence in Command, Control, Communications and Intelligence at George Mason University. A licensed Professional Engineer and a Fellow of the IEEE, he was previously with ARPA, where he managed networking research and led a major initiative in distributed simulation that is developing a worldwide internetted distributed simulation capability. He teaches courses in computer networking and has active research programs in networking for distributed interactive simulation and multimedia tools for both command and control and distance education.

Yakov Rekhter, currently of Cisco Systems, worked for over ten years at the T.J. Watson Research Center, IBM Corp. He was one of the leading architects and software developers for the NSFNET Backbone Phase II, and is a leading designer of the Border Gateway Protocol (BGP) and the Inter-Domain Routing Protocol ISO 10747 (IDRP). His present activities include work on: routing and addressing for IPv6, the Routing Arbiter, Classless Inter-Domain Routing (CIDR), the Unified Approach to Inter-Domain Routing, support for host mobility, autoconfiguration, and IP support for ATM. He actively participates in many activities of the Internet Engineering Task Force (IETF). Currently he is a member of the Internet Architecture Board (IAB), and a chairman of the Inter-Domain Routing Working Group.

Davide Salomoni is a network researcher at INFN, the Italian National Institute for Nuclear Physics. He is involved in planning and managing TCP/IP routing and infrastructure of the INFN network and of the Italian National Research Network.

William Allen Simpson is a very independent consultant, involved in wireless, IP router, network design, game networking, political database, real-time data collection and distribution, and many other projects. He has been known as "The DayDreamer" on networks for over 20 years.

Ron Skelton is responsible for Information Technology strategy development at the Electric Power Research Institute. Most recently he managed a project that defined the opportunities and risks for power utilities in creating the National Information Infrastructure. Formerly at Aetna Life & Casualty and at CONTEL, he worked to develop information systems and telecommunications infrastructure in the insurance and telecommunications industries. Much of his work now focuses on the future "real-time" information needs and standards for the power industry (the Vision of Information and Power). Ron is an active participant in the Cross Industry Working Team (XIWT).

Frank Solensky has eleven years of experience in the design and development of the Internet Protocol and related applications on computers, routers, and embedded systems. He works at FTP Software, Inc. and has been an active member of the IETF since 1989.

Susan Flynn Symington is a lead scientist at the MITRE Corporation where she heads a project designing and implementing mechanisms for deploying Internet Protocol multicasting in an Asynchronous Transfer Mode environment. Her previous activities were performing research and writing papers in high-performance networking, networking and communications support for modeling and simulation, and network security.

John Tavs currently leads IBM's TCP/IP Technical Strategy group. He joined IBM Boca Raton in 1982 as a Communications I/O Architect for the 9370 and AS/400 systems, focusing on inter-process communication, bus error recovery, and control program kernel design and implementation for those systems. In 1988 he transferred to the IBM Research Triangle Park facility where he has been instrumental in IBM's TCP/IP products including support for the following systems: 3172, 3745, 6611, MVS, OS/2, DOS, and Windows.

Mark Taylor is the Director of Research and Development in the Wireless Data Division of McCaw Cellular, where his team sets the technical direction for wireless data services. He led the specification team for Cellular Digital Packet Data (CDPD) releases 1.0 and 1.1 on behalf of the cellular industry. Prior to joining McCaw, Mr. Taylor was a lead architect of Motorola's Altair wireless Ethernet LAN product, and also worked with several architecture and development groups at AT&T Bell Laboratories.

Susan Thomson is a member of the internetworking research group at Bellcore. She joined Bellcore in 1991, where she has been actively involved in defining a new version of the internetworking protocol (IPv6) for the Internet, first as a contributor to the P. Internet Protocol (Pip) and the Simple Internet Protocol Plus (SIPP) proposals, and subsequently as a contributor to IPv6. She is co-director of the Internet Area in the IETF, and is chair of the IPv6 address configuration (ADDRCONF) working group.

Mario P. Vecchi is currently Vice President, Network Engineering at Time Warner Cable, Engineering and Technology, Englewood, CO, where he is working to develop the technology and products for the delivery of high-speed data services to home personal computers over the broadband hybrid fiber/coax network using multimegabit/s cablemodems. He is interested not only in the deployment of high-speed data applications to residential PCs, but also in the integration with telecommunications and interactive video entertainment, based on open, scalable, and extensible distributed systems architectures.

Cristina Vistoli is a network researcher at INFN, the Italian National Institute for Nuclear Physics. She is involved in planning and managing TCP/IP routing and infrastructure of the INFN network and of the Italian National Research Network.

David C. Wood, a Consulting Scientist at the MITRE Corporation, is involved in networking technology, distributed simulation, and standards policy. He has led MITRE's support in data networking to the Department of Defense for over twenty years, and is a member of the Distributed Interactive Simulation Communications Architecture standards group.

The Need for IPng

Part I

The Need for IPng

Even the most farseeing of the TCP/IP developers in the early 1980s could not begin to imagine the dilemma of scale that the Internet faces today. In 1987, estimates projected the need to address as many as 100,000 networks at some vague point in the future.[1] Now it appears that the Internet will reach that mark by 1996, and there are many realistic projections of millions of interconnected networks in the not too distant future.[2,3] The Internet is growing far faster than anyone could have possibly predicted even a few years ago.

Originally an experimental research network connecting a few dozen universities, military installations, and government contractors, the Internet has grown to become the prototype of the much touted Global Information Infrastructure. It already connects many millions of computers, and the infrastructure to support additional tens of millions of computers within the next year or two is now being put into place. As this is being written, the first concrete steps are being taken to enable safe and reliable commerce to take place over the Internet. With a potential of $2 trillion worth of business that could be conducted in this way—from ordering pizzas to exchanging orders and invoices between manufacturing companies—the development of Internet commerce will be a powerful driver for yet more growth.

Currently, most existing Internet connections are established using dial-up or leased telephone lines. However, new technologies are beginning to extend the connection options to include cable TV, electric power lines, and radio communications. As the providers of these alternatives compete with each other, the cost of connecting to the Internet will likely decrease rapidly at the same time that the speed of connection increases. These developments will make the Internet a viable information exchange medium for an ever larger number of businesses and individuals.

Interestingly, the growth of the Internet, both in terms of users and applications, has brought a number of social issues to the forefront. The Internet provides a very open forum for the exchange of ideas and data. The very nature of this open forum means that the content of information exchanged is becoming an issue. For example, the content of messages on an open network without national boundaries can challenge political, social, and moral assumptions. But even the stresses and confusion caused by reactions to some of the content now present on the Internet have yet to slow its growth.

The Internet's astounding growth has begun to stress the technology that supports it, namely the current Internet Protocol suite, IPv4. At first look IPv4 appears as if it should be able to handle an Internet of the scale projected for the next decade or two. Its 32-bit address structure can enumerate over 4 billion hosts on as many as 16.7 million networks. However, the actual address assignment efficiency is far less than that, even on a theoretical basis,[4] and this inefficiency is exacerbated by the division of IPv4 addresses into three separate classes, Class A, B, and C. Address assignments were made assuming that the Internet world consisted of numerous small organizations containing fewer than 250 computers each (Class C networks), a smaller number of larger organizations with up to 64,000 computers each (Class B networks), and a few very large companies with up to 15 million computers each (Class A networks).

Using this inefficient address assignment method, the Internet was running out of the most popular type of address assignment, Class B networks. At the 1991 rate of assignment, Class B address space was projected to be exhausted by March of 1994.

The obvious remedy of assigning multiple Class C addresses in place of Class B addresses introduced its own set of problems by further expanding the size of the routing tables in the backbone routers which were already growing at an alarming rate that was faster than memory technology would be able to support for long.

Therefore, the Internet community faced the dilemma of either limiting the Internet's rate of growth and ultimate size, or disrupting the network by switching to new techniques and technologies.

The Internet Engineering Task Force (IETF), the organization charged with developing the standards for the protocols used on the Internet, felt it had to explore these competing pressures.

Defining the IPng Process

Part II

The First Step

To explore these many issues and dilemmas, the IETF formed the Routing and Addressing (ROAD) group at the November 1991 Santa Fe meeting. At the following meeting in March 1992, the group reported on its work and offered several recommendations ranging from immediate to long term.[1] These recommendations included adopting CIDR route aggregation, a technology that would help reduce the rate of routing table growth, [2] and having the IETF call for proposals to explore new approaches for designing bigger addresses that would enable the Internet to grow.

Meanwhile, in the late spring of 1992, the Internet Architecture Board (IAB) issued its own recommendations for a new Internet Protocol, referred to as IPv7. This proposal also endorsed the use of CIDR. In addition, however, the IAB called for the IETF to prepare a detailed plan for using the International Standard Organization's (ISO) Connectionless Network Protocol (CLNP) as the basis for the next generation IP. After spirited discussion on this controversial proposal, the IETF decided to reject the IAB's recommendation and instead issued the call for proposals recommended by the ROAD group. The adoption of CLNP was not excluded, but instead could be explored along with other proposals. The call for IPng proposals went out in July 1992 at the Boston IETF meeting, and a number of working groups were formed in response.

After these initial efforts, it became clear that the Internet community needed to refocus attention on three very important topics: defining the technical criteria for a new Internet protocol; making a decision between the various candidates for IPng; and deciding who should lead the process and make the final recommendation to the community.[3] At the July 1993 Amsterdam IETF meeting, Phill Gross, chair of the IETF and IESG, led the participants toward a consensus on these issues and set in motion the process for deciding on a new Internet protocol.

Consensus, Charges, and Challenges

Phill Gross
MCI

A New Direction. The IPDecide BOF held at the Amsterdam IETF meeting explored several facets of the IPng process: What are the technical requirements and decision criteria for choosing the next generation IP? With the advent of CIDR and the possibility of instituting new, more stringent address assignment policies, what is the true level of urgency? Should the IETF or the marketplace make the final IPng decision?

Although the BOF was held in a productive atmosphere, it did not achieve what could be called a clear consensus among the attendees. In fact, despite its generally productive spirit, it did more to highlight the lack of a firm direction than to create it.

However, at the open IESG plenary held on the following evening, the IESG and attendees again discussed these IPng issues, and this time seemed to arrive at a consensus:

- The IETF should take active steps toward a technical decision, rather than waiting for the marketplace to decide.
- The IESG should provide the leadership. It should be responsible for developing an IPng recommendation for the Internet community and take specific actions to help move the IETF toward a technical decision.
- The procedures and process of choosing IPng should be open and published well in advance, and the networking community should have ample opportunity to comment prior to the final IESG recommendation.

The Process. Building on this consensus, the IESG set up a specific process intended to resolve many of these key issues and move the organization toward a final IPng recommendation. First of all, a temporary, ad hoc area, headed by Scott Bradner and Allison Mankin, was established to deal specifically with IPng issues. The charter for this new IETF area was to recommend which, if any, of the current proposals should be adopted as the next generation Internet Protocol. This recommendation would be submitted to the IESG and the Internet community for review and, following an adequate review period during which any community concerns could surface, the IESG would issue a final IPng recommendation.

All IETF areas are expected to have area directorates, groups of experts from various industries and technologies. For the IPng Area, a Directorate would be especially important to bring many different viewpoints into the process. As had been agreed on, the IPng process was to be completely open, so that reports and meeting notes from IPng Directorate meetings would be published in timely fashion.

Issues toward IPng Resolution. Two important questions needed to be answered by the Directorate before any progress could be made toward an IPng recommendation:

- What is the available time frame? Before the IESG could even begin to make an informed decision about the scope, we needed a better understanding of the urgency of time constraints facing us.
- What is the scope of the effort? Should IPng be limited to solving the well-known scaling and address exhaustion issues; or should IPng also include advanced features, such as resource reservation for real-time traffic? Migration to a new IP would (hopefully!) be a once-in-a-generation occurrence, and therefore all advanced features should at least be considered. However, the available time frame might not allow for this level of effort before the scaling and address exhaustion problems confronted us. Also, we might not have the necessary understanding and experience to make all the correct choices at this time.

Therefore, the new Area Directors were requested to accomplish the following specific tasks on their way to formulating their ultimate IPng recommendation:

- Develop an estimate for how much time is available for the development and implementation of IPng before IPv4 address space runs out. Factors to consider are:
  - Internet growth metrics, such as the current address assignment and utilization rates, and how more stringent assignment policies, reclaiming underutilized addresses, or renumbering significant portions of the Internet might affect those rates.
  - The impact of CIDR address aggregation on router table space.
  - The effect of classless Internet addressing on efficient use of addresses. Specific examples include guidelines for how to utilize

variable length subnet masks, and ways to utilize currently unused Class A and B addresses in a classless fashion in hosts and routers.

- The amount of time required for the development, fielding, and migration to a new IP.

- Based on the results of the time constraints study, recommend the scope for IPng—should IPng consider scaling issues only or advanced topics also?
- Develop a clear and concise set of technical requirements and decision criteria for IPng that reflects the recommended scope.
- Evaluate the current IPng candidates according to these technical requirements and criteria, and recommend which one to accept, if any.

Finally, the IPng Directorate was to make a detailed report at the opening plenary of the next IETF meeting in November 1994 on the progress of its work.

The IPng Directorate

The Internet Engineering Steering Group (IESG) accepted Phill Gross' recommendation and, as stipulated, the IPng Area Directors began the process of exploring the many unresolved issues relating to IPng. First, a Directorate was recruited. The members of this Directorate were chosen for both their general and specific technical expertise, and represented a wide spectrum of knowledge. The members were experts in security, routing, the needs of large users, end systems, UNIX and non–UNIX platforms, routers, theory, protocol architecture, and operating regional, national, and international networks. Several Directorate members were also deeply involved in each of the IPng proposal working groups. The members were then asked to be certain that their management understood the IETF process and that they authorized their participation in the process.

The directorate members (with their employers at the time) were: J. Allard (Microsoft), Steve Bellovin (AT&T), Jim Bound (Digital), Ross Callon (Bay Networks), Brian Carpenter (CERN), Dave Clark (Massachusetts Institute of Technology), John Curran (BBN Planet Corporation), Steve Deering (Xerox Corporation), Dino Farinacci (Cisco Systems), Eric Fleischman (Boeing Computer Services), Paul Francis (NTT), Mark Knopper (Ameritech), Greg Minshall (Novell, Inc.), Paul Mockapetris (USC/ISI), Rob Ullmann (Lotus Development Corporation), and Lixia Zhang (Xerox Corporation).

The Directorate engaged in biweekly conference calls, participated in an internal mailing list, and corresponded actively on the Big-Internet mailing list. It held open meetings during the March 1994 Seattle and July 1994 Toronto IETF meetings as well as two additional multi-day retreats. To ensure that the IPng process was as open as possible, the minutes of these meetings were published. The archives of the internal IPng mailing list were also placed on an anonymous ftp site.

The Directorate members were responsible for a two-phased review of the technical criteria for the IPng document, the many documents from each of the IPng proposals, and the papers received in response to RFC-1550.[4] In the first phase the documents were reviewed for verbal clarity, and in the second for technical soundness. The directorate also helped in the comparative evaluation of the IPng proposals and assisted in the development of the Area Directors' final recommendation.

How Long Do We Have?

Part III

The IPng Directorate's first task was to obtain a reasonable estimate of how much time remained before IPv4 address space would be exhausted so that we could determine the scope of the IPng effort. In October 1993, the IETF formed the Address Lifetime Expectations (ALE) Working Group, chaired by Tony Li of Cisco Systems and Frank Solensky of FTP Software, to develop an estimate for the remaining lifetime of the IPv4 space, based on currently known and available technologies. The IETF also charged the ALE Working Group to consider if developing more stringent address allocation and utilization policies might provide more time for the transition to IPng.

In the following section, Frank Solensky, co-chair of the ALE Working Group, explores more of the history leading to the realization within the IETF of the looming exhaustion of IPv4 addresses.

The ALE projections presented indicate that none of the more stringent assignment policies, such as reclaiming already assigned address space, was necessary. However, network service providers should offer to assist their new customers in renumbering their networks to conform to the providers' CIDR assignments. One other suggestion emerges from the ALE piece—that of assigning CIDR-type address blocks out of the unassigned Class A address space, a recommendation which is now being tested.

IPv4 Address Lifetime Expectations

Frank Solensky
FTP Software, Inc.

One of the factors considered in the selection of the IPng protocol was the available time frame in which a new network protocol could be developed and deployed throughout the Internet. It was imperative that this protocol be fully operational well in advance of the time that any network would be prevented from connecting to the Internet due to the lack of an available IPv4 network number. Unlike maintaining a computer program that tracks years using a two-digit field, however, the Internet community could not simply look at a calendar to determine its deadline for completing the transition effort. This section describes the efforts within the IETF that quantified this deadline and the steps that were taken to push it off into the future as far as both possible and practical.

While it would be pleasant to believe that the IETF had always been aware that it would eventually need to replace the network layer protocol all along, it could be said that the IETF's IPng effort was initiated by a humorous remark. In July 1990, a discussion about the growth of the Internet was taking place on the IETF mailing list. The Internet was then providing connectivity between 1700 networks which, as Mike St. Johns, a U.S. Air Force Major and current ARPA Program Manager, noted, was reasonably close to the number predicted by a formula he had worked out some months earlier. My reply to the message was that if his model was accurate, we would run out of 32-bit IP addresses some time in the year 2000, following this statement with the ubiquitous "smiley-face" since it seemed mildly implausible at the time.

The reasoning behind this prediction was fairly simple to those familiar with the format of IPv4 addresses at the time. The 32-bit IP address was composed of two separate fields: a network number and a host number. The length of each field depended on the first few bits of the address. Addresses where the first bit was "0" were known as "Class A" addresses; the network number was seven bits wide followed by a 24-bit host number. Addresses that began with "10" were "Class B" addresses with a 14-bit network number and a 16-bit host number. "Class C" addresses began with "110" and separated the network and host numbers into fields that were twenty-one and eight bits wide respectively. All addresses starting with "111" at the time were reserved for future experiments and were not factored in. Since there were a total of 128 possible Class A network numbers, 16,384 Class B network numbers and 2,097,152 Class C network numbers, the projection was simply a matter of determining when the formula approached the sum of these three values (more precisely, 2,113,661, since the three "all-zeros" network numbers are also reserved).

However, matters were not so simple as that. An analysis of data put together by researchers at SRI that tracked the count of assigned network numbers separated by class indicated that the demand for Class B addresses was increasing at a startling rate—over 20% of the possible Class B network numbers had already been assigned to various organizations, most of which had not yet connected to the rest of the Internet—and that the total was doubling approximately every 14 months. The analysis suggested that if that growth rate were to continue unabated, all of the possible Class B network numbers would be depleted by March 1994.

One explanation for the heavy demand for the Class B network numbers was the Goldilocks theory: when an organization applied for an IP network number, it would need to estimate how large it expected its network to eventually become and indicate which address class it would fall into based on that estimate. Many campuses and businesses would naturally conclude that a 256-node network would eventually prove to be too small while a network of over 16 million nodes would far exceed their most ambitious plans, so a Class B network number would be "just right."

However, while a model of exponential growth might suffice for some back-of-the-envelope calculations, one couldn't realistically extend this projection too far into the future without concluding that the number of Class B networks would eventually exceed the number of electrons in the universe. A better model for tracking this growth could be found in the logistic distribution. This function roughly resembles a flattened "S," starting off as an exponential curve but eventually growing less rapidly and approaching a fixed limiting value over time. This model had been used to predict the growth of the telephone network in the 1960s [1] and, later that year, in an effort independent from mine, the growth of BITNET. [2]

Another problem concerned the Internet's routers. If the current growth were to continue even for only a couple years, many of the routers that were commercially available at that time would soon be unable to keep track of all the connected networks. The first signs of this problem were already occurring in some of the older routers that had limited memory. Further, the number of routes that had to be carried in the routing update messages would soon exceed the capabilities of the older protocols.

By late 1991, it was becoming clear that the demand for Class B network numbers still showed no signs of subsiding and that more draconian actions would be necessary. As a result, the Network Information Center (NIC) instituted a new policy of being more discriminating when assigning Class B network numbers: unless it was apparent that the network was eventually going to become very large, a number of consecutive Class C network numbers would be assigned instead.

While it was anticipated that this strategy would have the desired effect of slowing the growth in the Class B portion of the address space, it was also recognized that this would further aggravate the growth of the routing tables: if a network that asked for a single Class B network number was instead assigned eight Class C numbers, the router that provided their connectivity would use eight times as much memory to keep track of those routes as compared with a single routing table entry. Further, each routing protocol update message was getting larger for the same reason. This was already making it difficult for some networks using older protocols to remain connected in a reliable manner since the routing table update messages were getting longer than their designers originally anticipated.

The need to tread the delicate balance between these two extremes led to the formation of the Routing and Addressing (ROAD) Working Group at the Santa Fe IETF in November 1991. After meeting several times over the following months, the group presented a recommendation for the use of Classless Inter-Domain Routing (CIDR) as a short-term solution to these two problems at the March 1992 IETF meeting in San Diego.

The CIDR proposal, as described in RFC-1519,[3] removed the implied separation of the IP address into network and host number components and required that the routing protocols and hosts explicitly include this delineation in the network mask. By way of example: if a router was providing connectivity for the fictitious network numbers 257.123.0 through 257.123.7, it would announce a route to 257.123.0/21 to its neighbors (The number after the '/' character indicates the width of the network mask and is used as a shorthand notation; internally a separate 32-bit field indicates which bits of the address are part of the network number). The neighboring routers would then hear, kept track of, and forwarded only a single route.

While CIDR meant that changes would have to be made to some of the existing routing protocols, another benefit of this proposal was that the existing end hosts required little or no modifications to use a network mask which was shorter than its default path since most hosts already had the capability to override the default network mask with a subnetwork mask that could be defined by the user. The host simply defined its subnet mask to be shorter than the default mask. As a result, these changes could be made transparently to most of the end systems and allowed CIDR deployment to take place much more easily than if it required coordinated updates to the host software.

In the same way that several consecutive network numbers would be aggregated to announce an individual network, the CIDR proposal also extended network aggregation up to the service provider level; providers could then announce their subscriber networks within a single routing table entry, allowing the routing tables to shrink even further. The manner in which IP addresses were assigned was changed in order to facilitate this. Instead of assigning network numbers to end customers in a sequential order, the NIC would instead delegate portions of the remaining IPv4 address space to the regional service providers. The service providers would then assign network numbers to their customers out of these blocks. A drawback to this scheme is that when customers decide to change network service providers, they would be required to renumber all of their hosts into the new provider's address space. While this drawback proved to be a very contentious point within the IETF, it was expected that it would be less of a concern as protocols and software eventually became available that would enable a server within an end network to dynamically assign IP addresses to requesting hosts. The end network in this case would simply reconfigure its server, and the hosts within that network would pick up new addresses directly.

While this approach looked good on paper, it was impossible to know ahead of time whether or not changes that allowed each individual network to take up a smaller proportion of the remaining IPv4 address space would cause the address space growth rates to slow sufficiently, or to what degree the routing tables would actually be reduced. Further, renumbering technology to this day is not much past the experimental stage; at the time, it wasn't at all clear that it could be deployed widely or quickly enough before IPv4 addresses ran out. While CIDR was getting deployed throughout the Internet to address the immediate problems within IPv4, the IPng Directorate would formulate the requirements and analyze proposals for what the next version of IP would entail and make a recommendation as soon as was reasonable.

The IPv4 Address Lifetime Estimation (ALE) Working Group was formed within the IPng Area to monitor the impact CIDR was having on the demand for the remaining IPv4 address space, to formulate some recommendations on how to keep IPv4 running as long as possible, and to estimate the year in which IPv4 address space was likely to run out. The two co-chairs of the Working Group, myself and Tony Li, had differing opinions about how to best estimate the Internet's future growth: while I felt the logistic "S" curve described earlier was a realistic model to follow, Tony Li felt that a graph of the historic data more closely resembled a straight line and preferred to use linear regression for his predictions. Since it would be impossible to know which model was the more accurate one until after the fact, each of us updated our different projections at subsequent meetings as more data became available.

One of the more interesting challenges we encountered during this time was factoring in those months when very large blocks of addresses were allocated to the network providers: each new data point that was much higher than prior trend lines had predicted would cause the new trend line to show a greater growth rate than before, leading us to revise our predictions for when IPv4 addresses would be exhausted by large amounts. We could smooth out the data so as to filter out the biasing effect caused by the new data point, but doing so would force us to assume that these sudden jumps were not going to be recurring events, an assumption that many were highly reluctant to take as a given. In addition, there were concerns that our predictions were based on the history of how widely the Internet Protocol was deployed within existing technologies and did not take into account the demands that future technologies might place on the remaining IPv4 address space. As a result of these assumptions, predictions made using this methodology could lead us to believe that there was much more time available to develop the new IP than was actually the case. While this was a valid concern, we felt that there was no way to make a reasonable estimate of the impact of future technologies that were so far totally unknown. Further, it was not inconceivable that new technologies might be created that would actually reduce the demand rather than increasing it. (As an example, RFC-1597 [4] presents a proposal for assigning IPv4 addresses that are not globally unique to devices that do not require full Internet connectivity. A related document, RFC-1627 [5], identifies some of the drawbacks of this approach.) Therefore, we felt that the most responsible action was to include caveats that noted these risks along with the predictions.

While the original problem — the growth rate within the Class B address space — now appears to be under control, consistently leveling off below its maximum, demand for the rest of the IPv4 address space is still growing. The ALE group recommended that the upper half of the Class A space (sometimes called "the A-sharp space") be made available so that portions of it could be delegated to the regional providers in the same manner as the rest of the address space. An operational experiment, documented in RFC-1797, [6] was initiated in 1995 to determine whether or not a single Class A network number can easily be subdivided among different providers. Also, changes have been made to the Router Requirements document standard to mandate that all routers be capable of recognizing CIDR-ized addresses. Assuming that the Class A experiment proves successful, the most recent data suggests that the remaining IPv4 address space will be depleted sometime in 2008 using the logistic model and 2018 under the linear growth model. It should be emphasized again that these estimates are very volatile.

The estimates for these time frames also assume that IPv4 addresses which are currently in use or assigned to the service providers will not be reused. The working group had considered the option of recycling those portions of the IPv4 address space which had been assigned at one time but were no longer in active use by any party. The group recommended that this be pursued for the unused network numbers in the lower portion of the Class A address space since this effort could be directed toward a small number of sites. In addition, each individual Class A network number represented a significantly larger portion of the total IPv4 address space and thus provided more time before the deployment of IPng became a necessity.

It was not known, however, whether or not this approach could be used for the Class B and C portions of the address space. To determine the answer to this question, I sent out a short survey in July 1994, to many network administrators to estimate approximately what portion of the address space could be reclaimed in this manner. A random sample of these responses suggested that while many of the addresses within the individual networks were not assigned to any particular system and were still available to the organizations that were using the network numbers (2.5% of the Class B addresses and 10.9% of Class Cs), only a small portion of them would be able to give up a contiguous block of the addresses without having to first assign new addresses to a significant portion of their existing hosts. Further, in order to again avoid enlarging the routing tables in the manner described earlier, the reclaimed addresses would need to be delegated back only to the organization's service provider. As a result of the great cost and low return, the group recommended that this approach should be used for Class B and C addresses only if it became absolutely necessary.

During the time that the ALE group focused on estimating and extending the life of the remaining IPv4 address space, the BGP Deployment (BGPD) Working Group, chaired by Vince Fuller of BARRNet and Jessica Yu of MERIT, directed its efforts to deploying the updates to the routing protocols and measuring the effect it had on the size of the routing tables. The updated protocols started to appear in the production networks of some of the European service providers by March 1994. Once the group was satisified that the revisions were, in fact, reducing the size of the routing tables without loss of connectivity, CIDR started to get deployed more widely. As a result, the routing tables shrank from approximately 20,000 entries in April 1994 to about 18,000 entries in July. While this might appear to have been only a moderate success, one also needs to recognize that the Internet was continuing to grow at the same time: during these four months, approximately 2% of the total IPv4 address space had been delegated either to the service providers or directly to the end networks.

The routing tables have continued to grow since CIDR was first deployed, reaching approximately 28,000 entries by August 1995 with about 56% of the service providers announcing at least some routes with CIDR aggregations. The effort to get CIDR deployed throughout the rest of the Internet continues under the auspices of the CIDR Deployment (CIDRD) Working Group, into which the ALE working group was merged.

The Role of IPng
in Communications
Technology

Part IV

Now that the IPng Area Directors had a better sense of the projected lifespan of IPv4 and the possible scope of IPng, it was time to begin developing the technical criteria. The IESG had provided the IPng Area with an outline of the type of criteria to be used in evaluating the IPng proposals. The IETF further refined this understanding of appropriate criteria with the recommendations passed down to us from a Selection Criteria BOF held during the November 1992 IETF meeting in Washington D.C.

However, it was becoming very apparent that the Internet and the supporting IPng technology were likely to play a major role in the development of many different technologies and industries. In order to develop technical criteria for a data-networking protocol that could support the broadest possible range of applications, the IETF felt that it needed input from outside its traditional constituency to help better understand the demands on the future Internet.

In the light of the Internet's growth, it was necessary to be sure that the depth and range of inquiry was extensive. Questions to be considered included:

- *What features should be in an IPng to facilitate security?*
- *What is a reasonable estimate for the scale of the future data networking environment?*

- *What are the requirements or concerns that affect how IPng should facilitate the use of resource reservations or flows?*
- *How important is policy based routing?*
- *How important a consideration should the ability to do accounting be in the selection of an IPng?*
- *How important is the proliferation of mobile hosts to the IPng selection process?*
- *Are there technologies that will pull the Internet in a way that should influence IPng? Can specific strategies be developed to encompass these?*
- *What are reasonable time estimates for the IPng selection, development, and deployment process or what should the timeframe requirements be?*

Therefore, the IPng Area put out a call for papers (issued as RFC-1550 [1]) into the wider networking and communications communities. In response, 21 papers were received. These papers, and several more besides, are represented (in modified form) in the next two sections of this book. They are divided into two groups: the first group (contained in Part IV) consists of papers addressing the general requirements for future data networking; and the second group (contained in Part V) focuses on specific features needed in the protocols themselves.

These papers reveal the kinds of technologies and features IPng needs to incorporate in order to serve the industries and markets of the future. Many of the requirements set forth in these papers were, in fact, reflected in the technical criteria for IPng and ended up in the final IPng specifications.

Internetworking in the Navy

R. Brian Adamson
Naval Research Laboratory

The U.S. Navy and other armed services have identified critical requirements for security, mobility, real–time data delivery applications, multicast, and quality–of–service and policy–based routing of the next generation of the Internet Protocol. Address scaling for military application of internet technology may include very large numbers of local (intraplatform) distributed information and weapons systems and a smaller number of nodes requiring global connectivity. The flexibility of the current Internet Protocol (IP) for supporting widely different communication media should be preserved to meet the needs of the highly heterogeneous networks of the tactical environment.

Compact protocol headers are necessary for efficient data transfer on the relatively low throughput radio frequency (RF) systems. Mechanisms which can enhance the effectiveness of an internet datagram protocol to provide resource reservation, priority, and service quality guarantees are also very important. The broadcast nature of many RF networks and the need for broad dissemination of information to war-fighting participants makes multicast the general case for information flow in the tactical environment.

Naval Research Efforts. The requirements for Internet Protocol next generation (IPng) candidates with respect to their application to military tactical RF communication networks need to be considered along with private concerns. The foundation for these requirements are experiences born of the Navy's research efforts in this area: the NATO Communication System Network Interoperability (CSNI) project; the Naval Research Laboratory Data/Voice Integration Advanced Technology Demonstration (D/V ATD), and the Navy Communication Support System (CSS) architecture development.

NATO Communication System Network Interoperability Project. The goal of the CSNI project is to apply internetworking technology to facilitate multinational interoperability for typical military communication applications (e.g., electronic messaging, tactical data exchange, and digital voice) on typical tactical RF communication links and networks.

The International Standard Organization (ISO) Open Systems Interconnect (OSI) protocol suite, including the Connectionless Network Protocol (CLNP), was selected for this project for policy reasons. There are design issues in meeting the project goals with this particular protocol stack.

Naval Research Laboratory's Data/Voice Integration Advanced Technology Demonstration. The D/V ATD is focused on demonstrating a survivable, self–configuring, self–recovering RF subnetwork technology capable of simultaneously supporting data delivery, including message transfer, imagery, tactical data, and real–time digital voice applications. Support for real–time interactive communication applications was extended to include a "white board" and other similar applications. IP datagram delivery is also planned as part of this demonstration system.

Navy Communication Support System Architecture Development. The CSS architecture will provide U.S. Navy tactical platforms with a broad array of user–transparent voice and data information exchange services. This will include support for sharing and management of limited platform communication resources among multiple war–fighting communities. Emphasis is placed on attaining interoperability with other military services and foreign allies. Utilization of commercial off–the–shelf communications products to take advantage of existing economies of scale is important to make any resulting system design affordable. It is anticipated that open, voluntary standards, and flexible communication protocols, such as IP, will play a key role in meeting the goals of this architecture.

IPng Requirements and RFC-1550. Before addressing any IPng requirements as applied to tactical RF communications, it is necessary to define what is meant by "IPng requirements." To maintain brevity, the criteria described in this section are specifically related to the design of an OSI model's Layer 3 protocol format and a few other areas suggested by RFC-1550. [2] There are also several additional areas of concern in applying internetwork protocols to the military tactical RF setting:

- routing protocol design
- address assignment
- network management
- resource management

Scale. The requirement that IPng should be able to deal with 10^{12} nodes is more than adequate in the face of military requirements. More importantly, with IPng it must be possible to assign addresses efficiently. For example, although a military platform may have a relatively small number of nodes with requirements to communicate with a larger, global infrastructure, there will likely be applications of IPng to management and control of distributed systems (e.g., specific radio communications equipment and processors, weapons systems) within the platform. This local expansion of address space requirements may not necessarily need to be solved by "sheer numbers" of globally unique addresses but perhaps by alternate delimitation of addressing to differentiate between globally unique and locally unique addressing. The advantages of a compact internet address header are clear for relatively low capacity RF networks.

Transition. The Navy and other armed services are currently (in the past few years) designing and deploying systems that use open systems internetworking technology. From this point of view, the time scale for selection of IPng must be somewhat rapid. Otherwise, two transition phases will need to be suffered: 1) the move from unique, "stove pipe" systems to open, internetworked (e.g., IP) systems, and 2) a transition from deployed IP–based systems to IPng. In some sense, if an IPng is quickly accepted and widely implemented, the transition for tactical military systems will be somewhat easier than the enterprise Internet where a large investment in current IP already exists. However, having said this, the Department of Defense as a whole already deploys a large number of IP–capable systems, and the issue of transition from IP to IPng remains significant.

Media Independence. The tactical communication environment includes a very broad spectrum of communication media from shipboard fiber–optic LANs to very low data rate (fewer than 2400 bps) RF links. Many of the RF links, even higher speed ones, can exhibit error statistics not necessarily well–serviced by higher layer reliable protocols (i.e., TCP). In these cases, efficient lower layer protocols can be implemented to provide reliable datagram delivery at the link layer, but at the cost of highly variable delay performance.

It is also important to recognize that RF communication cannot be viewed from the IPng designer as simple point–to–point links.

Often, highly complex, unique subnetwork protocols are utilized to meet requirements of survivability, communications performance with limited bandwidth, anti–jam and/or low probability of detection requirements.

It is understood that IPng cannot be the panacea of Layer 3 protocols, particularly when it comes to providing special mechanisms to support the endangered–species low data rate user. In some of these cases IPng will be one of several Layer 3 protocols sharing the subnetwork. However, note that there are potentially many low data rate, IP–based applications of value to the tactical user. Well–designed, efficient networking protocols, can allow many more users to share the limited available RF bandwidth. A significant portion of data traffic in the tactical environment may consist of short datagram messages (e.g., position reports, fire control, etc.). Also, relatively low data rate links will also likely utilize relatively small packet MTU sizes. As a result, any mechanisms which facilitate compression of network headers can be considered highly valuable in an IPng candidate.

Configuration, Administration, and Operation. The tactical military has very real requirements for multimedia services across its shared and interconnected RF networks. This includes applications from digital secure voice integrated with applications such as "white boards" and position reporting for mission planning purposes to low latency, high priority tactical data messages (target detection, identification, location, and heading information). Because of the limited capacity of tactical RF networks, resource reservation is extremely important to control access to these valuable resources. Resource reservation can play a role in "congestion avoidance" for these limited resources as well as ensuring that quality–of–service (QoS) data delivery requirements are met for multimedia communication.

Note that this requires more than can be met by simple QoS–based path selection and subsequent source–routing to get real–time data, such as voice, delivered. For example, to support digital voice in the CSNI project, a call setup and resource reservation protocol was designed. It was determined that the QoS mechanisms provided by the CLNP specification were not sufficient for our voice application path selection. Voice calls could not be routed and resources reserved based on any single QoS parameter (e.g., delay, capacity) alone. Some RF subnets in the CSNI test bed simply did not have the capability to support voice calls.

To perform resource reservation for the voice calls, the CLNP cost metric was "hijacked" as essentially a Type–of–Service identifier to let the router know which datagrams were associated with a voicecall. The cost metric, concatenated with the source and destination addresses, were used to form a unique identifier for voice calls in the router and subnet state tables. Voice call paths were to be selected by the router (i.e., the "cost" metric was calculated) as a rule–based function of each subnet's capability to support voice, its delay, and its capacity.

While source–routing provided a possible means for voice datagrams to find their way from router to router, the network address alone was not explicit enough to direct the data to the correct interface, particularly in cases where there were multiple communication media interconnecting two routers along the path. Fortunately, exclusive use of the cost QoS indicator for voice in CSNI was able to serve as a flag to the router for packets requiring special handling.

Flow Specification. While a simple Type–of–Service field as part of an IPng protocol can serve this purpose where there are a limited number of well known services (CSNI has a single special service: 2400 bps digital voice), a more general technique such as RSVP's Flow Specification can support a larger set of such services. And a field, such as the one sometimes referred to as a Flow Identification (Flow ID), can play an important role in facilitating internetworked data communication over these limited capacity networks.

For example, the D/V ATD RF sub–network provides support for both connectionless datagram delivery and virtual circuit connectivity. To utilize this capability, an IPng could establish a virtual circuit connection across this RF subnetwork which meets the requirements of an RSVP Flow Specification. By creating an association between a particular Flow ID and the subnetwork header identifying the established virtual circuit, an IPng gateway could forward data across the low–capacity link while removing most, if not all, of the IPng packet header information. The receiving gateway could re–construct these fields based on the Flow Specification of the particular Flow ID/virtual circuit association.

A field such as a Flow ID can serve at least two important purposes:

- It can be used by routers (or gateways) to identify packets with special, or pre–arranged delivery requirements. It is important to realize that it may not always be possible to "peek" at internet packet content for this information if certain security considerations are met (e.g., an encrypted transport layer).
- It can aid mapping datagram services to different types of communication services provided by specialized subnet/data link layer protocols.

Secure Operation. As with any military system, information security, including confidentiality and authenticity of data, is of paramount importance. With regard to IPng, network layer security mechanisms for tactical RF networks are generally important for authentication purposes, including routing protocol authentication, source authentication, and user network access control. Concerns for denial of service attacks, traffic analysis monitoring, etc., usually dictate that tactical RF communication networks provide link layer security mechanisms.

Compartmentalization and multiple levels of security for different users of common communication resources call for additional security mechanisms at the transport layer or above. In the typical tactical RF environment, network layer confidentiality, and in some cases even authentication, becomes redundant with these other security mechanisms.

The need for network layer security mechanisms becomes more critical when the military utilizes commercial telecommunications systems or has tactical systems interconnected with commercial internets. While the Network Encryption Server (NES) works in this role today, there is a desire for a more integrated, higher performance solution in the future. Thus, to meet the military requirement for confidentiality and authentication, an IPng candidate must be capable of operating in a secure manner when necessary, but also allow for efficient operation on low throughput RF links when other security mechanisms are already in place.

In either of these cases, key management is extremely important. Ideally, a common key management system could be used to provide key distribution for security mechanisms at any layer from the application to the link layer. As a result, it is anticipated, however, that key distribution is a function of management, and should not be dependent upon a particular IPng protocol format.

Multicast. Tactical military communication has a very clear requirement for multicast. Efficient dissemination of information to distributed war–fighting participants can be the key to success in a battle.

In modern warfare, this information includes imagery, the "tactical scene" via tactical data messages, messaging information, and real–time interactive applications such as digital secure voice. Many of the tactical RF communication media are broadcast by nature, and multicast routing can take advantage of this topology to distribute critical data to a large number of participants. The throughput limitations imposed by these RF media and the physics of potential electronic counter measures (ECM) dictate that this information be distributed efficiently. A multicast architecture is the general case for information flow in a tactical internetwork.

Extensibility. Quality of service and policy based routing are of particular importance in a tactical environment with limited communication resources, limited bandwidth, and possible degradation and/or denial of service. Priority is a very important criteria in the tactical setting. In the tactical RF world of limited resources (limited bandwidth, radio assets, etc.) there will be instances when there is not sufficient capacity to provide all users with their perception of required communication capability.

It is extremely important for a shared, automated communication system to delegate capacity to higher priority users. Unlike the commercial world, where everyone has more equal footing, it is possible in the military environment to assign priority to users or even individual datagrams. An example of this is the tactical data exchange. Tactical data messages are generally single–datagram messages containing information on the location, bearing, identification, etc., of entities detected by sensors. In CSNI, tactical data messages were assigned 15 different levels of CLNP priority. This ensured that important messages, such as a rapidly approaching enemy missile's trajectory, were given priority over less important messages, such as a friendly, slow–moving tanker's heading.

Applicability. There will be a significant amount of applicability to tactical RF networks. The current IP and CLNP are being given considerable attention in the tactical RF community as a means to provide communication interoperability across a large set of heterogeneous RF networks in use by different services and countries. The applicability of IPng can only improve with the inclusion of features critical to supporting QoS and policy–based routing, security, real–time multi–media data delivery, and extended addressing. It must be noted that it is very important that the IPng protocol headers not grow overly large. There is a sharp tradeoff between the value added by these headers (interoperability, global addressing, etc.) and the degree of communication performance attainable on limited capacity RF networks. Regardless of the data rate that future RF networks will be capable of supporting, there is always a tactical advantage in utilizing your resources more efficiently.

Support for Mobility. The definition of most tactical systems include mobility in some form. Many tactical RF network designs provide means for members to join and leave particular RF subnets as their position changes. For example, as a platform moves out of the RF line–of–sight (LOS) range, it may switch from a typical LOS RF media such as the ultra–high frequency (UHF) band to a long–haul RF media such as high frequency (HF) or satellite communication (SATCOM).

In some cases, such as the D/V ATD network, the RF subnet will perform its own routing and management of this dynamic topology. This will be invisible to the internet protocol except for subtle changes to some routing metrics (e.g., more or less delay to reach a host). In this instance, the RF subnetwork protocols serve as a buffer to the internet routing protocols and IPng will not need to be too concerned with mobility. In other cases, however, the platform may make a dramatic change in position and require a major change in internet routing. IPng must be able to support this situation. It is recognized that an internet protocol may not be able to cope with large, rapid changes in topology. Efforts will be made to minimize the frequency of this in a tactical RF communication architecture, but there are instances when a major change in topology is required.

Furthermore, it should be realized that mobility in the tactical setting is not limited to individual nodes moving about, but that, in some cases, entire subnetworks may be moving. An example of this is a Navy ship with multiple LANs on board, moving through the domains of different RF networks. In some cases, the RF subnet will be moving, as in the case of an aircraft strike force, or Navy battlegroup.

Datagram Service. The datagram service paradigm provides many useful features for tactical communication networks. The "memory" provided by datagram headers, provides an inherent amount of survivability essential to the dynamics of the tactical communication environment. The availability of platforms for routing and relaying is never 100% certain in a tactical scenario. The efficiency with which multicast can be implemented in a connectionless network is highly critical in the tactical environment where rapid, efficient information dissemination can be a deciding factor. And, as has been proven with several different Internet applications and experiments, a datagram service is capable of providing useful connection–oriented and real–time communication services.

Consideration should be given in IPng to how it can co–exist with other architectures such as switching fabrics which offer demand–based control over topology and connectivity. The military owns many of its own communication resources and one of the large problems in managing the military communication infrastructure is directing those underlying resources to where they are needed. Traditional management (SNMP, etc.) is of course useful here, but RF communication media can be somewhat dynamically allocated.

Circuit switching designs offer some advantages here. Dial–up IP routing is an example of an integrated solution. The IPng should be capable of supporting a similar type of operation.

Supporting ATM Services in IPng

Christina Brazdziunas
Evolving Systems, Inc.

The future internet will be comprised of both conventional and sophisticated link technologies. The sophisticated features of link layers like ATM need to be incorporated into an internet where data travels not only across an ATM network but also across several existing LAN and WAN technologies. Future networks are likely to be a combination of subnetworks providing best–effort link–level service, such as Ethernet, and sophisticated subnetworks, that can support QoS–based connections like ATM. Data could originate from an Ethernet, pass through an ATM network, a Fiber Distributed Data Interface (FDDI) network, another ATM network, and finally arrive at its destination, which resides on a (High Performance Parallel Interface) HiPPI network. IPng packets will need to be able to travel through such interconnected networks when ATM is incorporated in the future internet.

Asynchronous Transfer Mode (ATM) is a "sophisticated" link–level technology which provides the potential capability for applications at the TCP/UDP level to map to a single virtual circuit that has been customized for the performance and traffic requirements of that application. This is a step above many of today's existing link technologies which can only support a single level of network performance that must be shared by all applications operating on a single endpoint. IPng should provide support for existing and emerging link technologies that it will be transported over. Link technologies like Ethernet simply multiplex traffic from upper layer protocols onto a single channel. Sophisticated link technologies such as ATM allow multiple, performance–sensitive virtual channels to be established over a single wire (or fiber).

ATM Virtual Circuits. Support for both sophisticated (ATM) and existing link technologies needs to be considered in IPng. End–to–end applications will communicate through a network where IPng packets travel across subnetworks such as Ethernet and HiPPI and also more sophisticated link levels such as ATM. Though initial support for IPng over ATM subnetworks will not facilitate a virtual circuit per application, the hooks to provide such a mapping should be in place from the first.

Application support for quality–of–service–based (QoS–based) link–level service requires that the following types of ATM information be mappable (or derivable) from the higher level protocol(s) such as IPng:

- source and destination(s) addresses
- connection QoS parameters
- connection state
- ATM virtual circuit identifier

Some of these mappings may be derivable from information provided by proposed resource reservation protocols supporting an integrated services Internet.[3] However, the ATM virtual circuit identifier should be efficiently derivable from IPng packet information.

Any IPng candidate should provide evidence that the mapping from an application's IPng packets to ATM virtual circuit(s) can be accomplished in a heterogeneous internet architecture keeping in consideration the gigabit/sec rates that IPng/ATM subnetworks will eventually be operating at.

Terminology. The term application refers to a process or set of collective processes operating at the TCP/UDP level or above in the protocol stack, for example, each instance of Telnet or each FTP session running on an end station is a distinct application.

Characteristics of ATM Service. ATM has several characteristics that differentiate it from current link–level technologies. First, ATM has the capability of providing many virtual channels to transmit information over a single wire, or fiber. This is very similar to X.25 where many logical channels can be established over a single physical media. Unlike X.25, ATM allows for each of these channels or circuits to have a customizable set of performance and QoS characteristics. Link–level technologies like Ethernet provide a single channel with a single performance and a single QoS characteristic. In a sense, a single ATM link–level media appears as an array of link–level technologies, each with customizable characteristics.

ATM virtual circuits can be established dynamically, using ATM's signaling protocol. ATM signaling establishes a hard state in the network for a call. Hard state implies that the state of a connection in intermediate switching equipment can be set, and once established, it will be maintained until a message is received by one of the ends of the call requesting a change in state for the connection.[4] As a result, an ATM end system (this could be either a workstation with an ATM adapter or a router with an ATM interface) receives guaranteed service from the ATM network. The ATM network is responsible for maintaining the connection state. The price the ATM termination points pay for this guarantee is the responsibility for changing the state of the connection, specifically for informing the ATM network to establish, alter, or tear down the connection.

ATM User–Network Interface (UNI). The ATM User–Network Interface (UNI) signaling protocol based on the International Telecommunication Union (ITU) TS Q.2931 allows many different service parameters for describing connection characteristics:

- ATM adaptation layer (AAL) information
- Network QoS objectives
- Connection traffic descriptor
- Transit network selector[5]

The AAL information specifies negotiable parameters such as type and maximum packet sizes.

The network QoS objectives describe the service that the ATM user expects from the network. Q.2931 allows for one of four service classes to be selected by the ATM user. The service classes are defined as general traffic types, Constant Bit Rate (CBR), Variable Bit Rate (VBR), Available Bit Rate (ABR), and Unspecified Bit Rate (UBR). Each of these categories are further specified through network provider objectives for various ATM performance parameters which may include cell transfer delay, cell delay variation, and cell loss ratio.

The connection traffic descriptor specifies characteristics of the data generated by the user of the connection. This information allows the ATM network to commit the resources necessary to support the traffic flow with the quality of service the user expects. Characteristics defined in the ATM Forum UNI specification include peak cell rate, sustainable cell rate, and maximum and minimum burst sizes.[6]

The transit network selection parameter allows an ATM user to select a preferred network provider to service the connection.[7]

Parameters Required to Map IPng to ATM. As mentioned earlier, the mapping of IPng to ATM will require IPng to provide four types of parameters:

- addressing parameters
- connection QoS–related parameters
- connection management information
- ATM virtual circuit identifier

The first three categories, addressing parameters, connection QoS–related parameters, and connection management information, provide support for ATM signaling. The last parameter, a connection identifier that maps IPng packets to ATM virtual circuits, provides support for an ATM virtual circuit per application when the end–to–end connection travels across an ATM subnetwork. This does not assume that ATM is the only type of subnetwork that an end–to–end connection can travel across.

Addressing. ATM supports routable addresses to each ATM endpoint to facilitate the dynamic establishment of connections. These addresses need to be derived from a higher level address such as an IPng address and IPng routing information. This type of mapping is not novel. It is a mapping that is currently done to support the current IP over link technologies such as Ethernet. An IP–over–ATM address resolution protocol (ARP) has been described in the Internet Standard, "Classical IP and ARP over ATM." In addition, support for IP routing over large ATM networks is being worked in the IETF's "Routing over Large Clouds" working group.[8]

Connection Quality of Service (QoS). As described above, an ATM virtual circuit is established based upon a user's traffic characteristics and network performance objectives. These characteristics which include delay and throughput requirements can only be defined by the application level (at the transport level or above) as opposed to the internetworking (IPng) level. For instance, a file transfer application transferring a 100 MB file has very different link–level performance requirements than a network time application. The former requires a high throughput and low error rate connection whereas the latter could perhaps be adequately serviced utilizing a best–effort service. Current IP does not provide much support for a quality of service specification and provides no support for the specification of link–level performance needs by an application directly. This is due to the fact that only a single type of link–level performance is available with link technologies like Ethernet. As a result, all applications over IP today receive the same level of link service.

IPng packets need not explicitly contain information parameters describing an application's traffic characteristics and network performance objectives (e.g., delay = low, throughput = 10 Mb/s). This information could potentially be mapped from resource reservation protocols that operate at the IP (and potentially IPng) level.

Connection Management. The establishment and release of ATM connections should ultimately be controlled by the applications utilizing the circuits, ATM signaling establishes a "hard state" in the network which is controlled by the ATM termination points.[9] Currently, IP provides no explicit mechanism for link–level connection management. Future support for link–level connection management could be accomplished through resource reservation protocols and need not necessarily be supported directly via information contained in the IPng protocol.

Connection Identifier. A mapping function needs to exist between IPng packets and ATM so that application flows map one–to–one to ATM virtual circuits. Currently, application traffic flows are identified at the transport level by UDP/TCP source and destination ports and IP protocol identifiers. This level of identification should also be available at the IPng level so that information in the IPng packets identifies an application's flow and maps to an ATM virtual circuit supporting that flow when the IPng packets travel across an ATM subnetwork.

Using the current IP protocol, identifying an application's traffic flow requires the combination of the following five parameters:

- source IP addresses
- destination IP addresses
- source UDP/TCP ports
- destination UDP/TCP ports
- IP protocol identifier

This application connection identifier for IP is complex and could potentially be costly to implement in IP end stations and routers. The IPng connection identifier should be large enough so that all application level traffic from an IPng end point can be mapped into the IPng packet. Currently, ATM provides 24 bits for virtual circuit identification (VPI and VCI). This provides sufficient capacity for 2^{24} (16,777,216) connections.[10] The actual number of bits that are used for the ATM virtual circuit however is established through negotiation between the ATM endpoint and

ATM network. This number is useful as an upper bound for the number of mappings that are needed to be supported by IPng.

An IPng candidate should be able to identify how IPng packets from an application can map to an ATM virtual circuit. In addition, this mapping should be large enough to support a mapping for every IPng application on an end system to an ATM virtual circuit. Careful consideration should be given to complexity of this mapping for IPng to ATM since it needs to eventually support gigabit/sec rates.

IPng in Large Corporate Networks

Edward Britton
John Tavs
IBM Corporation

As more and more corporations are using TCP/IP for their mission-critical applications, they are specifying additional requirements. The satisfaction of these requirements would make TCP/IP even more appealing to businesses. Since these are requirements, rather than solutions to existing network problems, we have included capabilities that might be provided in protocol layers other than the one that IPv4 occupies; i.e., these items might lie outside the scope typically envisioned for IPng, but we'll refer to them as IPng requirements nonetheless. When we mention potential solutions, it is not to suggest that they are the best approach, but merely to clarify the requirement.

The major requirements of business users are:

- predictable service for predictable costs
- smooth transition from, and coexistence with, IPv4
- secure operation
- heterogeneity

Robust Service. If a corporation depends on its network for applications that are critical to its business (such as airlines do for reservations, and brokerages do for stock and bond trades), then the corporation insists that the network provide the needed level of service for a predictable cost, so they can budget for it ahead of time. A service level agreement (SLA) is a contract between a network's provider and users that defines the service level which a user will see and the cost associated with that level of service. Measurements in an SLA may include response times (average and maximum), availability percentages, number of active sessions, throughput rates, etc. Businesses need to be able to predict and guarantee the service levels and associated costs (routing capacity, link bandwidth, etc.) for their traffic patterns on a TCP/IP network.

IPng should provide for control of the cost of networking, a major concern for corporations. Teleprocessing lines are a significant cost in corporate networks. Although the cost per bit–per–second tends to be lower on higher bandwidth links, high bandwidth links can be hard to get, particularly in emerging nations. In many places it is difficult to acquire a 64 kpbs line, and T1 service might not exist. Furthermore, lead times can be more than six months. Even in the U.S. the cost of transcontinental T1 service is high enough to encourage high utilization. Cost–conscious businesses want IPng to allow high utilization of teleprocessing links, but without requiring excessive processing power to achieve the high utilization. There has been considerable speculation concerning the rate of actual data flow through congested routes when using the Internet's current congestion control algorithms; instead, it should be measured in a range of realistic cases. If peak–busy–hour goodput under congestion is near the theoretical maximum, publicize the data and move on to other requirements. If not, then the IETF should seek a better standard (e.g., they might explore XTP's adaptive rate–based approach and other proposals).

Functions, such as class of service and priority, that let an enterprise control use of bandwidth also may help meet service level agreements. On the one hand, the absence of these functions may inhibit TCP/IP usage in corporate networks, especially when predictable interactive response times are required. On the other hand, few vendors have felt motivated to implement TCP's architected type–of–service, and priority tends to be handled in a non–standard way (e.g., to assure that interactive well–known ports, such as Telnet, get faster response times than non–interactive well–known ports, such as file transfer). The IETF should address these conflicting issues. If the ad hoc techniques can be demonstrated to be adequate, then they should be standardized; otherwise, effective techniques should continue to be developed and then standardized. The performance of TCP is not part of IPng, however, the IPng transition should include work on transports being able to assure very high utilization of network access links and otherwise assured end–to–end service characteristics.

Commercial users often require the options of a higher level of service for a higher cost, or a lower level of service for a lower cost (e.g., some businesses pay top dollar to assure fast response time during business hours, but choose less expensive satellite services for data backup during the night). Pervasive use of IPv4's type–of–service markings might satisfy this requirement.

To discourage waste of bandwidth and other expensive resources, corporations want to account for their use. Direct cost recovery would let an entity measure and benchmark its efficiency with minimal economic distortion. Alternatives, such as placing these costs into corporate over-head or charging per connection, make sense when the administrative cost of implementing usage–based accounting is high enough to intro-duce more economic distortion than the alternatives would. For example, connection–based costs alone may be adequate for a resource (such as LAN bandwidth) that is not scarce or expensive, but a combination of a connection cost and a usage cost may be more appropriate for a more scarce or expensive resource (such as WAN bandwidth). Balance must be maintained between the overhead of accounting and the granularity of cost allocation.

Transition. As the use of IPv4 continues to grow, the day may come when no more IPv4 network addresses are available, and no additional networks will be able to connect to the Internet. Classless Inter–Domain Routing (CIDR) and careful gleaning of the address space will postpone that cutoff for several years. The hundreds of millions of people on net-works that do get IPv4 addresses won't be affected directly by the exhaustion of the address space, but they will miss the opportunity to communicate with those less lucky.

Because the Internet is too large for all of its users to cutover to IPng quickly, IPng must coexist well with IPv4. Furthermore, IPv4 users won't spend the time, effort, and money to upgrade to IPng without a compel-ling reason. Access to new services will not be a strong enough motiva-tion, since new services will want to support both the IPng users and the IPv4 users. Only services that cannot exist on IPv4 will be willing to use IPng exclusively. Moreover, if IPng requires significantly more resources (e.g., storage, memory, or administrative complexity) than does IPv4, users will not install IPng unless it has clear benefits over IPv4. Indeed, the millions of users of low–end systems (DOS, sub–notebooks) might not ever be able to use IPng if it takes much more memory. Thus there will be a long period of coexistence between IPng and IPv4, so coexistence needs to be quite painless, and not be based on any assumption that IPv4 use will diminish quickly, if ever.

Secure Operation. Many corporations will stick with their private net-works until public ones can guarantee equivalent confidentiality, integrity, and availability. It is not clear that additional architecture is needed to satisfy this requirement; perhaps more widespread use of exist-ing security technology can suffice. For example, the IETF could encourage wide deployment of Generic Security Service, and then solicit feedback on whether additional security requirements need to be satisfied. Note that businesses are so concerned about network cost control mechanisms that they want them secured against tampering. IPng should not interfere with firewalls, which many corporations consider essential.

Heterogeneity. Corporate users want the Internet to accommodate multiple protocol suites. Several different protocol suites are growing in use, and some older ones will be used for many more years. Although many people wish there were only one protocol in the world, there is little agreement on which one it should be.

Since the marketplace has not settled on one approach to handling multiple protocols, IPng should be flexible enough to accommodate a variety of technical approaches to achieving heterogeneity. For example, most networking protocols assume they will be the dominate protocol that transports all others; protocol designers should pay more attention to making their protocols easily transported by others. IPng needs to be flexible enough to accommodate the major multiprotocol trends, including multiprotocol transport networking (X/OPEN document G306), tunneling (both IP being the tunnel and being tunneled), and link sharing (e.g., point–to–point protocol and frame relay). Fair sharing of bandwidth by different protocols is especially important.

Additional Requirements. Corporate users have other specific requirements and interests. They are, however, lower priorities than are robust service, transition, secure operation, and heterogeneity.

Scale. If IPng satisfies the scaling requirement of the Internet, then it satisfies it for corporate networks *a fortiori*.

Topological Flexibility. Today a TCP/IP host moved to a different subnet needs a new IP address. Such moves and changes can become a significant administrative cost. Moreover, mobile hosts require flexible topology. Note how the wireless world is trying to defeat the subnet model of addressing either by proxy or by IP address servers. Perhaps IPng needs an addressing model more flexible than subnetting, both to reduce the administrative burden and to facilitate roaming users.

The need to eliminate single points of failure drives the business requirement for multi–tail attachment of hosts to networks. Corporate users complain that TCP/IP can non–disruptively switch a connection from a broken route to a working one only if the new route leads to the same adapter on the end system.

Flow and Resource Reservation. Corporate users are becoming more interested in transmitting both non–isochronous and isochronous information together across the same link. IPng should coexist effectively with the isochronous protocols being developed for the Internet.

The Internet protocols should take advantage of services that may be offered by an underlying fast packet switching service. Constant–bit–rate and variable–bit–rate services typically require specification of, and conformance to, traffic descriptors and specification of quality–of–service (QoS) objectives from applications or users. The Internet's isochronous protocols should provide mechanisms to take advantage of multimedia services that will be offered by fast packet–switching networks, and must ensure that QoS guarantees are preserved all the way up the protocol stacks to the applications. Protocols using available bit–rate services may achieve better bandwidth utilization if they react to congestion messages from a fast packet–switching network, and if they consider consequences of cell discard (e.g., if one cell of an IP datagram is discarded, it would be a waste to continue forwarding the rest of the cells in that datagram; also, selective retransmit should be revisited in this context).

When the Internet protocol suite allows mixing of non–isochronous and isochronous traffic on one medium, it should provide mechanisms to discourage inappropriate reservation of resources; e.g., a Telnet connection probably doesn't need to reserve 45 Mbps. Accounting, class–of–service, and well–known port distinctions are possible ways to satisfy that requirement.

Configuration, Administration, and Operation. Businesses would like dynamic but secure updating of Domain Name System (DNS) servers, both to ease moves and changes and to facilitate cutover to backup hosts. In this vein, secure and dynamic interaction between DNS and Dynamic Host Configuration Protocol is required.[11] The IETF should encourage wide deployment of DHCP, and solicit feedback on whether additional configuration requirements need to be satisfied.

Support for Mobility. Wireless technology opens up opportunities for new TCP/IP applications that are specific to mobile hosts. In addition to coordinating with organizations developing wireless standards, the IETF also should encourage the specification of new TCP/IP applications enabled by wireless, such as connectionless messaging.

IPng should deal well with the characteristics peculiar to wireless (delay, error rates, etc.).

Policy–Based Routing. Policy–based routing is more a solution than a requirement. Businesses rarely require a general purpose policy architecture, although they do state requirements that policy–based routing could satisfy. For example, corporations do not want to carry for free the transit traffic of other enterprises, and they may not want their sensitive data to flow through links controlled by certain other enterprises. Policy–based routing is one possible way to satisfy those requirements, but there seems to be a concern that general purpose policy–based routing may have high administrative costs and low routing performance.

Summary. Enhancements to the Internet Protocol suite, together with wider deployment of some of its existing architectures, could satisfy the requirements of commercial customers while retaining IPv4. Expansion of the address space eventually will be necessary to allow continued Internet growth, but from a technical perspective the addressing issue of IPng is not an immediate concern.[12]

Nevertheless, the TCP/IP community should establish a direction for enlargement of the address space, because unfounded publicity about the address space is scaring away potential TCP/IP users. If the IETF does not provide direction on how its address space will grow, then people may use non–standard, and probably incompatible, approaches.

Evolutionary Possibilities for the Internetwork Layer

J. Noel Chiappa

Background and Context. A project called Nimrod, which aims to produce a next-generation routing architecture for the Internet, has produced, as part of its work, a somewhat different perspective on the potential future evolutionary path of the internetwork layer. This perspective is based on an established school of thought about how to design large-scale systems. This section both explains that thinking to some degree, and uses it to describe what the future evolution of the internetwork layer might look like.

Basic Principles of Large-Scale System Design. The Nimrod routing architecture springs, in part, from a design vision that sees the entire internetwork layer, although distributed across all the hosts and routers of the internetwork, as a single system.

Approaching the internetwork layer from this direction, one would naturally take a typical system designer point of view, and think of the modularization of the system: choosing the functional boundaries that divide the system up into functional units, and defining the interaction between these units. This modularization is the key part of the system design process. Thinking about the interaction is part of the modularization process, as it affects the placement of the functional boundaries. Poor placement leads to overly complex interaction, or to interaction that is needed but cannot be realized.

These issues are even more important in a system which is expected to have a long lifetime. Correct placement of the functional boundaries, to clearly and simply break up the system into its truly fundamental units, is a necessity if the system is to endure and serve the internetwork community well. It will be readily appreciated that a global communication system presents a particular challenge along these lines, since not only is the installed base substantial, but the inherent need for interoperability means that making changes, even in an evolutionary way, is more difficult than it would be with a similarly-sized overall investment in many independent smaller systems.

The Internetwork Layer Service Model. Let us return to the view of the internetwork layer as a system. That system provides certain services to its clients; that is, it instantiates a "service model." Without a definition of the service model that the internetwork layer is supposed to provide, it will be impossible to select the specific mechanisms at the internetwork level which are needed to provide that service model.

To answer the question of what the service model ought to be, one can view the internetwork layer itself as a subsystem of an even larger system-the entire internetwork itself. From that point of view, the issue of the service model of the internetwork layer is clearer. The services provided by the internetwork layer are no longer purely abstract, but can be thought of as the external module interface of the internetwork layer module. If it becomes clear what overall services the internetwork as a whole should provide, and then where to put the functional boundaries of the internetwork layer as a whole, the service model of the internetwork layer should be easier to define.

In general terms, it seems that the unreliable packet ought to remain the fundamental building block of the internetwork layer. The design principle which says that one can take any packet and discard it with no warning or other action, or take any router and turn it off with no warning, and have the system continue to work, seems very powerful. The simplicity of component design (since routers don't have to take extraordinary measures to retain a packet of which they have the only copy) and overall system robustness resulting from these two assumptions are absolutely necessary.

In detail, however, particularly in areas that are still the subject of research and experimentation (such as resource allocation, security, etc.), it is difficult to provide a finished definition of exactly what the service model of the internetwork layer ought to be. However, in any event, by viewing the internetwork layer as a large system, one starts to think about what subsystems are needed to implement it and provide its service model, and what the interaction among them should look like. Until the service model of the internetwork layer is more clearly visible, though, such a discussion is necessarily rather nebulous.

State and Flows in the Internetwork Layer. The internetwork layer as a whole contains a variety of information, of diverse lifetimes. Taken together, this information is the internetwork layer's "state." Some of the information comprising this state is stored in the routers, and some is stored in the packets flowing through the network, etc.

The internetwork layer's state can be characterized by several different classifications of that state. For example, the term "forwarding state" is used here to refer to information in the packet which records something about the progress of this individual packet through the network (such as the hop count, or the pointer into a source route). Other kinds of state, some described below, contain various kinds of information about what service the user wants from the network (such as the destination of the packet, etc.).

User and Service State. "User state" is the term used here for state which reflects the service requests of the user. This is information which can be sent in each packet, or stored in the router and applied to multiple packets, depending on which makes the most engineering sense. It is still called user state, even when a copy is stored in the routers.

User state can be divided into two classes; "critical" (such as destination addresses), without which the packets cannot be forwarded at all, and "non-critical" (such as a resource allocation class), without which the packets can still be forwarded, although probably not quite in the way the user would most prefer. There are a range of possible mechanisms for getting this user state to the routers; it may be put in every packet, or placed there by a setup. In the latter case, there is a whole range of possibilities for how to get it back when it is lost, such as periodically placing a copy in a normal data packet.

However, another kind of state, which cannot be stored in each packet, needs to be defined. Called "server state" here, it describes the longer term situation, across the life of many packets. In other words, the server state is inherently associated with a number of packets over some timeframe (for example, how much of a resource allocation has been used), and is meaningless for a single packet.

The existence of server state apparently contradicts the commonly accepted stateless model of routers somewhat, but this contradiction is more apparent than real. The routers already contain state, such as routing table entries, without which it is virtually impossible to handle user traffic. All that is being changed is the amount, granularity, and lifetime, of state in the routers, so the change is not really that radical.

Some of this service state may need to be installed in a fairly reliable fashion; for example, if there is service state related to routing, or to billing or allocation of resources for a critical application, one more or less needs to be guaranteed that this service state has been correctly installed.

To the extent that state is included in the routers (either as service state or as user state), one has to be able to associate that state with the proper packets. The fields in the packets used for this purpose are called "tags" here.

Flows. It is useful to step back a bit at this point, and think about the traffic in the network. Some of it will be from applications that are basically transactions; that is, they require only a single packet, or a very small number of them. (The term "datagram" refers here to such applications, and the term "packet" describes the unit of transmission through the network.) However, other packets are part of longer-lived communications, which have been termed "flows." [13]

From the user's point of view, a flow can be seen as a sequence of packets that are related, usually by virtue of having originated from a single application instance. In an internetwork layer with a more complex service model (for example, one which supports such features as resource allocation), the flow would have service requirements to pass on to some or all of the subsystems which provide those services.

To the internetworking layer, a flow can be seen as a sequence of packets that share all the attributes that the internetworking layer cares about. This includes, but is not limited to: source/destination, path, resource allocation, accounting/authorization, authentication/security.

There is not necessarily a one-to-one mapping from flows to anything else, be it a TCP connection or an application instance. A single flow might contain several TCP connections (for example, with the file transfer application, where one has the control connection and a number of data connections), or a single application might have several flows (for example, multimedia conferencing, with one flow for the audio, another for a graphic window, etc., each having different resource requirements in terms of bandwidth, delay, etc.)

Flows are not inherently unicast. They may also be multicast constructs, having multiple sources and destinations. Multicast flows are somewhat more complex than unicast, as there is a larger pool of state distributed across the network which must be made coherent, but the concepts are similar.

Practical Details of Flows. There is an interesting architectural issue here. To begin, there will probably be many different internetwork level subsystems (such as routing, resource allocation, security/access-control, and accounting). Now, there are two choices:

- First, to allow each individual subsystem which uses the concept of flows to define for itself what it thinks a flow is, and determine which values in which fields within the packet define a given flow for that subsystem. Presumably, one would then have to allow 2 flows for subsystem X to map onto 1 flow for subsystem Y to map onto 3 flows for subsystem Z; that is, users can mix and match flows as they wish.
- Second, to define a standard flow mechanism for the internetwork layer, along with a single means within the packet of identifying the flow. Then, if two streams of packets have different requirements in any subsystem, one would need a separate flow everywhere for each.

The former option has the advantage of being a little easier to deploy incrementally, since there is no need to agree on a common flow mechanism. It may also save on replicated state (if there are 3 flows which are the same for subsystem X, but different for Y, there only needs to be one set of X state). This option also has a lot of flexibility. The latter option is simple and straightforward.

The engineering choice of which is the better option is not trivial; the analysis of the cost and benefits of each depends on conditions which cannot yet be determined, such as the percentage of flows that will need to share the same state in certain subsystems. In general, however, simple and straightforward seems to be better. This system is quite complex already, and the benefits of being able to mix and match may not be worth the added complexity. It seems that any place it is possible to make things simpler, that should be the preferred choice. So, for the moment, the assumption here is that there will be a single, systemwide, definition of flows.

The packets which belong to a flow could be identified by a tag consisting of a number of fields (such as addresses, ports, etc.). However, it may be more straightforward and foolproof to simply identify which flow a packet belongs to by means of a specialized tag field (the "flow-id") in the internetwork header. Given that one can seemingly always find situations where the existing fields alone don't do the job, and thus still need a separate field to do the job correctly, it seems best to take this simple, direct approach.

The simplicity of globally-unique flow-id's (or at least a flow-id which is unique along the path of the flow) is also desirable; although it may take more bits in the header, one doesn't have to worry about all the mechanism needed to remap locally-unique flow-id's. From the perspective of designing a widely-deployed system with a long lifetime, simplicity and directness is the only way to go. That consideration translates into the strategy of having flows named solely by unique flow-id's, rather than by some complex semantics using existing fields.

However, the issue of how to recognize which packets belong to flows is somewhat orthogonal to the issue of whether the internetwork level should recognize flows at all. Is this a good idea?

Flows and State. To the extent that service state exists in the routers, one has to be able to associate that state with the related packets. In fact, this represents a fundamental reason for the explicit recognition of flows. However, while access to a service state is one reason to explicitly recognize flows at the internetwork layer, it is not the only one.

If the user has requirements in a number of areas (for example, routing and access control), they can theoretically communicate these requirements to the routers by placing a copy of all the relevant information in each packet within the internetwork header. If many subsystems of the internetwork are involved and the requirements are complex, this information could take up many bits.

There are two schools of thought on how to proceed. The first says that for reasons of robustness and simplicity, all user state ought to be repeated in each packet. For efficiency reasons, the routers may cache such information, probably along with precomputed data derived from the user state. (It makes sense to store such cached information along with any applicable server state, of course.)

The second school says that if a client is going to generate many packets, it makes engineering sense to give all this information to the routers once, and from then on place a tag (the flow-id) in the packet which tells the routers where to find that information. It is simply going to be too inefficient to carry all the user state around all the time. This is purely an engineering efficiency reason, but it is a significant one. (There is clearly no point in storing in the routers any user state about packets that are providing datagram service; the datagram service has usually come and gone in the same packet, and this discussion is about state retention.)

There is a somewhat more fundamental line of thinking which argues that the routers will inevitably come to contain more and more information about the user state. (In fact, this is already starting to happen; most high-performance routers include caches of such information as the preferred means of gaining that speed.) The question is whether that information will be installed by means of an explicit mechanism, or whether the routers will simply infer it from watching the packets that pass through them. To the extent that retention of user state in the routers is inevitable, there are obvious benefits to be gained from recognizing that fact, and explicitly designing an installation mechanism for that purpose. This strategy is far more likely to give satisfactory results than a more ad hoc mechanism.

It seems unlikely that there is any benefit to an intermediate position, in which one subsystem installs user state in the routers, and another carries a copy of its user state in each packet. It appears to make little sense to design a system in which one internetwork layer subsystem, such as resource allocation, carries user state in all packets (perhaps with a hint in the packets to help find potentially cached copies in the router), and have another subsystem, such as routing, use a direct installation technique with a flow-id tag in the packets. This seems to have the disadvantages of both, without the advantage in simplicity of having only one. We should do one or the other, based on a consideration of the efficiency/robustness/complexity tradeoffs.

There are also other intermediate positions that incorporate both mechanisms, but it is unclear at this point how useful they might be. In one scenario, a flow might use one of these techniques for all the subsystems it uses, and another flow might use the other technique for all of them. There is potentially some use to this, although the cost in complexity of supporting two separate mechanisms for handling user state may not be worth the benefits. In another scenario, a flow might use one mechanism with one particular router along its path, and another for a different router. A number of different reasons exist as to why one might do this, including the possibility that not all routers will support the same mechanisms simultaneously.

In addition, if there is a way of installing such flow-associated state, it makes sense to have only one, which all subsystems use, instead of building a separate one for each flow.

It is difficult to make this choice—between direct installation in the routers, and placing the information in each packet—without a better idea of exactly how much user state the network is likely to use in the future. For example, it might turn out that 500-byte headers are needed to include the full source route, resource reservation, and other user state in every header.

It is also difficult to make the choice without consideration of the actual mechanisms involved. As a general principle, it is best if the process of recovering lost state is as local as possible, and the number of entities which have to become involved is fairly limited. For instance, currently, when a router crashes, traffic is rerouted around it without needing to open a new TCP connection. From this perspective, the installation option looks a lot more attractive if it is simple and relatively cheap to reinstall user state when a router crashes, without otherwise causing a lot of work.

However, given the likely growth in user state, the necessity for server state, the requirement for reliable installation, and a number of similar considerations, it seems that direct installation of the user state, and explicit recognition of flows, through a unified definition and tag mechanism in the packet, is the best design choice.

Ramifications of Flows. Once the idea of flows has been accepted as a basic element of the architecture—one that presumably will carry a large share of the traffic—one then has to examine the ramifications of that design decision. These begin with the basic internetwork packet format. For example, should there be separate packet formats for the two service modes, flow and datagram, and if only one format, what optimizations, if any, should it include for the flow mode?

Another ramification of explicit support for flows at the internetwork layer that needs to be considered is its impact on the internal organization of the internetwork layer. Given that the internetwork layer provides two distinctly different services, should those services be provided independently by the internetwork layer, or should one be built on top of the other, using the facilities provided by the base service?

There is an excellent case that one service should be built on top of the other, leading to a simpler internetwork layer than if completely separate mechanisms must be provided. If this is the case, then which service should be the base? It seems inescapable that datagram service should be built on top of flows, and not the other alternative, since one can provide datagram service on top of flows, but not the other way around.

Conclusion. This discussion should show that, although to many people the current basic structure and services provided by the internetwork layer appear to approach some final ideal, it is in fact quite possible that future developments will include radical departures from past practice. In particular, the supposition that the basic internal mechanism of the internetwork layer should be flows is quite novel, and accepted far less widely than support for flows as a service provided to the user.

Hopefully, the analysis above will have also shown that such speculations are not merely "change for the sake of change," but are grounded in a hard look at inescapable fundamentals, such as how much information the system will need to operate—an amount which will have to grow over time in order to provide the increased capabilities needed both by the users and by new applications; where information is in the overall system; and how it gets from where it is created to where it is needed, and how much overhead is involved in that transfer.

Market Viability as an IPng Criteria

John Curran
BBN Planet Corporation

In an open marketplace, adoption of new technology is driven by consumer demand. New technologies that wish to succeed in the marketplace must provide new capabilities or reduced costs to gain consumer confidence. Internetworking technologies can be particularly difficult to deploy and must provide a correspondingly high return on investment. In order to determine market viability of new internetworking technology, it's necessary to compare the required deployment effort against the potential benefits as seen by the customer. Viability in the marketplace is an important requirement for any IPng candidate, and this perspective summarizes some important factors in determining market viability of IPng proposals.

"Pushing" Internetworking Technology. The adoption of a single IPng protocol by the computing industry could generate general acceptance in the networking industry. There is ample evidence to support this view; for example, some of today's more prevalent networking protocols gained initial market acceptance through bundling with computer operating systems (e.g., IP via UNIX, DECnet via VMS, etc.) It should be noted, however, that this approach to technology deployment is by no means assured, and some of today's most popular internetworking software (Novell, etc.) have thrived despite alternatives bundled by computing manufacturers. Given that IPng will have to compete against a well–established and mature internetworking protocol (IPv4), promotion of IPng by computer system manufacturers should be recognized as highly desirable, but not as sufficient on its own to ensure IPng acceptance in the marketplace.

Can IPng Compete Against IPv4? Given the large installed base of IPv4 systems, computer system manufacturers will need to continue to provide IPv4 capabilities for the foreseeable future. With both IPng and IPv4 support in their new systems, users will be facing a difficult choice between using IPv4 and IPng for internetworking. Existing IPv4 users will migrate to IPng for one of three possible reasons:

New Functionality Not Found in IPv4. IPng needs to provide functionality equivalent to that currently provided by IPv4. It remains to be seen whether additional functionality (such as resource reservation, auto–configuration, auto–registration, support for mobility, or secure operation) will be included in the default profile for IPng hosts. In order to provide motivation for users to migrate to IPng, it will be necessary for IPng to offer capabilities beyond those already provided by IPv4.

Costs of Using IPng. It is quite unlikely that migration to IPng will result in cost savings in any organization. Migration to IPng will certainly result in an increased need for training and engineering, and hence increased costs.

Connectivity to Otherwise Unreachable IPng Hosts. For existing sites with valid IPv4 network assignments, connectivity is not affected until address depletion occurs. Systems with globally–unique IPv4 addresses will have complete connectivity to any systems, since backwards–compatible communication is required of new IPng hosts.

From the perspective of an existing IPv4 site, IPng provides little tangible benefit until IPv4 address depletion occurs and organizations reachable only via IPng appear. Given the absence of benefits for migrating, it is uncertain whether a significant base of IPng sites will occur prior to IPv4 address depletion.

Sites which are not yet running IP have little motivation to deploy IPng for the immediate future. As long as IPv4 network assignments are available, new sites have the choice to use IPv4, which provides the sufficient internetworking capabilities (measured in functionality, cost, and connectivity) for many organizations today. Given the parity in IPng and IPv4 capabilities, IPv4 (as a more mature internetworking protocol) is the more probable choice for organizations just now selecting an internetworking protocol.

Once IPv4 address assignments are no longer available, sites wishing to participate in the global Internet will have a very difficult decision in selection of an internetworking protocol. Use of the IPng protocol alone does not ensure complete internetworking between IPng–only sites and IPv4–only sites since, by definition, there will be insufficient space to map all IPng addresses into the IPv4 address space, and yet an IPv4–only host must have an IPv4 address equivalent to refer to any given IPng host. In the absence of standard dynamic mapping algorithms between IPng–only hosts and a pool of IPv4 addresses, it appears that IPng–only sites will only have access to a partial set of IPv4 sites at any given moment.

Internetworking services which do not allow complete access to the global Internet (IPv4 and IPng in the post–IPv4–address–depletion world) are clearly not as valuable as services which offer complete Internet access. Sites which are unable to obtain IPv4 network assignments will be seeking services which can provide complete Internet service. Additionally, some sites will have privately numbered IPv4 networks and will desire similar Internet services which provide transparent access to the entire Internet. This will lead to the development of dynamic network address translation (NAT) services.

Summary. No internetworking vendor (whether host, router, or service vendor) can afford to deploy and support products and services which are not desired in the marketplace. Given the potential proliferation of NAT devices, it is not clear that IPng will secure sufficient following to attain market viability. In the past, we have seen internetworking protocols fail in the marketplace despite vendor promotion. IPng will not succeed if it is not actively deployed. As currently envisioned, IPng may not be ambitious enough in the delivery of new capabilities to compete against IPv4 and the inevitable arrival of NAT devices. In order to meet the requirement for viability in the marketplace, IPng needs to deliver superior functionality over IPv4 while offering some form of transparent access between the IPv4 and IPng communities once IPv4 address depletion has occurred.

IPng and Corporate Resistance to Change

Eric Fleischman
Boeing Computer Services

Fortune 100 corporations which have heavily invested in TCP/IP technology in order to achieve their (non–computer–related) business goals do not generally view the coming of IPng with excitement. The IETF community should be warned that their own enthusiasm for IPng is generally not shared by end users, and that it may be difficult to convince end users to deploy IPng technologies internally within their own networks. This is due to a difference in perspective and goals between the IETF and the large corporate end user.

The Internet and TCP/IP Protocols Are Not Identical. The Internet Engineering Task Force (IETF) community closely associates TCP/IP protocols with the Internet. In many cases it is difficult to discern from the IETF perspective where the worldwide Internet infrastructure ends and the services of the TCP/IP Protocol Suite begin—they are not always distinguishable from each other. Historically they both stem from the same roots: the Advanced Research Projects Agency (ARPA) of the U.S. Department of Defense (DoD) was the creator of TCP/IP and of the seminal Internet. The services provided by the Internet have been generally realized by the TCP/IP protocol family. The Internet has, in turn, become a primary vehicle for the definition, development, and transmission of the various TCP/IP protocols in their various stages of maturity. Thus, the IETF community has a mindset which assumes that there is a strong symbiotic relationship between the two.

End users do not share this assumption—despite the fact that many end users have widely deployed TCP/IP protocols and extensively use the Internet. It is important for the IETF community to realize that TCP/IP protocols and the Internet are generally viewed to be two quite dissimilar things by the large corporate end user. That is, while the Internet may be a partial selling point for some TCP/IP purchases, it has historically rarely been a significant motivation for the majority of purchases. This historical trend is in the process of changing since the advent of the World Wide Web (WWW) and the recent growth of Internet–based electronic commerce. However, until very recently, surprisingly many end users had sizable internal TCP/IP infrastructures but no Internet connectivity at all. For this reason, many end users view the relationship between the Internet and TCP/IP protocols to be tenuous at best.

More importantly, many corporations have made substantial investments in external (non–Internet) communications infrastructures. A variety of reasons account for this, including that, until recently, the Internet was excluded from the bilateral agreements and international tariffs necessary for international commerce. In any case, end users today are not (in general) dependent upon the Internet to support their business processes. This is not to deny that many Fortune 100 employees are directly dependent upon the Internet to fulfill their job responsibilities: The Internet has become an invaluable tool for many corporations' research and education activities. However, it is rarely used today for activities which directly affect the corporations' financial bottom line: commerce. By contrast, large end users with extensive internal TCP/IP deployments may perhaps view TCP/IP technology to be critically important to their corporation's core business processes.

Secure Operation. Another core philosophical difference between large end users and the IETF is concerning the importance of security islands (i.e., firewalls). The prevalent IETF perspective is that security islands are A Bad Thing. The basic IETF assumption is that the applications they are designing are universally needed and that security islands provide undesirable filters for that usage. That is, the IETF generally has a world view which presupposes that data access should be unrestricted and widely available.

By contrast, corporations generally regard data as being a sensitive corporate asset which, if compromised, may in some cases damage the corporation's business. Corporations, therefore, presuppose that data exchange should be restricted.

Large corporate end users also tend to believe that each class of their employees has differing data access needs. Factory workers have different computing needs than accountants who have different needs than aeronautical engineers who have different needs than research scientists. A corporation's networking department seeks to ensure that each class of employee actually receives the type of services they require. A firewall is one of the mechanisms by which the appropriate service levels may be provided to the appropriate class of employee, particularly in regard to external access capabilities.

More importantly, there are differing classes of computer resources within a corporation. A certain percentage of these resources are critical to the continuing viability of that corporation. These systems should not be accessible from outside of the company. These "corporate jewels" must be protected by viable security mechanisms. Firewalls are one very important component within a much larger total security solution.

For these reasons we concur with the observation made by Yakov Rekhter of IBM and Bob Moskowitz of Chrysler in their joint electronic mail message to the Big–Internet mail list on January 28, 1994. They wrote:

> "Hosts within sites that use IP can be partitioned into three categories: Hosts that do not require Internet access. Hosts that need access to a limited set of Internet services (e.g., Email, FTP, net news, remote login) which can be handled by application layer relays. Hosts that need unlimited access (provided via IP connectivity) to the Internet."

The exact mechanism by which a corporation will satisfy the differing needs of these three classes of devices must be independently determined by that corporation based upon a number of internal factors. Each independent solution will determine how that corporation defines their own version of firewalls.

Thus, if corporate end users use the Internet at all, they will generally do so through a security island of their own devising. The existence of the security island is yet another element to (physically and emotionally) decouple the end user from the Internet. That is, while the end user may use the Internet, their networks (in the general case) are neither directly attached to it, nor are their core business processes today critically dependent upon it. As previously mentioned, this orientation may be in the process of changing with the advent of the WWW and the growth of Internet–based electronic commerce.

Networking. The following five key characteristics describe Boeing's environment, and are probably generally representative of other large TCP/IP deployments. An understanding of these characteristics is very important for obtaining insight into how the large corporate end user is likely to view IPng.

Host Ratio. Many corporations explicitly try to limit the number of their TCP/IP hosts that are directly accessible from the Internet. This is done for a variety of reasons, chief among them, security. While the ratio of those hosts that have direct Internet access capabilities to those hosts without such capabilities will vary from company to company, ratios ranging from 1:1,000 to 1:10,000 (or more) are not uncommon. The implication of this host ratio is that the state of the worldwide (IPv4) Internet address space only directly impacts a tiny percentage of the currently deployed TCP/IP hosts within a large corporation. This is true even if the entire population is currently using Internet–assigned addresses.

Router–to–Host Ratio. Most corporations have significantly more TCP/IP hosts than they have IP routers. Ratios ranging between 100:1 to 600:1 (or more) are common. The implication of this routers–to–host ratio is that a transition approach which solely demands changes to routers is generally much less disruptive to a corporation than an approach which demands changes to both routers and hosts.

Business Factor. Large corporations exist to fulfill some business purpose such as the construction of airplanes, baseball bats, cars, or some other product or service offering. Computing is an essential tool to help automate business processes in order to more efficiently accomplish the business goals of the corporation. Automation is accomplished via applications. Data communications, operating systems, and computer hardware are the tools used by applications to accomplish their goals. Thus, users actually buy applications, not networking technologies. The central lesson of the business factor is that IPng will be deployed according to the applications which use it and not because it is a better technology.

Integration Factor. Large corporations currently support many diverse computing environments. This diversity limits the effectiveness of a corporation's computing assets by hindering data sharing, application interoperability, application portability, and software reusability. The net effect is stunted application life cycles and increased support costs. Data communications is but one of the domains which contribute this diversity. For example, the Boeing Company currently has deployed at least sixteen different protocol families within its networks (e.g., TCP/IP, SNA, DECnet, OSI, IPX/SPX, AppleTalk, XNS, etc.). Each distinct protocol family population potentially implies unique training, administrative, support, and infrastructure requirements. Consequently, corporate goals often exist to eliminate or merge diverse data communications protocol family deployments in order to reduce network support costs and to increase the number of devices which can communicate together (i.e., foster interoperability). This results in a basic abhorrence to the possibility of introducing "Yet Another Protocol" (YAP).

Subsequently, an IPng solution which introduces an entirely new set of protocols will be negatively viewed simply because its by–products are more roadblocks to interoperability coupled with more work, greater expense, and greater risk to support the end users' computing resources and business goals. Having said this, it should be observed that this abhorrence may be partially overcome by extenuating circumstances such as applications using IPng which meet critical end–user requirements or by broad (international) commercial support.

Inertia Factor. There is a natural tendency to continue to use the current IP protocol, IPv4, regardless of the state of the Internet's IPv4 address space. Motivations supporting inertia include the following: existing application dependencies (including Application Programming Interface (API) dependencies); opposition to additional protocol complexity; budgetary constraints limiting additional hardware/software expenses; additional address management and naming service costs; transition costs; support costs; training costs; etc. As the number of Boeing's deployed TCP/IP hosts continues to grow toward the 100,000 mark, the inertial power of this population becomes increasingly strong. However, inertia even exists with smaller populations simply because the cost to convert or upgrade the systems are not warranted. Consequently, pockets of older "legacy system" technologies often exist in specific environments (e.g., we still have pockets of the archaic BSC protocol). The significance of this inertia is that unless there are significant business benefits to justify an IPng deployment, economics will oppose such a deployment. Thus, even if the forthcoming IPng protocol proves to be "the ultimate and perfect protocol," it is unrealistic to imagine that the entire IPv4 population will ever transition to IPng. This means that should we deploy IPng within our networks, there will be an ongoing requirement for our internal IPng deployment to be able to communicate with our internal IPv4 community. This requirement is unlikely to go away with time.

Address Depletion Doesn't Resonate with Users. The central, bottom–line question concerning IPng from the large corporate user perspective is: What are the benefits which will justify the expense of deploying IPng? At this time we can conceive of only four possible causes which may motivate us to consider deploying IPng:

Possible Cause:	**Possible Corporate Response:**
1. Many remote (external) peers solely use IPng.	Gateway external systems only.
2. Internet requires IPng usage.	Gateway external systems only.
3. "Must–have" products are tightly coupled with IPng (e.g., flows for real–time applications).	Upgrade internal corporate network to support IPng where that functionality is needed.
4. Senior management directs IPng usage.	Respond appropriately.

It should explicitly be noted that the reasons which are compelling the Internet Community to create IPng (i.e., the scalability of IPv4 over the Internet) are not themselves adequate motivations for users to deploy IPng within their own private networks. That is, should IPng usage become mandated as a prerequisite for Internet usage, a probable response to this mandate would be to convert our few hosts with external access capabilities to become IPng–to–IPv4 application–layer gateways. This would leave the remainder of our vast internal TCP/IP deployment unchanged. Consequently, given gateways for external access, there may be little motivation for a company's internal network to support IPng.

User's IPv4 "Itches" Need Scratching. The end user's loyalty to IPv4 should not be interpreted to mean that everything is necessarily perfect with existing TCP/IP deployments and that there are therefore no "itches" which an improved IPv4 network layer—or an IPng—can't "scratch." The purpose of this section is to address some of the issues which are very troubling to many end users. Should IPng provide a solution to these problems then it may become viewed with increasing favor by the end user:

Security. TCP/IP protocols are commonly deployed upon broadcast media (for example, Ethernet Version 2). However, TCP/IP mechanisms to encrypt passwords or data which traverse this media are inadequate. This is a very serious matter which needs to be expeditiously resolved. An integrated and effective TCP/IP security architecture needs to be defined and become widely implemented across all vendors' TCP/IP products.

User Address Space Privacy. Current IPv4 network addressing policies require that end users go to external entities to obtain IP network numbers for use in their own internal networks. These external entities often determine whether these network requests are "valid" or not. It is our belief that a corporation's internal addressing policies are their own private affair—except in the specific instances in which they may affect others. Consequently, a real need exists for two classes of IPv4 network numbers: those which are (theoretically) visible to the Internet today and thus are subject to external requirements and those which will never be connected to the Internet and thus are strictly private. We believe that the concept of local addresses is a viable compromise between the justifiable need of the Internet to steward scarce global resources and the corporate need for privacy. Local addresses by definition, are non-globally unique addresses which should never be routed (or seen) by the Internet infrastructure. An alternative solution to local addresses would be to have a global address space so large that end users could receive all of the addresses they need without repeatedly having to go to an outside entity to obtain additional addresses as their addressing needs grow.

Self–Defining Networks. Large end users have a pressing need for plug–and–play TCP/IP networks which auto–configure, auto–address, and auto–register. End users have repeatedly demonstrated our inability to make the current manual methods work (that is, heavy penalties for human error). The existing DHCP technology is a good beginning in this direction.

APIs and network integration: End users have deployed many differing complex protocol families. We need tools by which these diverse deployments may become integrated together, along with viable transition tools to migrate proprietary alternatives to TCP/IP–based solutions. We also desire products to use open multi–vendor, multi–platform, exposed APIs which are supported across several data communications protocol families to aid in this integration effort.

International Commerce. End users are generally unsure as to what extent TCP/IP can be universally used for international commerce today, and whether this is a cost–effective and safe option to satisfy our business requirements. Several reliability, security, and quality–of–service questions still surround the business use of the Internet.

Technological Advances. We have ongoing application needs which demand a continual pushing of the existing technology. Among these needs are viable (for example, integratable into our current infrastructures) solutions to the following: mobile hosts, multimedia applications, real–time applications, very high–bandwidth applications, improved very low–bandwidth (for example, radio–based) applications, standard–TCP/IP–based transaction processing applications (for example, multi–vendor distributed databases).

Motivations for Users to Deploy IPng.

Despite this list of IPv4 problem areas, we suspect that there are only two causes which may motivate users to widely deploy IPng:

Add Critical Functionality. If IPng products add critical functionality which IPv4 can't provide (for example, real time applications, multimedia applications, genuine (scalable) plug–and–play networking, etc.), users would be motivated to deploy IPng where that functionality is needed.

However, these deployments must combat the Integration Factor and the Inertia Factor forces which have previously been described. This implies that there must be a significant business gain to justify such a deployment. While it is impossible to predict exactly how this conflict would play out, it is reasonable to assume that IPng would probably be deployed according to an as–needed–only policy. Optimally, specific steps would be taken to protect the remainder of the network from the impact of these localized changes. Of course, should IPng become bundled with "killer applications" (that is, applications which are extremely important to significantly many key business processes) then all bets are off: IPng will become widely deployed. However, it also should be recognized that virtually all (initial) IPng applications, unless they happen to be "killer applications," will have to overcome significant hurdles to be deployed simply because they represent risk and substantially increased deployment and support costs for the end user.

Foster a Convergence. Should IPng foster a convergence between Internet standards and international standards (OSI, for example), this convergence could change IPng's destiny. That is, the networks of many large corporations are currently being driven by sets of strong, but contradictory, requirements: one set demanding compliance with Internet standards (that is, TCP/IP) and another set demanding compliance with international standards.

Worldwide commerce is regulated by governments in accordance with their treaties and legal agreements. Worldwide telecommunications are regulated by the ITU (a United Nations chartered/authorized organization). International Standards (that is, OSI) are the only government–sanctioned method for commercial data communications. While government regulations and restrictions upon TCP/IP–based international commerce have been loosened, the inertia formed during the former era still is being felt. This results in the continuance (in some cases) of OSI infrastructural deployments and plans. This, in turn, must support their own products in order to fulfill their customers' needs.

Also, certain industries (for example, the Electrical Industry (EPRI)) have requirements to address vast numbers of newly networked devices—devices which historically were not networked. This corresponds to a general trend in which previously "dumb" devices (for example, security passes on doors and elevators, thermostats, light switches, etc.) are becoming networked. This trend is called "toasternet" and represents the theoretical possibility of quickly saturating the remaining IPv4 address space. Since IPng products do not yet exist, many believe that the best way in which entities needing large addresses may have their needs met today is via OSI's Connectionless Network Protocol (CLNP).

These factors represent a continuing tension between the very popular and ubiquitous IPv4 protocol and its OSI equivalent, CLNP. Thus, if a means could be found to achieve greater synergy (integration/adoption) between Internet standards and international standards (for example, CLNP) then corporate management may be inclined to mandate internal deployment of the merged standards and promote their external use. Optimally, such a synergy should offer the promise of reducing currently deployed protocol diversity (that is, supports the Integration Factor force). Depending on the specific method by which this convergence is achieved, it may also partially offset the previously mentioned Inertia Factor force, and especially if IPng proves to be a protocol which has already been deployed.

Finally, it should be observed that if IPng could be transparently deployed within an IPv4 community (for example, like the Multicast Backbone (MBONE) is transparently (more or less) deployed within the Internet today) then much of the force of the Integration Factor and the Inertia Factor would be diminished. Current transition plans and approaches for IPng include capabilities which offer the hope that this may be accomplished. To the extent to which IPng can be truly transparent to IPv4 will the deployment of IPng be eased and the natural push–back against it reduced.

User–based IPng Requirements. From this one can see that a mandate to use IPng to communicate over the Internet does not correspondingly imply the need for large corporate networks to generally support IPng within their networks. Thus, while the IPv4 scalability limitations are a compelling reason to identify a specific IPv4 replacement protocol for the Internet, other factors are at work within private corporate networks. These factors imply that large TCP/IP end users will have a continuing need to purchase IPv4 products even after IPng products have become generally available.

However, since the IETF community is actively engaged in identifying an IPng solution, it is desirable that the solution satisfy as many end user needs as possible. For this reason, we would like to suggest that the following are important "user requirements" for any IPng solution:

- The IPng approach must permit users to slowly transition to IPng in a piecemeal fashion. Even if IPng becomes widely deployed, it is unrealistic to expect that users will ever transition all of the extensive IPv4 installed base to IPng. Consequently, the approach must indefinitely support corporate–internal communication between IPng hosts and IPv4 hosts regardless of the requirements of the worldwide Internet.
- The IPng approach must not hinder technological advances from being implemented.
- The IPng approach is expected to eventually foster greater synergy (integration/adoption) between Internet standards and international standards (that is, OSI). (Note that this may be accomplished in a variety of ways including having the Internet standards adopted as international standards or else having the international standards adopted as Internet standards.)
- The IPng approach should have self–defining network (that is, plug–and–play) capabilities. That is, large installations require device portability in which one may readily move devices within one's corporate network and have them auto–configure, auto–address, auto–register, etc., without explicit human administrative overhead at the new location—assuming that the security criteria of the new location have been met.

- The approach must have network security characteristics which are better than existing IPv4 protocols.

Summary. The key factor which will determine whether—and to what extent—IPng will be deployed by large end users is whether IPng will become an essential element for the construction of applications which are critically needed by our businesses. If IPng is bundled with applications which satisfy critical business needs, it will be deployed. If it isn't, it is of little relevance to the large end user. Regardless of what happens to IPng, the large mass of IPv4 devices will ensure that IPv4 will remain an important protocol for the foreseeable future and that continued development of IPv4 products is advisable.

High Performance Networking in the Navy

Dan Green
Phil Irey
Dave Marlow
Karen O'Donoghue
Naval Surface Warfare Center-Dahlgren Division

The U.S. Navy has set up a program through the Space and Naval Warfare Systems Command called the Next Generation Computer Resources (NGCR) Program. The purpose of this program is to identify the evolving needs for information system technology in Navy mission critical systems. The NGCR High Performance Network (HPN) working group was recently established by the NGCR program to examine high performance networks for use on future Navy platforms (aircraft, surface ships, submarines, and certain shore–based applications). This working group is currently reviewing Navy needs. The requirements provided below are based on the HPN working group's current understanding of these Navy application areas. The application areas of interest are further examined below. The time frame for design, development, and deployment of HPN based systems and subsystems is 1996 into the twenty–first century.

We have identified three general problem domains within the mission critical environment that are of interest to the HPN working group. The first is a distributed combat system environment which is analogous to a collection of workstations involved in many varied applications involving multiple sources and types of information. Analog, audio, digital, discrete, graphic, textual, video, and voice information must be coordinated in order to present a single concise view to a commander, operator, or any end user.

The second problem area is the condition of the general internetworking environment. The task of moving information to many heterogeneous systems over various subnetworks is of major concern to the Navy.

Finally, the problem of providing a high–speed interconnect for devices such as sensors and signal processors is important.[14]

These assumptions include accommodation of current functionality, commercial viability, and transitioning. The general requirements include addressing, integrated services architecture, mobility, multicast, and rapid route reconfiguration. Finally, the additional considerations include fault tolerance, policy–based routing, security, and time synchronization. We are interested in participating with the IETF in the development of standards which would apply to mission critical systems. In particular, we are interested in the development of multicast functionality, an integrated services architecture, and support for high performance sub-networks.

Information types required by the HPN working group include voice, live and pre–recorded audio ranging from voice to CD quality (e.g., from sensors), video (1 to 30 frames–per–second in both monochrome and color), image data (static or from real–time sensors), reliable and connec-tionless data transfer, and very high bandwidth (gigabits–per–second) unprocessed sensor data.

Services. Another way of categorizing the HPN application area is by considering the user services that need to be supported. Some of these services are the following:

- process–to–process message passing
- distributed file and database manipulation
- email (within the platform, between platforms, and across the Inter-net)
- teleconferencing (within the platform, between platforms, and across the Internet)
- video monitoring of various physical environments
- voice distribution (as a minimum between computer processes and people)
- image services
- time synchronization
- name or directory services
- network and system management
- security services (support of multilevel data security, privacy and protection)

Assumptions. These assumptions are concerns that we have faith will be accommodated in the IPng process. However, they are of enough importance to this working group to merit identification.

Based on the interests of the HPN working group, we have identified a number of requirements for the IPng protocol set. Many of the necessary capabilities exist in current Internet and ISO network protocols; however, certain capabilities that are beyond the existing standards are needed. Three categories of topics have been identified: Assumptions (topics that we believe will be solved without specific Navy input); general requirements (capabilities that are insufficiently addressed in existing network protocols and of key importance to Navy mission critical applications); and additional considerations (issues that are important, however, no guidance or specific requests are provided at this time).

Application Area. The application area of HPN is the communication network which is a component of the mission critical systems of Navy platforms. The expected endpoints or users of the HPN include humans, computers, and the many devices (cameras, etc.) found on such platforms. The function of these endpoints includes sensor input, signal processors, operator consoles, navigation systems, etc. The endpoints are typically grouped into systems both on platforms and at shore–based sites. These systems perform functions including long–range planning, analysis of sensor information, and machinery control in real time.

We perceive these requirements for an IPng protocol set. Many of the necessary capabilities exist in current Internet and ISO network protocols; however, certain capabilities that are beyond the existing standards are needed.

Accommodation of Current Functionality. The IPng protocols need to provide for at least the existing functionality, in particular:

- The IPng protocols need to provide for the basic connectionless transfer of information from one endpoint to another.
- The IPng protocols need to support multiple subnetwork technologies. This includes but is not limited to Ethernet, FDDI, Asynchronous Transfer Mode (ATM), Fiber Channel, and Scalable Coherent Interface (SCI). These are the subnetwork technologies that are important to the Navy. Ideally, IPng protocols should be subnetwork–independent.
- The IPng protocols need to support hosts that may be multi–homed. Multi–homed implies that a single host may support multiple subnetwork technologies. Multi–homed hosts must have the capability to steer the traffic to selected subnetworks.
- The IPng process needs to recognize that IPng may be only one of several network protocols that a host utilizes.

- The IPng process needs to provide for appropriate network management in the finished product. Network management is of vital importance to Navy applications.

Commercial Viability. The IPng protocols should be commercially viable. This includes, but is not limited to, the following issues:

- The IPng protocols must function correctly. The Navy cannot afford to have network protocol problems in mission critical systems. There must be a high degree of confidence that the protocols are technically sound and multi–vendor interoperability is achievable.
- The IPng protocols must have the support of the commercial/industrial community. This may first be demonstrated by a strong consensus within the IETF community.

Transition Plan. The Navy has a large number of existing networks including both Internet and ISO protocols as well as a number of proprietary systems. As a minimum, the IPng effort must address how to transition from existing IP-based networks. Additionally, it would be desirable to have some guidance for transitioning from other network protocols including, but not limited to, CLNP and other commonly used network protocols. The transition plan for IPng needs to recognize the large existing infrastructure and the lack of funds for a full scale immediate transition. There will, in all likelihood, be a long period of coexistence that should be addressed.

General Requirements. The general requirements documented below are topics of vital importance in a network protocol solution. The IPng solution should address all of these issues.

Addressing. The initial addressing requirements follow: first, a large number of addresses are required. In particular, the number of addressable entities on a single platform will range from the 100s to 100,000. The number of large platforms (ships, submarines, shore–based sites) will range from a few hundred to several thousand. In addition, there will be 500 to 1000 or more small platforms, primarily aircraft. Since it is expected that in the future many of these platforms will be connected to global networks, the addresses must be globally unique.

The second requirement is for some form of addressing structure. It is felt that this structure should be flexible enough to allow for logical structures (not necessarily geographical) to be applied. It is also felt that this is important for the implementation of efficient routing solutions. In addition, the addressing structure must support multicast group addressing. At a minimum 2^{16} globally unique multicast groups must be distinguishable per platform.

Integrated Services Architecture. An important goal of the HPN working group is to identify existing and emerging technologies which provide mechanisms for integrating the services required by mission critical Navy systems. Two classes of problems exist under the general category of integrated services. The first is to provide for the multiple types of services pointed out above. It is required to support these services in an integrated fashion in order to be able to correlate (in time) related streams of information.

The second class of problems relates to the predictable management of the various traffic flows associated with the above–identified services. While many of these services require the delivery of a PDU within a specified time window, the applications in a mission critical environment can demand more stringent requirements. In areas where real–time systems are in use, such as machinery control, narrower and/or more predictable delivery windows may be required than in the case of the delivery of audio or video streams. The mission critical environment also requires the ability to assign end–to–end importance to instances of communications (i.e., invocations of a particular service). For example, an ongoing video stream may need to yield to machinery control commands to ensure that the commands are received before their deadline. The expense of this action is to degrade temporarily the video stream quality. We are looking for mechanisms in the IPng protocols to provide for both of these classes of problems in an integrated fashion. An integrated services architecture reduces design and integration complexities by providing a uniform set of tools for use by the mission critical system designer and application developer. Finally, the integrated services architecture must be flexible and scalable so that new services can be added in the future with minimum impact on systems using it. We have intentionally avoided mentioning particular mechanisms that can be used to solve some of these problems in order to avoid requiring a particular solution.

Mobility. Two classes of mobility exist for the Navy mission critical environment. First, most platforms are themselves mobile. As these platforms move from port to port or from flight deck to flight deck, it is important that they are able to communicate with a number of defense installations via a general infrastructure. Additionally, it is feasible that systems within a single platform may be mobile. Maintenance and damage assessment requires large amounts of information at numerous locations on a platform. This information could possibly be made available through mobile terminals.

Multicast. Multicast transfer is a very critical IPng requirement for the Navy's mission critical systems. Aboard a Naval platform there are many hosts (e.g., workstations) connected via numerous subnetworks. These hosts are all working different aspects of the problem of keeping the platform operational to perform its mission. In support of this environment, multicast transfer is needed to share data that is required by multiple hosts. For example, aboard a ship platform, environmental data (roll, pitch, heading...) is needed by almost all systems. Video conferencing may be used for communication among operational personnel at multiple places aboard this ship. Video conferencing could also be used for communicating with personnel on other platforms or at shore facilities. Both of these examples, in addition to a number of DoD and NATO studies, have highlighted the need for multicast functionality in mission critical systems.

One of the limiting factors with the present IPv4 multicast is the optional nature of this multicast, particularly with respect to routers. The use of tunnels, while enabling the initial deployment of multicast in the Internet, appears to limit its potential. The best approach to provision of multicast functionality is to consider it as a basic functionality to be provided by IPng. In addition, sensible mechanisms are needed to control multicast traffic (i.e., scope control). Finally, support is required to enable multicast functionality in IPng in areas such as group addressing and scalable multicast routing.

Rapid Route Reconfiguration. The HPN project will be using very high bandwidth subnetwork technology. In the mission–critical environment one very important problem is placing a very low bound on the time it takes to identify a subnetwork problem and to complete the necessary route reconfigurations. The Navy's mission critical environment needs to be able to trade off bandwidth to enable a short detection/reconfiguration time on subnetwork faults. A maximum bound on this time is felt to be less than 1 second.

Additional Considerations. This section represents additional concerns of the mission critical environment which may impact IPng. These issues are important for the mission critical environment; however, it was not clear how or whether it is necessary to accommodate them in IPng solutions. It may suffice that designers of IPng are aware of these issues and therefore do not preclude reasonable solutions to these problems.

Fault Tolerance. The mission critical environment is particularly sensitive to the area of fault tolerance. Any mechanisms that can be accommodated within the IPng protocol set, including routing and management, to support various levels of fault tolerance are desirable. In particular, the following features should be supported: error detection, error reporting, traffic analysis, and status reporting.

Policy–based Routing. There may be some uses for policy–based routing within the Navy's mission critical systems. The primary interest is in support of a very capable security facility. Other uses discussed are as a means for keeping certain types of data on certain subnetworks (for multi–homed hosts) and providing for automatic reconfiguration in the event of particular subnetwork failures.

Secure Operation. Security is an important requirement for most Navy applications and thus the ability for the network functions to be designed to support security services are essential. The network function should be able to support the following security services: rule–based access control, labeling, authentication, audit, connection-oriented and connectionless confidentiality, selective routing, traffic flow confidentiality, connection-oriented and connectionless integrity, denial of service protection, continuity of operations, and precedence/preemption. In addition to these services, the network function should also support the security management of these security services. In particular, key management is of importance.

Currently, the IPSEC of the IETF has several draft memos being considered to incorporate various security services in the network functions. The IPng should be able to support the concepts currently being developed by the IPSEC and also provide the ability for the addition of future security services.

Time Synchronization. Time synchronization among the various components of mission critical systems is of vital importance to the Navy. It is desirable to be able to synchronize systems on multiple subnetworks via a network layer infrastructure. Some hooks for time synchronization can be envisioned in the network layer. However, as a minimum, efficient time synchronization algorithms must be able to function above an IPng infrastructure. For HPN systems, it is desirable that a time–of–day synchronization capability be supported of at least an accuracy of one microsecond among all hosts in a platform or campus network. The IPng protocols should not arbitrarily prevent this type of synchronization capability.

Summary. The HPN working group is interested in participating with the IETF in the development of standards which would apply to mission critical systems. In particular, we would like to join in the development of multicast functionality, an integrated services architecture, and support for high performance subnetworks.

Lessons from Other Transition Experiences

Denise Heagerty
CERN, European Laboratory for Particle Physics

The IPng decisions and transition tasks should be broken down into smaller parts so they can be tackled early by the relevant experts. Specialized debates such as address structure, naming issues, or routing protocols can be carried out in parallel by the experts in those fields. Decisions on the critical path of the overall IPng specifications should be identified and taken in a timely manner, while other details can wait until ideas mature.

Timescales. In order to allow key decisions to be made early, IPng decisions and timescales should be broken down into smaller parts, for example:

- address structure and allocation mechanism
- name service changes
- host software and programming interface changes
- routing protocol changes

Although interrelated, not all details need to be defined by the same date. Identify which decisions will be hard to change and which can be allowed to evolve. All changes should be worked on in parallel, but the above list indicates the urgency of a decision. Administrative changes (as may be required for addressing changes) need the greatest elapsed time for implementation, whereas routing protocol changes need the least.

An early decision on address structure is advisable so service managers have enough information to start planning their transitions. Some hosts will never be upgraded and will need to be phased out or configured with reduced connectivity. A lead time of 10 years or more will help managers to make good long term technical decisions and ease financial and organizational constraints.

Transition and Deployment. Transition requires intimate knowledge of the environment (financial, political, and technical). The task of transition needs to be broken down so that service managers close to their clients can take IPng decisions and make them happen.

- Let the service managers adapt solutions for their environments by providing them with a transition toolbox and scenarios of their uses based on real–life examples. Clearly state the merits and limitations of different transition strategies.
- Provide for transition autonomy. Let systems and sites transition at different times as convenient.
- Identify what software needs to be changed, and keep an up–to–date list.
- Identify what is essential to have in place so that service managers can transition at their own pace.
- Allow for a feedback loop to improve software based on experience.

Configuration, Administration, and Operation. IP runs on a wide range of equipment and operating systems at CERN. We need an easy way to (re)configure all our IP capable systems. The systems need to be sent their IP parameters (e.g., their address, address of their default router, address of their local name servers) and we need to obtain data from the system (e.g., contact information for owner, location, and name of system). We also need an easy way to update Domain Name System (DNS) servers.

In our environment systems are regularly moved between buildings, and we therefore find the tight coupling of IP address to physical subnet overly restrictive. Automatic configuration could help overcome this. We would like to efficiently load–balance users of various IP-based services (e.g., Telnet, FTP, locally–written applications) across a number of systems.

The ability to break down addresses and routing into several levels of hierarchy is important to allow the delegation of network management into subdomains. As the network grows, so does the desire to increase the number of levels of hierarchy.

IPng Transition in Science Internetworking

Antonia Ghiselli
Davide Salomoni
Cristina Vistoli
INFN

The problems that should be solved with IPng are: address exhaustion; flat address space; and routing efficiency, flexibility, and capacity. The aim of the IPng selection process should be to define a plan that solves all these problems as a whole and not each of them separately.

The general requirements for this transition are:

- transparency to the final user: user applications should not be influenced.
- flexibility: simplify the suitability to new communication technology and to topology changes due to new services provided or to different users' needs.

Application and Transport Level. Starting from the top of the OSI model, the users' applications should not be influenced by the migration plan. TCP (the transport layer) must maintain the same interfaces and services to the upper layers. It is also necessary to foresee the use of different transport services. The possibility of using a different transport should be offered to the applications, so a transport selector field is needed.

Datagram Service. The network layer must continue to provide the same datagram service as does IPv4. CLNP could be a solution and a reliable starting point for the IPng. The main advantage is that this solution has been profitably tested and is already available on many systems. It is not, of course, deployed as widely as IPv4 since it is a newer technology, but it is widely configured and there is already operational experience. The corresponding address, the NSAP, is 20 bytes long. It is long enough to scale the future data network environment. Its hierarchical format can be organized in a really flexible way, satisfying hierarchical routing and policy-based routing needs and simplifying distributed administration and management. A lot of work has already been done in the majority of countries in order to define NSAP formats satisfying the requirements of both administrative delegation and routing performances.

Routing Protocols. The decision about the routing protocol to be adopted for the IPng is not a fundamental one. Even if this choice is very important to obtain good performance, the routing protocols can be changed or improved at any time because there is no influence into the end system configuration. Relationships between NSAP aggregation, hierarchical topology, and hierarchical routing algorithm must be taken into account in any IPng plan. These issues could improve administration and topological flexibility of the IPng and solve the existing flat routing problem of IPv4. The IPng routing protocols should include policy-based features. The IPv4 network topology is very complex, and it will continue to enlarge during the transition. It would be very difficult or impossible to manage it without "policy" tools. The multicast capability (as well as any other new features that fit in a datagram network) should be supported. Regarding the source routing feature, since we think that it deeply modifies the aim and the "philosophy" of a connectionless network and also introduces a heavy complication in the end node and router software, we don't consider it a major issue.

Layer 2 or Communication Infrastructure Media Support. This is a rapidly changing open field, so it must be left open to any evolution but remain compatible with the above network layer.

Transition and Deployment. We faced the problem of the transition of the DECnet global network to DECnet/OSI over Connectionless Network Service (CLNS). This activity is now almost complete, and based on this experience, we would underline some points that are important during the transition and deployment. The transition must be planned and developed in a distributed way. Every organization should have the ability to plan and start its network migration without losing connectivity with the existing global Internet. Of course, compatibility with the IPv4 world must be maintained, so the next generation system must work with both the IPv4 and IPng nodes using the same applications.

It is important, however, to define a deadline for the backward compatibility in order to avoid huge software maintenance in user systems and multiple topology management. A dual-stack approach could simplify the transition very much, whereas a translation mechanism would need a broad and deep coordination in order to maintain global connectivity during the transition period. The dual stack is simpler and could be easily developed, but it is important to push for a pure IPng with global connectivity as soon as possible. This may happen only when there are no more IPv4-only hosts.

Indeed, the drawback of the dual stack configuration is that the community continues to suffer IPv4 address space exhaustion, and we must continue to support the IPv4 routing protocols and infrastructure. The tunnel solution to interconnect the IPv4 islands will not provide good performance for users. It is most important to maintain IPv4 connectivity and dual-stack software support in the end system software in a determined timeframe or else the transition will never end.

An Electric Power Industry View of IPng

Ron Skelton
Electric Power Research Institute (EPRI)

Because of its success and open nature, future evolution of the Internet Protocol (IP) is an issue of national and international concern. It is critical to the building of a National Information Infrastructure (NII), comparable to the adoption of basic standards for electricity, railroads, and highways in the industrial era.

The Electric Power Research Institute (EPRI) is a non–profit organization made up of 700 volunteer members. EPRI manages a program of research and development, including information technologies, for the electric utility industry to improve power production, distribution, and use. We have a vital interest in our internal information infrastructure, as well as a role in building the future NII and Global Information Infrastructure (GII).

While the electric utility industry today is a heavy user of the Internet Protocol, it is also following a long–term strategic architecture based on international standards developed by ISO, CCITT, and other national bodies (including the IEEE and ANSI). We look to these organizations which employ formal review and voting procedures to extend standards that will achieve end–to–end data and application interoperability.

Utility Industry Infrastructure Needs. Our need for a comprehensive information architecture is based on a survey of all aspects in the electrical power supply enterprise. These needs comprise one of the nation's largest and most demanding real–time communications networks, ranging from very low bit rate dispersed telemetry to industrial automation and video applications. The infrastructure must extend across all elements of the power generation, transmission, and distribution system to the load devices on the customers' premises.

In highly competitive industries there is a well–grounded maxim, "Never let your competitor come between you and your customer." This is now becoming a fact of life for utilities as they enter the era of competition. While customer communications can come in many forms, utilities will be driven to differentiate themselves from their competitors, in what will ultimately become a commodity market, by providing energy–related services for power consumers. Also, by leveraging information network technology, utilities can simultaneously increase the ability of local communities to attract new business. Areas of EPRI customer research and demonstration projects include two–way communications for real–time energy pricing, non–intrusive load monitoring, and custom power conditioning.

National Information Infrastructure (NII) Potential. While the power industry has routinely used data networks of all kinds for more than 100 years, the impact of deregulation, open access, and competition in the industry will make investments in the information infrastructure a survival issue for utilities in the near future. The challenge of building an NII comes at a time when the electric utility industry is facing unprecedented change. The utilities industry is transforming from a regulated monopoly to an industry based on market economics and commerce.

A set of issues surround the legal and regulatory factors facing utility involvement in building any information infrastructure that exceeds their internal requirements. However, a study commissioned by the U.S. Department of Energy, published in November 1994, suggests that because of internal needs and the prospect of obtaining compensating revenues from unused network capacity, "the electric utilities may be the key to achieving important social and economic needs—in particular, universal service." [15]

Strategic Technology Assessment. Comparing vendor–specific options to vendor–neutral options, the needs of the industry will be met more effectively by the current suite of OSI protocols and several international standards, or vender–neutral options, that are now under development. In particular, the future needs of the utilities industry at the network level would be met most effectively by the OSI CLNP protocol. The bottom line is: How will we be able to meet the electric power industry goals in an international standards framework? Alternatively, CLNPng, based on the convergence envisioned by the U.S. Federal Internetworking Requirements Panel, might be adopted as part of our overall communications architecture.

EPRI has, to date, developed the Utility Communications Architecture (UCA) specification for communications and the Database Access Integrated Services specification for data exchange. Both are based on the

OSI model and other international standards. The UCA specifications have been incorporated into the Industry Government Open Systems Specification (IGOSS). They are receiving favorable response from, and are being applied by, the electric industry and its suppliers. The UCA specifications also have the support of the natural gas and water industries. These specifications will be revised from time to time as international standards mature and as de facto standards emerge in the marketplace.

The management of growth toward ubiquitous, general–purpose data networks is critical to the utilities and to the NII Agenda. For an IPng to achieve this goal it must be acceptable from both private and public sector viewpoints, and both nationally and internationally. It is also important that new requirements be achieved by convergence of efforts to develop additional standards. Security, directory services, network management, software object architectures, and the ability to support distributed real–time applications are examples of where new convergent standards efforts are urgently required.

Just as society could not accept multiple standards for the gauge of railroads, we can no longer accept multiple platform standards for information transport and distributed processing. Standard communications and processing platforms minimize the cost of system integration, enlarge the market, and free resources to create new wealth.

Engineering Considerations–Mandatory Requirements. Internetworking must evolve to provide an industrial strength computing and communications environment for multiple uses of globally connected network resources. Specifically, the underlying transport must provide a standard programmatic interface and high integrity support for upper layer industrial OSI applications, including Manufacturing Messaging Specification (MMS), Transaction Processing (TP), Remote Data Access (RDA), and Open Distributed Processing, ISO Reference Model (ODP–RM). Use of interface layers such as RFC-1006 [16] is not acceptable except as a transition strategy.

Engineering Considerations–Basic Requirements. There are a few features that must be considered basic requirements for an IPng:

Scalability. The addressing scheme must have essentially an unlimited address space to encompass an arbitrarily large number of information objects. Specifically it must solve the fundamental limitations of 32–bit formats. The need for pervasive addressable information objects within the utility industry alone may well exceed 10^9.

Routing Table Economy. Network addressing must achieve significant economy in routing database size with very large networks. The burden of routing must be alleviated in some manner so that the administrative problem doesn't grow linearly (or worse) in obtaining an untethered and ubiquitous infrastructure. The existing internetworking paradigm and existing OSI and IPS applications are to be supported.

Key Engineering Considerations.

In addition, there are a number of things that should be taken into consideration during the IPng development process.

Prompt Availability. The solution must be available now using mature, internationally agreed standards and off–the–shelf implementations for hosts and routers. The solution must leverage existing investments in standards development, deployment, and experience, while at the same time providing for the basic requirements of a vendor–independent platform.

Ease of Transition. Any solution must provide an evolutionary transition path.

An IP dual network layer strategy must be achievable without modifications to existing inter–domain routing protocols, while providing the ability to support proprietary protocols such as IPX and Appletalk. The scheme must provide the ability to encompass other addressing schemes such as X.121 and E.164. Existing SNMP and CMIP MIBs must be applicable and available. Internet domain names need to be retained.

Routing Effectiveness. This key objective requires features such as route aggregation, service selection, and low frequency host advertisements; host routing intelligence should not be required.

Flexible Efficient Administration. Operational needs will need to be met in a pragmatic, economic, and flexible manner. Some form of administration of address allocations needs to be provided. This can be based on geography, carrier ID, or both, and will be administered by policy, not by network topology. Simplified and robust configurability is required, including the ability to identify resources (e.g., multi–homed hosts and applications), instead of interfaces.

Mobility. Dynamic addressing is required where hosts have the ability to learn their own network address with the minimum of human intervention. The technologies inherent in open distributed systems are a special case which requires the ability for servers to advertise their capabilities in a process defined by the ISO ODP–RM as "Trading."

Use of IPng in Combat Simulation

Susan Symington
David Wood
MITRE Corporation
J. Mark Pullen
George Mason University

The Defense Modeling and Simulation (M&S) community is a major user of packet networks and as such has a stake in the definition of IPng. We will summarize the Distributed Interactive Simulation environment that is under development, with regard to its real-time nature, scope, and magnitude of networking requirements. The requirements for real-time response, multicast, and resource reservation are set forth, based on our best current understanding of the future of Defense Modeling and Simulation.

Introduction. The Internet Engineering Task Force (IETF) is now in the process of designing the Internet Protocol next generation (IPng). IPng is expected to be a driving force in the future of commercial off-the-shelf (COTS) networking technology. It will have a major impact on what future networking technologies are widely available, cost-effective, and multi-vendor interoperable. Applications that have all of their network layer requirements met by the standard features of IPng will be at a great advantage, whereas those that don't will have to rely on protocols that are not as widely available and more costly, that may have limited interoperability with the ubiquitous IPng-based COTS products.

We will specify the network layer requirements of Defense M&S applications. It is important that the M&S community make its unique requirements clear to IPng designers so that mechanisms for meeting these requirements can be considered as standard features for IPng. The intention is to make IPng's benefits have wide COTS availability, multi-vendor interoperability, and cost-effectiveness, all fully available to the M&S community.

Overview of Distributed Interactive Simulation. The Defense M&S community requires an integrated, wide area, wideband internetwork to perform Distributed Interactive Simulation (DIS) exercises among remote, dissimilar simulation devices located at worldwide sites. The network topology used in current M&S exercises is typically that of a high-speed cross-country and trans-oceanic backbone running between wideband packet switches, with tail circuits running from these packet switches to various nearby sites. At any given site involved in an exercise, there may be several internetworked local area networks on which numerous simulation entity hosts are running. Some of these hosts may be executing computer-generated semi-automated forces, while others may be manned simulators. The entire system must accommodate delays and delay variance compatible with human interaction times in order to preserve an accurate order of events and provide a realistic combat simulation. While the sites themselves may be geographically distant from one another, the simulation entities running at different sites may themselves be operating and interacting as though they are in close proximity to one another in the battlefield. Our goal is that all of this can take place in a common network that supports all Defense M&S needs, and hopefully is also shared with other Defense applications.

In a typical DIS exercise, distributed simulators exchange information over an internetwork in the form of standardized packets. The DIS protocols and packet formats are currently under development. The first generation has been standardized as IEEE 1278.1 and used for small exercises (around 100 hosts), and development of a second generation is underway. The current Communications Architecture for DIS specifies use of Internet protocols.

The amount, type, and sensitivity level of information that must be exchanged during a typical DIS exercise drives the communications requirements for that exercise, and depends on the number and type of participating entities and the nature and level of interaction among those entities. Future DIS exercises now in planning extend to hundreds of sites and tens of thousands of simulation platforms worldwide. For example, an exercise may consist of semi-automated and individual manned tank, aircraft, and surface ship simulators interacting on predefined geographic terrain. The actual locations of these simulation entities may be distributed among sites located in Virginia, Kansas, Massachusetts, Germany, and Korea. The packets that are exchanged among simulation entities running at these sites must carry all of the information necessary to inform each site regarding everything relevant that occurs with regard to all other sites that have the potential to affect it within the simulation. Such information could include the location of each entity, its direction and speed, the orientation of its weapons systems, if any, and the frequency on which it is transmitting and receiving radio messages. If an entity launches a weapon, such as a missile, a new entity representing this missile will be created within the simulation and it will begin transmitting packets containing relevant information about its state, such as its location, and speed.

A typical moving entity would generate between one and two packets per second, with typical packet sizes of 220 bytes and a maximum size of 1400 bytes, although rates of 15 packets/second and higher are possible. Stationary entities must generate some traffic to refresh receiving simulators; under the current standard this can be as little as 0.2 packets per second. Compression techniques reducing packets size by 50% or more are being investigated but are not included in the current DIS standard.

With so much information being exchanged among simulation entities at numerous locations, multicasting is required to minimize network bandwidth used and to reduce input to individual simulation entities so that each entity receives only those packets that are of interest to it. For example, a given entity need only receive information regarding the location, speed, and direction of other entities that are close enough to it within the geography of the simulation that it could be affected by those entities. Similarly, an entity need not receive packets containing the contents of radio transmissions that are sent on a frequency other than that on which the entity is listening.

Resource reservation mechanisms are also essential to guarantee performance requirements of DIS exercises: reliability and real-time transmission are necessary to accommodate the manned simulators participating in an exercise.

M&S exercises that include humans in the loop and are executed in real-time require rapid network response times in order to provide realistic combat simulations. For DIS, latency requirements between the output of a packet at the application level of a simulator and input of that packet at the application level of any other simulator in that exercise have been defined as:

- 100 milliseconds for exercises containing simulated units whose interactions are tightly coupled
- 300 milliseconds for exercises whose interactions are not tightly coupled[17]

The reliability of the best-effort datagram delivery service supporting DIS should be such that 98% of all datagrams are delivered to all intended destination sites, with missing datagrams randomly distributed.[18]

While these numbers may be refined for some classes of simulation data in the future, latency requirements are expected to remain under a few hundred milliseconds in all cases. It is also required that delay variance (jitter) be low enough that smoothing by buffering the data stream at the receiving simulator does not cause the stated latency specifications to be exceeded.

There are currently several architectures under consideration for the M&S network of the future. Under fully distributed models, all simulation entities rely directly on the network protocols for multicasting and are therefore endowed with much flexibility with regard to their ability to join and leave multicast groups dynamically, in large numbers.

In some cases, the M&S exercises will involve the transmission of classified data over the network. For example, messages may contain sensitive data regarding warfare tactics and weapons systems characteristics, or an exercise itself may be a rehearsal of an imminent military operation. This means the data communications used for these exercises must meet security constraints defined by the National Security Agency (NSA). Some such requirements can be met in current systems by use of end-to-end packet encryption (E3) systems. E3 systems provide adequate protection from disclosure and tampering, while allowing multiple security partitions to use the same network simultaneously.

Currently the M&S community is using the experimental Internet Stream protocol version 2 (ST2) to provide resource reservation and multicast. There is much interest in converting to IPv4 multicast as it becomes available across the COTS base, but this cannot happen until IPv4 has a resource reservation capability. The RSVP work ongoing in the IETF is being watched in expectation that it will provide such a capability. Also some tests have been made of IPv4 multicast without resource reservation; results have been positive, now larger tests are required to confirm the expected scalability of IPv4 multicast. But issues remain, for security reasons, some M&S exercises will require sender-initiated joining of members to multicast groups. In addition, it is not clear that IPv4 multicast will be able to make use of link-layer multicast available in ATM systems, which the M&S community expects to use to achieve the performance necessary for large exercises.

Specific Requirements. It is recognized that some of the capabilities described below may be provided not from IPng but from companion protocols, e.g., RSVP [19] and IGMP. The M&S requirement is for a compatible suite of protocols that are available in commercial products.

Real-time Response. DIS will continue to have requirements to communicate real-time data, therefore the extent to which IPng lends itself to implementing real-time networks will be a measure of its utility for M&S networking.

Multicasting. M&S requires a multicasting capability and a capability for managing multicast group membership. These multicasting capabilities must meet the following requirements:

- Scalable to hundreds of sites and, potentially, to tens of thousands of simulation platforms.
- It is highly desirable that the network-layer multicasting protocol be able to use the multicasting capabilities of link-level technologies, such as broadcast LANs, Frame Relay, and ATM. (By highly desirable, we mean that the capabilities are not essential, but they will enable more direct and cost-effective networking solutions.)
- The group management mechanics must have the characteristics that thousands of multicast groups consisting of tens of thousands of members each can be supported on a given network and that a host should be able to belong to hundreds of multicast groups simultaneously.
- Multicast group members must be able to be added to or removed from groups dynamically, in less than one second, at rates of hundreds of membership changes per second. It is not possible to predict what special cases may develop, thus this requirement is for all members of all groups.
- The network layer must support options for both sender- and receiver-initiated joining of multicast groups.

Resource Reservation. The M&S community requires performance guarantees in supporting networks. This implies that IPng must be compatible with a capability to reserve bandwidth and other necessary allocations in a multicast environment, in order to guarantee network capacity from simulator-to-simulator across a shared network for the duration of the user's interaction with the network. Such a resource reservation capability is essential to optimizing the use of limited network resources, increasing reliability, and decreasing delay and delay variance of priority traffic, especially in cases in which network resources are heavily used. The resource reservations should be accomplished in such a way that traffic without performance guarantees will be re-routed, dropped, or blocked before reserved bandwidth traffic is affected.

In addition, it would be highly desirable for the resource reservation capability to provide mechanisms for:

- Invoking additional network resources (on-demand capacity) when needed.
- The network to feed back its loading status to the applications to enable graceful degradation of performance.

A Cellular Industry View of IPng

Mark Taylor
McCaw Cellular Communications, Inc.

The chief requirements for IPng, as envisioned by the service providers of the Cellular Digital Packet Data (CDPD) Forum, are support for mobility, scalability, route selectivity, addressability, security, accountability, data efficiency, and transition capability. Currently, CDPD provides the capability for mobility of native mainstream connectionless Network Layer–based applications.

Support for Mobility. Since we offer mobile services, our primary requirement is that IPng not inhibit our support of mobility of connectionless Layer 3 protocols. IPng must not impede hosts from being able to operate anywhere at anytime. Applications on mobile devices must look and feel the same to the user regardless of location. Network Layer packets should be self–contained and not disallow the redirection inherent to our mobility solution (i.e., IPng must be connectionless).

Further, since IPng provides an opportunity for design enhancements above and beyond IPv4, native support for mobility should be regarded as an explicit IPng requirement. Local area and wide area wireless technology creates new opportunities for both TCP/IP and the Internet. Although the capability for mobility is orthogonal to the wired/wireless nature of the data link in use, the rapid deployment of wireless technology amplifies the requirement for topological flexibility.

As a by–product of mobility, the significance of occasionally connected hosts increases. The ability to accommodate occasionally connected hosts in IPng is a requirement.

Scalability. In terms of scale, we envision 20 to 40 million users in North America alone by the year 2007. In this context a user is anything from a vending machine to a "road warrior." Worldwide, IPng should be able to support billions of users. Of course, the sparseness of network address assignments which is necessary for subnetting, etc., dictates that IPng should support at least tens or hundreds of billions of addresses. With the inherent difficulty of guessing how much address space to allocate to any user's network, network address assignments will have to leave extra address spaces.

Route Selectivity. In the voice communications arena, equal access and selection of an interexchange carrier (IXC) are required. Similar requirements for data also exist.

Source– and policy–based routing for inter–domain traffic can address this requirement. IPng must allow the selection of at least the first transit network service provider based on the source host (address).

Addressability. We would expect addresses to be hierarchical. In addition, a node with multiple links should require only a single address, although more than one address should also be possible. The mapping of names to addresses should be independent of location; an address should be an address, not a route. Variable–length addressing is also ideal to ensure continued protocol (IPng) extensibility. Administration of address assignments should be distributed and not centralized as it is now.

Security. IPng should also support security mechanisms, which will grow increasingly important on the proverbial information highway for commercial users. Security services which may be expected from a Layer 3 entity such as IPng include peer entity authentication, data confidentiality, traffic flow confidentiality, data integrity, and location confidentiality.

Accountability. The ability to do accounting at Layer 3 is a requirement. The CDPD specification could be used as a model of the type of accounting services that we need.

Data Efficiency. The bandwidth of wide area wireless networks is a precious resource, the use of which must be optimized. IPng must allow optimal use of the underlying Layer 2 medium. Layer 3 Protocol Control Information should be as condensed as possible. The protocol should be optimized for data efficiency.

Packet prioritization must also be supported by IPng in order to optimize the use of low speed networks. This requirement includes both class and grade of service definitions for flexibility.

Transition Capability. The final requirement for IPng is that it must interoperate with IPv4 for the foreseeable future. Bridging mechanisms must be supported, and a strategy for the transition from IPv4 to IPng must be defined. Use of options fields, etc., is one mechanism to support the requirement for IPng protocols to support IP addresses and headers.

A Cable TV Industry View of IPng

Mario P. Vecchi
Time Warner Cable

The IPng requirements and selection criteria from a cable television industry viewpoint are unique. The perspective taken is to position IPng as a potential internetworking technology to support the global requirements of the future integrated broadband networks that the cable industry is designing and deploying. I will include a description of the cable television industry and an outline of the network architectures to support the delivery of entertainment programming and interactive multimedia digital services, as well as telecommunication and data communication services.

Cable networks touch residences, in addition to campuses and business parks. Broadband applications reach the average, computer-shy person. The applications involve a heavy use of video and audio to provide communication, entertainment, and information-access services. The deployment of these capabilities to the homes will represent tens of millions of users. Impact on the network and the IPng requirements that are discussed include issues of scalability, reliability and availability, support for real-time traffic, security and privacy, and operations and network management, among others.

Cable Television Industry Overview. Cable television networks and the Internet are discovering each other. It looks like a great match for a number of reasons, the available bandwidth being the primary driver. Nonetheless, it seems that the impact of the cable television industry in the deployment of broadband networks and services is still not fully appreciated. This section will provide a quick (and simplified) overview of cable television networks, and explain the trends that are driving future network architectures and services.

Cable television networks in the U.S. pass by approximately 90 million homes, and have about 56 million subscribers, of a total of about 94 million homes. There are more than 11,000 headends, and the cable TV industry has installed more than 1 million network-miles. Installation of optical fiber proceeds at a brisk pace, the cable fiber plant in the U.S.

going from 13,000 miles in 1991 to 23,000 miles in 1992. Construction spending by the cable industry in 1992 was estimated to be about $2.4 billion, of which $1.4 billion was for rebuilds and upgrades. Cable industry revenue from subscriber services in 1992 was estimated to be more than $21 billion, corresponding to an average subscriber rate of about $30 per month (Source: Paul Kagan Associates, Inc.). These figures are based on "conventional" cable television services, and are expected to grow as the cable industry moves into new interactive digital services and telecommunications. [20]

The cable industry's broadband integrated services network architecture is based on a hierarchical deployment of network elements interconnected by broadband fiber optics and coaxial cable links. In a very simplified manner, the following is a view of this architecture. Starting at the home, a coaxial cable tree-and-branch plant provides broadband two-way access to the network. The local access coaxial cable plant is aggregated at a fiber node, which marks the point in the network where fiber optics becomes the broadband transmission medium. Current deployment is for approximately 500 homes passed by the coaxial cable plant for every fiber node, with variations (from as low as 100 to as many as 3000) that depend on the density of homes and the degree of penetration of broadband services. The multiple links from the fiber nodes reach the headend, which is where existing cable systems have installed equipment for origination, reception, and distribution of television programming. The headends are in buildings that can accommodate weather protection and powering facilities, and hence represent the first natural place in the network where complex switching, routing, and processing equipment can be conveniently located. Traffic from multiple headends can be routed over fiber optics to regional hub nodes deeper in the network, where capital-intensive functions can be shared in an efficient way.

The cable networks are evolving quite rapidly to become effective two-way digital broadband networks. Cable networks will continue to be asymmetric, and they will continue to deliver analog video. But digital capabilities are being installed very aggressively and a significant upstream bandwidth is rapidly being activated. The deployment of optical fiber deeper into the network is making the shared coaxial plant more effective in carrying broadband traffic in both directions. For instance, with fiber nodes down to where only about 100 to 500 homes are passed by the coaxial drops (down from tens of thousands of homes passed in the past), an upstream bandwidth of several MHz represents a considerable capacity. The recent announcement by Continental Cablevision and

PSI of Internet access services is but one example of the many uses of these two-way broadband capabilities.

The cable networks are also rapidly evolving into regional networks. The deployment of fiber optic trunking facilities (many based on SONET) will provide gigabit links that interconnect regional hub nodes in regional networks spanning multiple cable systems. These gigabit networks carry digitized video programming, but will also carry voice (telephone) traffic, and, of course, data traffic. There are instances in various parts of the country where these regional networks have been in successful trials. And given that compressed digital video is the way to deliver future video programs (including interactive video, video on demand, and a whole menu of other applications like computer-supported collaborative work, multiparty remote games, home shopping, customised advertisement, multimedia information services, etc.), one can be guaranteed that gigabit regional networks will be put in place at an accelerated pace.

The cable networks are evolving to provide broadband networking capabilities in support of a complete suite of communication services. The Orlando network being built by Time Warner is an example of a Full Service Network™ that provides video, audio, and data services to the homes. For the trial, ATM is brought to the homes at DS3 rates, and it is expected to go up to OC-3 rates when switch interfaces are available. This trial in Orlando represents a peek into the way of future cable networks. The Full Service Network uses a "set-top" box in every home to provide the network interface. This set-top box, in addition to some specialized modules for video processing, is a powerful computer in disguise, with a computational power comparable to high-end desktop workstations. The conventional analog cable video channels will be available, but a significant part of the network's RF bandwidth will be devoted to digital services. There are broadband ATM switches in the network (as well as 5E-type switches for telephony), and video servers that include all kinds of movies and information services. An important point to notice is that the architecture of future cable networks maps directly to the way networked computing has developed. General purpose hosts (i.e., the set-top boxes) are interconnected through a broadband network to other hosts and to servers.

The deployment of the future broadband information superhighway will require architectures for both the network infrastructure and the service support environment that truly integrate the numerous applications that will be offered to the users. Applications will cover a very wide range of scenarios. Entertainment video delivery will evolve from the current core services of the cable industry to enhanced offerings like interactive video, near video-on-demand and complete video-on-demand functions. Communication services will evolve from the current telephony and low-speed data to include interactive multimedia applications, information access services, distance learning, remote medical diagnostics and evaluations, computer supported collaborative work, multiparty remote games, electronic shopping, etc. In addition to the complexity and diversity of the applications, the future broadband information infrastructure will combine a number of different networks that will have to work in a coherent manner. Not only will the users be connected to different regional networks, but the sources of information—in the many forms that they will take—will also belong to different enterprises and may be located in remote networks. It is important to realize from the start that the two most important attributes of the architecture for the future broadband information superhighway are integration and interoperability. The Internet community has important expertise and technology that could contribute to the definition and development of these future broadband networks.

Engineering Considerations. The following comments represent expected requirements of future cable networks, based on the vision of an integrated broadband network that will support a complete suite of interactive video, voice and data services.

Scale. The current common wisdom is that IPng should be able to deal with 10^{12} nodes. Given that there are on the order of 10^8 households in the U.S., we estimate a worldwide number of households of about 100 times as many, giving a total of about 10^{10} global households. This number represents about 1 percent of the 10^{12} nodes, which indicates that there should be enough space left for business, educational, research, government, military, and other nodes connected to the future Internet.

One should be cautious, however, not to underestimate the possibility of multiple addresses that will be used at each node to specify different devices, processes, services, etc. For instance, it is very likely that more than one address will be used at each household for different devices such as the entertainment system (i.e., interactive multimedia "next generation" television(s)), the data system (i.e., the home personal computer(s)), and other new terminal devices that will emerge in the future (such as networked games, PDAs, etc.). Finally, the administration of the address space is important. If there are large blocks of assigned, but unused, addresses, the total number of available addresses will be effectively reduced from the 10^{12} nodes that have been originally considered.

Timescale. The cable industry is already making significant investments in plant upgrades, and the current estimates for the commercial deployment indicate that, by the year 1998, tens of millions of homes will be served by interactive and integrated cable networks and services. This implies that during 1994, various trials will be conducted and evaluated, and the choices of technologies and products will be well under way by the year 1995. That is to say, critical investment and technological decisions by many of the cable operators, and their partners, will be made by the end of 1995 or 1996.

These time estimates are tentative, of course, and subject to variations depending on economic, technical, and public policy factors. Nonetheless, the definition of the IPng capabilities and the availability of implementations should not be delayed beyond the end of 1995, in order to be ready at the time during which many of the early technological choices for the future deployment of cable networks and services will be made. The full development and deployment of IPng will require, of course, a long period. However, availability of early implementations will allow experimentation in trials to validate IPng choices and to provide early buy-in from the developers of networking products that will support the planned roll out.

The effective support for high-quality video and audio streams is one of the critical capabilities that should be demonstrated by IPng in order to capture the attention of network operators and information providers of interactive broadband services (e.g., cable television industry and partners). The currently accepted view is that IP is a great networking environment for the control side of an interactive broadband system. It is a challenge for IPng to demonstrate that it can be effective in transporting the broadband video and audio data streams, in addition to providing the networking support for the distributed control system.

Transition and Deployment. The transition from the current version to IPng has to consider two aspects: support for existing applications and availability of new capabilities. The delivery of digital video and audio programs requires the capability to do broadcasting and selective multicasting efficiently. The interactive applications that the future cable networks will provide will be based on multimedia information streams that will have real-time constraints. That is to say, both the end-to-end delays and the jitter associated with the delivery across the network have to be bounded. In addition, the commercial nature of these large private investments will require enhanced network capabilities for routing choices, resource allocation, quality-of-service controls, security, privacy, etc. Network management will be an increasingly important issue in the future. The extent to which the current IP fails to provide the needed capabilities will provide additional incentive for the transition to occur, since there will be no choice but to use IPng in future applications.

It is very important, however, to maintain backwards compatibility with the current IP. There is the obvious argument that the installed technological base developed around IP cannot be neglected under any reasonable evolution scenario. But in addition, one has to keep in mind that a global Internet will be composed of many interconnected heterogeneous networks, and that not all subnetworks, or user communities, will provide the full suite of interactive multimedia services. Internetworking between IPng and IP will have to continue for a very long time in the future.

Secure Operation. The security needed in future networks falls into two general categories: protection of the users and protection of the network resources. The users of the future global Internet will include many communities that will likely expect a higher level of security than is currently available. These users include business, government, research, and military, as well as private subscribers. The protection of the users' privacy is likely to become a hot issue as new commercial services are rolled out. The possibility of illicitly monitoring traffic patterns by looking at the headers in IPng packets, for instance, could be disturbing to most users that subscribe to new information and entertainment services.

The network operators and the information providers will also expect effective protection of their resources. One would expect that most of the security will be dealt with at higher levels than IPng, but some issues might have to be considered in defining IPng as well. One issue relates, again, to the possibility of illicitly monitoring addresses and traffic patterns by looking at the IPng packet headers. Another issue of importance will be the capability of effective network management under the presence of benign or malicious bugs, especially if both source routing and resource reservation functionality is made available.

Configuration, Administration, and Operation. The operations of these future integrated broadband networks will indeed become more difficult, and not only because the networks themselves will be larger and more complex, but also because of the number and diversity of applications running on or through the networks. It is expected that most of the issues that need to be addressed for effective operations support systems will belong to higher layers than IPng, but some aspects should be considered when defining IPng.

The area where IPng would have most impact would be in the interrelated issues of resource reservation, source routing and quality of service control. There will be a push to maintain high quality of service and low network resource usage simultaneously, especially if the users can specify preferred routes through the network. Useful capabilities at the IPng level would enable the network operator, or the user, to effectively monitor and direct traffic in order to meet quality and cost parameters. Similarly, it will be important to dynamically reconfigure the connectivity among end points or the location of specific processes (e.g., to support mobile computing terminals), and the design of IPng should either support, or at least not get in the way of, this capability. Under normal conditions, one would expect that resources for the new routing will be established before the old route is released in order to minimize service interruption. In cases where reconfiguration is in response to abnormal (i.e., failure) conditions, then one would expect longer interruptions in the service, or even loss of service.

The need to support heterogeneous, multiple administrative domains will also have important implications on the addressing schemes that IPng should support. It will be both a technical and a business issue to have effective means to address nodes, processes, and users, as well as choosing schemes based on fair and open processes for allocation and administration of the address space.

Support for Mobility. The proliferation of personal and mobile communication services is a well-established trend by now. Similarly, mobile computing devices are being introduced to the market at an accelerated pace. It would not be wise to disregard the issue of host mobility when evaluating proposals for IPng. Mobility will have impact on network addressing and routing, adaptive resource reservation, security, and privacy, among other issues.

Flows and Resource Reservation. The largest fraction of the future broadband traffic will be due to real-time voice and video streams. It will be necessary to provide performance bounds for bandwidth, jitter, latency, and loss parameters, as well as synchronization between media streams related by an application in a given session. In addition, there will be alternative network providers that will compete for the users and that will provide connectivity to a given choice of many available service providers. There is no question that IPng, if it aims to be a general protocol useful for interactive multimedia applications, will need to support some form of resource reservation or flows.

Two aspects of flow and resource reservation are worth mentioning. First, the quality of service (QoS) parameters are not known ahead of time, and hence the network will have to include flexible capabilities for defining these parameters. For instance, MPEG-2 packetized video might have to be described differently than G.721 PCM packetized voice, although both data streams represent real-time traffic channels. In some cases, it might be appropriate to provide soft guarantees in the quality parameters, whereas in other cases hard guarantees might be required. The trade-off between cost and quality could be an important capability of future IPng-based networks, but much work needs to be advanced on this.

A second important issue related to resource reservations is the need to deal with broken or lost end-to-end state information. In traditional circuit-switched networks, a considerable effort is expended by the intelligence of the switching system to detect and recover resources that have been lost due to misallocation. Future IPng networks will provide resource reservation capabilities by distributing the state information of a given session into multiple nodes of the network. A significant effort will be needed to find effective methods to maintain consistency and recover from errors in such a distributed environment. For example, keep-alive messages to each node where a queuing policy change has been made to establish the flow could be a strategy to make sure that network resources do not remain stuck in some corrupted session state. One should be careful, however, not to assume that complex distributed algorithms can be made robust by using timeouts. This is a problem that might require innovation beyond the reuse of existing solutions.

It should be noted that some aspects of the requirements for recoverability are less stringent in this networking environment than in traditional distributed data processing systems. In most cases it is not needed (or even desirable) to recover the exact session state after failures, but only to guarantee that the system returns to some safe state. The goal would be to guarantee that no network resource is reserved that has not been correctly assigned to a valid session. The more stringent requirement of returning to old session state is not meaningful since the value of a session disappears, in most cases, as time progresses. One should keep in mind, however, that administrative and management state, such as usage measurement, is subject to the same conventional requirements of recoverability that database systems currently offer.

Policy-based Routing. In future broadband networks, there will be multiple network operators and information providers competing for customers and network traffic. An important capability of IPng will be to specify, at the source, the specific network for the traffic to follow. The users will be able to select specific networks that provide performance, feature or cost advantages. From the user's perspective, source routing is a feature that would enable a wider selection of network access options, enhancing their ability to obtain features, performance, or cost advantages. From the network operator and service provider perspective, source routing would enable the offering of targeted bundled services that will cater to specific users and achieve some degree of customer lock-in. The information providers will be able to optimize the placement and distribution of their servers, based on either point-to-point streams or on multicasting to selected subgroups. The ability of IPng to dynamically specify the network routing would be an attractive feature that will facilitate the flexible offering of network services.

Topological Flexibility. It is hard to predict what the topology of the future Internet will be. The current model developed in response to a specific set of technological drivers, as well as an open administrative process reflecting the non-commercial nature of the sector. The future Internet will continue to integrate multiple administrative domains that will be deployed by a variety of network operators.

It is likely that there will be more "gateway" nodes (at the headends or even at the fiber nodes, for instance) as local and regional broadband networks will provide connectivity for their users to the global Internet.

Applicability. The future broadband networks that will be deployed, by both the cable industry and other companies, will integrate a diversity of applications. The strategies of the cable industry are to reach the homes, as well as schools, business, government, and other campuses. The applications will focus on entertainment, remote education, telecommuting, medical, community services, news delivery, and the whole spectrum of future information networking services. The traffic carried by the broadband networks will be dominated by real-time video and audio streams, even though there will also be an important component of traffic associated with non-time-critical services such as messaging, file transfers, remote computing, etc. The value of IPng will be measured as a general internetworking technology for all these classes of applications. The future market for IPng could be much wider and larger than the current market for IP, provided that the capabilities to support these diverse interactive multimedia applications are available.

It is difficult to predict how pervasive the use of IPng and its related technologies might be in future broadband networks. There will be extensive deployment of distributed computing capabilities, both for the user applications and for the network management and operation support systems that will be required. This is the area where IPng could find a firm stronghold, especially as it can leverage on the extensive IP technology available. The extension of IPng to support video and audio real-time applications, with the required performance, quality, and cost to be competitive, remains a question to be answered.

Datagram Service. The "best-effort," hop-by-hop paradigm of the existing IP service will have to be reexamined if IPng is to provide capabilities for resource reservation or flows. The datagram paradigm could still be the basic service provided by IPng for many applications, but careful thought should be given to the need to support real-time traffic with (soft and/or hard) quality of service requirements.

Accounting. The ability to do accounting should be an important consideration in the selection of IPng. The future broadband networks will be commercially motivated, and measurement of resource usage by the various users will be required. The actual billing may or may not be based on session-by-session usage, and accounting will have many other useful purposes besides billing. The efficient operation of networks depends on maintaining availability and performance goals, including both on-line actions and long-term planning and design. Accounting information will be important on both scores. On the other hand, the choice of providing accounting capabilities at the IPng level should be examined with a general criterion to introduce as little overhead as possible. Since fields for "to," "from," and time stamp will be available for any IPng choice, what other parameters in IPng could be useful to both accounting and other network functions should be examined, so as to keep IPng as lean as possible.

Media Independence. The generality of IP should be carried over to IPng. It would not be an advantage to design a general internetworking technology that cannot be supported over as wide a class of communications media as possible. It is reasonable to expect that IPng will start with support over a few select transport technologies, and rely on the backwards compatibility with IP to work through a transition period. Ultimately, however, one would expect IPng to be carried over any available communications medium.

Robust Service. Service availability, end-to-end, and at expected performance levels, is the true measure of robustness and fault-tolerance. In this sense, IPng is but one piece of a complex puzzle. There are, however, some vulnerability aspects of IPng that could decrease robustness. One general class of bugs will be associated with the change itself, regardless of any possible enhancement in capabilities. The design, implementation, and testing process will have to be managed very carefully. Networks and distributed systems are tricky. There are plenty of horror stories from the Internet community itself to make us cautious, not to mention the brief but dramatic outages over the last couple of years associated with relatively small software bugs in the control networks (i.e., CCS/SS7 signaling) of the telephone industry, both local and long distance.

A second general class of bugs will be associated with the implementation of new capabilities. IPng will likely support a whole set of new functions, such as larger (multiple?) address space(s), source routing, and flows, just to mention a few. Providing these new capabilities will require in most cases designing new distributed algorithms and testing implementation parameters very carefully. In addition, the future Internet will be even larger, have more diverse applications and have higher bandwidth. These are all factors that could have a multiplying effect on bugs that in the current network might be easily contained. The designers and implementers of IPng should be careful. It will be very important to provide the best possible transition process from IP to IPng. The need to maintain robustness and fault-tolerance is paramount.

Technology Pull. The strongest "technology pull" factors that will influence the Internet are the same that are dictating the accelerated pace of the cable, telephone, and computer networking world. The following is a partial list: higher network bandwidth, more powerful CPUs, larger and faster (static and dynamic) memory, improved signal processing and compression methods, advanced distributed computing technologies, open and extensible network operating systems, large distributed database management and directory systems, high-performance and high-capacity real-time servers, friendly graphical user interfaces, and efficient application development environments. These technology developments, coupled with the current aggressive business strategies in our industry and favorable public policies, are powerful forces that will clearly have an impact on the evolution and acceptance of IPng. The current deployment strategies of the cable industry and their partners do not rely on the existence of commercial IPng capabilities, but the availability of new effective networking technology could become a unifying force to facilitate the interworking of networks and services.

Summary. The potential for IPng to provide a universal internetworking solution is a very attractive possibility, but there are many hurdles to be overcome. The general acceptance of IPng for supporting future broadband services will depend on more than the IPng itself. There is need for IPng to be backed by the whole suite of Internet technology that will support the future networks and applications. These technologies must include the adequate support for commercial operation of a global Internet that will be built, financed, and administered by many different private and public organizations.

The Internet community has taken pride in following a nimble and efficient path in the development and deployment of network technology. And the Internet has been very successful up to now. The challenge is to show that the Internet model can be a preferred technical solution for the future. Broadband networks and services will become widely available in a relatively short future, and this puts the Internet community in a fast track race. The current process to define IPng can be seen as a test of the ability of the Internet to evolve from its initial development—very successful but also protected and limited in scope—to a general technology for the support of a commercially viable broadband marketplace. If the IPng model is to become the preferred general solution for broadband networking, the current IPng process seems to be a critical starting point.

Features, Technologies, and Issues for IPng

Part V

The Advantages of Many Addresses per Host

Steven M. Bellovin
AT&T Bell Laboratories

Currently, most hosts have only one address. With comparatively rare exceptions, hosts acting as hosts (as opposed to hosts acting as routers or PPP servers) are single–homed. Address space calculations reflect this one–host–one address; we assume that we can estimate the size of the address space by counting hosts. But this may be a serious error in planning for the IPng address space. The one–host–one address model may and should change.

For these ideas, I do not claim that multiple addresses per host is the only, or even the best, way to accomplish the goal in each case. The following ideas are at the very least plausible, and I expect that many of them will be tried.

Encoding Services. More and more often, services are being encoded in the host name. One can fetch files from ftp.research.att.com, look up an IP address on ns.uu.net, or synchronize clocks from ntp.udel.edu. Should this practice be generalized to the IP address domain?

In some cases such encoding is a very good idea. Certain services need to be configured by IP address; they are either used when the Domain Name System (DNS) is being bootstrapped (such as in glue records and root server cache records), or when its unavailable (i.e., when booting after a power hit, and local name servers are slower to reboot than their diskless clients).

Security is another reason for encoding services in addresses, in some cases. Address–based authentication is generally inadequate; relying on the name service adds another layer of risk. An attacker can go after the DNS, in that case. A risk–averse system manager might prefer to avoid the extra exposure, instead granting privileges (i.e., rlogin or NFS) by address instead of name. But that, of course, leads to all the usual headaches of manual configuration when the location of the service changes. If the address for the service could be held constant, there would be much more freedom to move it to another machine. One way to do that is by assigning the serving host a secondary address.

A related notion comes from the need to offer different views of a service from a single host. For example, research.att.com has long offered two distinct FTP archives with slightly different access policies. It would be nice if both could live on the same machine, with a different host address and name to distinguish them.

Many Internet service providers are already doing this for World Wide Web sites. In order to host two companies, foo.com and bar.com, and give them each their natural Web presence points—www.foo.com and www.bar.com—an extra IP address is often configured for the machine. This trend will only increase.

Archie is an even better example. There are three principal ways to use Archie: use a special protocol, and hence a special application program, on a dedicated port and host that is probably named archie.foo.bar; Telnet to archie.foo.bar and go through an extra and gratuitous login as archie; or Telnet to some special port on archie.foo.bar. The latter two are examples of using a standard protocol (Telnet) to offer a different service.

It would be better if archie.foo.bar provided the Archie service, while host.foo.bar provided a login prompt. Again, an easy way to do this would be to assign the host a separate IP address for its extra service. Users would be accessing not just different host names, but different IP addresses as well. Note that there are security advantages here, too. A firewall could be configured to allow access to the address associated with the Archie server, but not the other addresses on that host. That would provide a high degree of safety, assuming, of course, that the other servers on that host were bound to its primary addresses, and not the exposed address.

Another way to implement this concept would be to extend the DNS to return port number information as well as IP addresses. Thus, netlib.att.com might return 192.20.225.3:221. But that would necessitate changing every FTP client program, a daunting task.

MX records are very valuable, but they apply only to mail, and they don't supply port numbers. We could also look on use of multiple IP addresses as the extension of the MX concept.

Accounting and Billing. For better or worse, some parts of the Internet are moving toward usage–sensitive charging. At least four charging schemes seem possible now; doubtless, the marketeers in charge of such things can and will come up with more.

The first charging scheme is the traditional "pay as you go" approach. Each host is responsible for its own packets. Of course, that means that in a typical conversation both parties pay, and therefore, the providers of free FTP archives will end up paying dearly for their beneficence. This scheme seems unlikely. That leads to our second charging model: caller pays. The third charging scheme is to "make collect calls," much as is done on the telephone today. Finally, there might be the equivalent of American "900" numbers: the caller pays a premium to the server. This is not at all far–fetched; UUNET already has a 900 number for anonymous uucp clients. There is no need to register in advance; just dial in, and let the phone company act as your agent.

Given all these charging schemes, it is vital that the caller and recipient know in advance who will pay. It is not acceptable for users to learn after the fact that they have incurred a cost. We could envision use of IP options to convey cost information, but then again, that would preclude use of today's standard clients.

It is not sufficient to present a message at connection time warning of the charges, because many interfaces do not provide a hook for user interaction. And there are security concerns—suppose that someone puts up a gopher server that redirects a caller to some pay-to-play address, without displaying the required warning. A scam? Sure—but it's already happened with the phone network, and there is no reason to think that the Internet will be far behind.

My suggestion, of course, is to encode the charge algorithm in the destination address (and perhaps in the DNS name space as well). The bits themselves would determine who pays. Organizational border routers could implement policies on pay services; the anonymous workstations in a dorm computer lab wouldn't be allowed to call collect.

An extension of this scheme would use a comparatively large number of bits, letting the address act not just as a policy indicator, but also as an index to a charge algorithm table.

One Address per User. It may be useful to assign each user on a host a separate IP address for the duration of the login session. This has a number of advantages.

The first advantage ties to the charging scheme given above. The host would simply have to record the address assignments; billing could be done offline.

Similarly, different classes of users could have different forms of addresses. For example, those with hard–money accounts might have some bits set in the address that would allow for access to costly services.

Using today's technology, the border routers could make this sort of distinction.

One IP address per user also fits in well with encryption. There is a lot of attention today focused on network–layer encryption. But that provides host–level granularity of protection, which is sometimes insufficient. Transport–layer encryptors provide finer–grained protection, but does the Internet need two different low–level encryption schemes? If each user had a separate IP address and perhaps had it only on hosts that cared about such matters we could provide user–level protection and accountability with the same infrastructure used to support host–level accountability.

Low–grade Mobility. Several schemes under discussion for mobile IP hosts are aimed at a fairly general model of hosts moving anywhere. While moving hosts anywhere is important, there is also some need for limited mobility, within a subnet. This could be used for load–balancing. A mail relay that had just been asked to send a large message to a huge mailing list could offload some of its IP addresses to its peers. That would divert future incoming messages without invalidating thousands of cached MX records and their associated IP addresses. Similarly, servers for low–speed X terminals could reside on different physical machines, all the while not disturbing sessions in progress.

Merging Subnets. There has long been some need to merge subnets. Sometimes this is due to organizational changes; other times, bridges have been installed when routers would have been a more appropriate choice. Some hosts need to live on both logical networks at once, to avoid an extra hop through a router. It would be useful to be able to assign them multiple addresses per host to reflect the subnet structure.

How Many Addresses Do We Need? Assuming that these ideas bear fruit, how many addresses per host do we need?

Most of these schemes are fairly cheap. Few people would offer more than a handful of distinct service views per system. But the one–host–one address notion could be quite costly. We also have to account for address mask assignment policies. In many of today's networks, enough bits of host address have to be allocated to allow for the largest subnet in an organization. Even if we assume that IPng's routing protocols will be smarter about such things, foresight in address allocation will be needed to allow headroom for some networks to grow, while still maintaining a contiguous netmask. This in turn will contribute to sparse utilization of the address space. Accordingly, I recommend that we allow for 2^6, and perhaps as many as 2^8, extra addresses per host, to leave room for the ideas presented here.

Security Implications for IPng

Steven M. Bellovin
AT&T Bell Laboratories

A number of the candidates for IPng have some features that are worrisome from a security perspective. While it is not necessary that IPng be an improvement over IPv4, it must not make things worse. In some cases, there are features that would have a negative impact on security if we do not take certain precautions. It may be desirable to adopt the features anyway as the least of all evils, but in that case the corrective action is mandatory.

Firewalls. For better or worse, firewalls are very much a feature of today's Internet. They are not primarily a response to network protocol security problems per se. Rather, they are a means to compensate for failings in software engineering and system administration. As such, firewalls are not likely to go away any time soon; IPng will do nothing to make host programs any less buggy. Anything that makes firewalls harder to deploy will make IPng less desirable in the market.

Firewalls impose a number of requirements. First, there must be a hierarchical address space. Many address–based filters use the structure of IPv4 addresses for access control decisions. Fortunately, this is a requirement for scalable routing as well. Routers, though, only need access to the destination address of the packet. Network–level firewalls often need to check both the source and destination address. A structure that makes it harder to find the source address is a distinct negative.

There is also a need for access to the transport–level (i.e., the TCP or UDP) header. This may be for the port number field, or for access to various flag bits, notably the ACK bit in the TCP header. This latter field is often used to distinguish between incoming and outgoing calls.

In a different vein, at least one of the possible transition plans uses network–level packet translators (See *Transition and Other Critical Issues for IPng*). Organizations that use firewalls will need to deploy their own translators to aid in converting their own internal networks. They cannot rely on centrally located translators intended to serve the entire Internet community. It is thus vital that translators be simple, portable to many common platforms, and cheap; we do not want to impose too high a financial barrier for converts to IPng.

By the same token, it is desirable that such translation boxes not be usable for network–layer connection–laundering. It is difficult enough to trace back attacks today; we should not make it harder. (Some brands of terminal servers can be used for laundering. Most sites with such boxes have learned to configure them so that such activities are impossible.) Comprehensive logging is a possible alternative; when translators are developed they should preserve the originating addresses as far as possible.

Encryption and Authentication. A number of people are starting to experiment with IP–level encryption and cryptographic authentication. This trend will (and should) continue. IPng should not make this harder, either intrinsically or by imposing a substantial performance barrier. Encryption can be done with various different granularities: host–to–host, host–to–gateway, and gateway–to–gateway. All of these have their uses; IPng must not rule out any of them. Encapsulation and tunneling strategies are somewhat problematic, as the packet may no longer carry the original source address when it reaches an encrypting gateway. (This may be seen more as a constraint on network topologies, but we should warn people of the limitation.)

Dual–stack transition approaches imply multiple addresses for each host. The encryption and access control infrastructure needs to know about all addresses for a given host belonging to whichever stack. It should not be possible to bypass authentication or encryption by asking for a different address for the same host.

Source Routing and Address–based Authentication. The dominant form of host authentication in today's Internet is address–based. That is, hosts often decide to trust other hosts based on their IP addresses. (Actually, it's worse than that; much authentication is name–based, which opens up new avenues of attack. But if an attacker can spoof an IP address, there's no need to attack the name service.) To the extent that it does work, address–based authentication relies on the implied accuracy of the return route. That is, though it is easy to inject packets with a false source address, replies will generally follow the usual routing patterns and be sent to the real host with that address. This frustrates most, though not all, attempts at impersonation.

Problems can arise if source–routing is used. A source route, which must be reversed for reply packets, overrides the usual routing mechanism, and hence destroys the security of address–based authentication. For this reason, many organizations disable source–routing, at least at their border routers. To the extent that source–routing is used, it will break address–based authentication. This may not be bad; in fact, it is probably good. But it is vital that a more secure cryptographic authentication protocol be defined and deployed before any substantial cutover to source–routing on the Internet.

Accounting. A significant part of the Internet world would like to see usage–sensitive accounting. Usage–sensitive accounting has advantages for billing and for quality–of–service. For both uses definitive knowledge of the relevant address fields is needed. To accommodate relevant address fields, IPng should have a non–intrusive packet authentication mechanism. Non–intrusive means that it should (a) present little or no load to intermediate hops that do not need to do authentication, (b) be deletable (if desired) by the border gateways, and (c) be ignorable by end–systems or billing systems to which it is not relevant.

Implementing IPng on a BSD Host

Jim Bound
Digital Equipment Corporation

A host is a system that contains an operating system supporting a network subsystem as one of its parts, and an interprocess communications facility to access that network subsystem. These hosts are often referred to as workstations, servers, PCs, super computers, mainframes, or embedded systems (real-time devices). IPng will require changes to a host's network software architecture. Those changes should be as transparent as possible to the existing IPv4 applications executing on hosts.

After discussing the network software architecture for hosts based on the Berkeley Standard Distribution (BSD), Release 4.3/4.4 software, the paper will discuss the perceived network software alterations, extended capabilities, transition software, and a deployment consideration for IPng hosts.

Network Software Architecture. The BSD host network software architecture consists essentially of three components: the interprocess communications facility, the network communications subsystem, and the network protocols supported by the host. These three components are tightly coupled and must be integrated in a way that affords high performance for the applications that are dependent on these components to interoperate efficiently. A BSD host implementation view of the TCP/IP protocol suite is depicted in Figure 1.

Interprocess Communications Facility. The interprocess communications (IPC) facilities include three critical parts:

- IPC system calls themselves
- Mechanisms to support particular network protocols
- Data structures to support network communication

The IPC facility has two implementation parts: the part in user space, and the part in kernel space within the operating system. This distinction is often not made. This is why, in Figure 1, sockets appear in both user and kernel space. An IPC supports in user space an application program

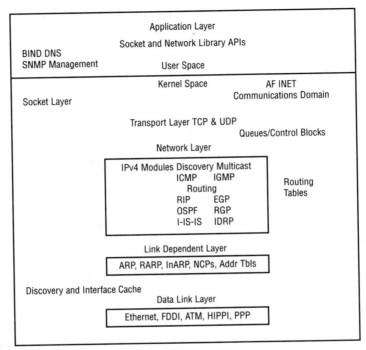

Figure 1. BSD Host Diagram

interface (API) which application developers use to access the network communications features of the host. These APIs have corresponding functions in the kernel space which execute the functions requested by the user space requests through the APIs.

The sockets paradigm on a BSD host defines the data structure of the network address within a selected protocol family (communications domain) in the network subsystem. This data structure consists of an address family, a port for the protocol selected, and a network address.

The IPC facility on a host is dependent upon its interface to the Domain Name System (DNS) application, usually the Berkeley BIND program. This is the standard method of turning host names into network addresses.

Other interfaces that may be required by applications to properly set up the network connection within the IPC facility include: setting and getting options for the protocols used; obtaining and accessing information about networks, protocols, and network services; and sending and transmitting datagrams.

Network Communications Subsystem. The ultimate purpose of the network communications subsystem is to send large amounts of data, known as datagrams, over a data network, and to receive datagrams from the data network.

The network communications subsystem consists of the following generic parts as depicted in Figure 1: transport layer, network layer, link dependent layer, and data link layer. However, these four are not implemented as truly distinct layers on BSD hosts. The transport layer supports the application interface into the network communications subsystem and sets up the parametric pieces to initiate and accept connections. The transport layer performs these functions through requests to the lower layers of the network communications subsystem. The transport layer also supports the queues and protocol control blocks for specific network connections.

The network layer supports the modules to build and extend the network layer datagram, the control protocol datagrams, and the routing abstraction on the host. This layer of the network communications subsystem on a BSD host is often extended to provide both interior and exterior routing functionality.

The link dependent layer supports the modules that provide an interface for the network communications subsystem to map network addresses to physical addresses, and build the necessary cache so this information is available to the host network software.

On a BSD host the network layer and link dependent layer together provide system discovery for hosts and routers. The data link layer supports the modules that define the structures for communicating with the hardware media used by the host on the local network.

Network Protocols. The TCP/IP protocol suite as defined by the IETF RFC specifications is a set of currently deployed network protocols and is referenced here for comparison.

Network Software Alterations. Alterations to a BSD host for IPng network software will be expected in the following:

- Applications Embedding IPv4 Addresses
- Transport Interfaces and Network APIs
- Socket Layer and Structures
- Transport Layer
- Network Layer Components
- Link Dependent Layer

Applications Embedding IPv4 Addresses. Internet–style applications are the set of protocols defined for an end user using TCP/IP to exchange messages, transfer files, and establish remote login sessions.

Applications use the sockets' network APIs to maintain an opaque view of the network addresses used to support connections across a network. Opaque in this context means that the application determines the network address for the connection and then binds that address to a socket. The application then uses the reference defined for that socket to receive and transmit data across a network, rather than continuing to use the network address itself.

An application that embeds an IPv4 network address within its datagram has made an underlying assumption that the format of that address is permanent. This will cause a great problem when the transition to IPng causes addresses to change. The prominent example of an application embedding IPv4 addresses is FTP. Other applications that have IP addresses embedded in their data include SNMP, the DNS, Kerberos, and many software license servers.

Transport Interfaces and Network APIs. The transport interface and network API enhancements that must take place on a BSD host because of IPng are alterations that affect the size of the network address used by the socket data structure. Depending on how the address data structure in the socket is implemented, supporting both IPv4 and IPng could require existing IPv4 applications to be recompiled. In the worst case scenario, supporting both could also require modifications to existing IPv4 applications software which accesses the network communications subsystem.

There will have to be enhancements to the network APIs that an application uses to retrieve DNS records to differentiate between IPv4 and IPng address requests. The network API enhancements and how they are implemented will affect the ability of IPng on a BSD host to inter-operate among IPv4 only, IPng only, and IPng–IPv4 dual–host systems.

For IPng, the network options, services, and management objects will have to be extended at the transport interface so those features can be accessed by applications software.

Socket Layer and Structures. The socket layer and structures will require changes to support the IPng addresses. In addition, new or removed options and services will need to be incorporated into the socket abstraction within the network communications subsystem.

Transport Layer. The transport layer will become more overloaded to support the binding of either the IPv4 or IPng network layer components to differentiate the services and structures available to a host application. The overload will also take place to support functionality removed in the network layer and moved to the transport layer.

It will also take some design thought to implement IPng so the hundreds of person–years invested in performance improvements in the host transport layer are maintained. For example, much has been invested to make header compression per TCP connection over a slow link worthwhile and efficient. The implementations of this must be modified for IPng. This must be analyzed in depth, and should be part of the operational testing of IPng.

Network Layer Components. The network layer components for IPng will require the greatest alterations on a host. In addition, a host will be required to maintain an integrated network layer below the transport layer software to support either the IPng or IPv4 network layer and associated components. Depending on the IPng selected, the host alterations to the network layer components will range from complete replacement with new protocols to extensions to existing IPv4 network layer protocols to support IPng. All IPng proposals will affect the BSD host routing abstraction to maintain host software that supports interior and exterior routing. Depending on the proposal selected, those changes can cause either a complete new paradigm or an update to the existing IPv4 paradigm. System discovery of nodes on the local subnetwork or across an internetwork path in all IPng proposals will require changes to the BSD host software network layer component.

Link Dependent Layer. The link dependent layer on a host will need to accommodate new IPng addresses and the system discovery models of any IPng proposal.

Extended Capabilities with IPng. Extended capabilities that could be implemented by BSD hosts are listed below. Many of these capabilities exist today with IPv4, but may require changes with the implementation of IPng. Some of them will be new capabilities.

Autoconfiguration and Autoregistration. Today hosts can provide autoconfiguration with Dynamic Host Configuration Protocol (DHCP) using IPv4 addresses. IPng hosts will be faced with having to provide support for existing IPv4 addresses and the new IPng addresses. In addition, the boot–strap protocol (BOOTP) used to boot minimal BSD host configurations (e.g., diskless nodes) will need to be supported by IPng hosts.

Network Management. Network management for IPng will have to support new network objects as defined by the IPng proposal. In addition, the data structures in the BSD host network kernel used as information to display network topology will be altered by a new network layer datagram and associated components.

Other extended capabilities are:

- PATH Maximum Transition Unit (MTU) Discovery
- Multicast
- Flow Specification and Handling
- System Discovery
- Translation and Encapsulation
- Network Layer Security
- Socket Address Structure
- Network APIs

Transition Software. Transition software is the alterations to the network software on a host to support both IPv4 and IPng for applications and the host's operating system network kernel. (See *Transition and Other Critical Issues for IPng.*)

Transition software on a host will be required to maintain compatibility between IPv4 and IPng, and to manage both the existing IPv4 and IPng environments as follows:

- DNS record updates and handling by the application
- SNMP management interface and monitoring of host network structures
- APIs supporting IPv4 and IPng differentiation for the application
- Network tools supporting IPv4 and IPng (e.g., tcpdump...)
- System discovery with IPng methods in lieu of IPv4 Address Resolution Protocol
- BOOTP diskless node support for IPng
- DHCP integration with IPng auto–configuration
- Routing table configuration on the BSD host (e.g., `route` and `ifconfig` commands)
- Selection of the network layer (IPv4 or IPng) at the transport layer

- New options and services provided by an IPng protocol through IPng
- IPv4 and IPng routing protocols in the network layer
- IPv4 and IPng system discovery in the network layer

These are only the highlights of the transition software that a host will have to deal with in its implementation of IPng. (See *Transition Overview* for more software components, such as configured tunneling.) The host network architecture shown in Figure 1 will require software enhancements to each labeled item in the figure.

It should also be a requirement that existing IPv4 binaries be preserved on hosts that have both IPv4 and IPng network layers, insofar as possible. Two options would be that

- binaries without interest in IPng on dual hosts may run over IPv4 as if IPng was not implemented there, or
- binaries without interest in new features of IPng may run either over IPv4 or IPng without being recompiled.

It is desirable that, when a host implements an IPv4 network layer, an IPng network layer, and associated components, there is no performance degradation on the host compared to the performance of an existing IPv4-only host.

It should not be a requirement by IPng that an IPng host must support both an IPv4 and an IPng network layer.

Transition and Other Critical Issues for IPng

Brian E. Carpenter
CERN

Some general requirements for IPng in selected areas are outlined. Firstly, the following features are required for stepwise transition:

- Interworking at every stage and every layer
- Header translation considered harmful
- Coexistence
- IPv4–to–IPng address mapping
- Dual–stack hosts
- Domain Name Service (DNS)
- Smart dual–stack code
- Smart management tools.

Transition and Deployment. It is clear that the transition to IPng will take years and that every Internet site will have to decide its own staged transition plan. Only the very smallest sites could envisage a single step ("flag day") transition, presumably under pressure from their Internet service providers. Furthermore, once the IPng is decided upon, the next decade (or more) of activity in the Internet and in all private networks using the Internet suite will be strongly affected by the process of IPng deployment. User sites will look at the decision whether to change from IPv4 in the same way as they have looked at changes of programming language or operating system in the past. It is not a foregone conclusion that all sites will change to IPng. The main concern for Internet users is to minimize both the cost of change and the risk of lost production.

These concerns immediately define strong constraints for transition and deployment of IPng. Some of these constraints, with short explanations, are listed below.

Interworking at Every Stage and Every Layer. Interworking at every stage and every layer is the major constraint on IPng. Vendors of computer systems, routers, and applications software will certainly not coordinate their product release dates with that of IPng. Users will go on running their old equipment and software. Therefore, any combination of

IPv4 and IPng hosts and routers must be able to interwork (i.e., participate in UDP and TCP sessions). IPv4 hosts and IPv4 routers are hosts and routers that run exactly what they run today, with no maintenance releases and no configuration changes. IPng hosts and IPng routers are hosts and routers that have a new version of IP, and have been reconfigured. An IPv4 packet must be able to find its way from any IPv4 host, to any other IPv4 or IPng host, or vice versa, through a mixture of IPv4 and IPng routers, with no modifications to the IPv4 hosts. IPv4 routers must internetwork with no modifications. Additionally, an application package which is "aware" of IPv4, but still "unaware" of IPng must be able to run on a computer system which is running IPv4, but communicating with an IPng host. For example an old PC in Europe should be able to access an NIC server in the United States, even if the NIC server is running IPng and the transatlantic routing mechanisms are partly converted; or a Class C network in one department of a company should retain full access to corporate servers which are running IPng, even though nothing whatever has been changed inside the Class C network.

An IPv4–only application should not be required to run on an IPng host. Some hosts cannot be upgraded until all their applications are IPng–compatible. In other words, the API may change to some extent. Some vendors, however, may want to strictly preserve the IPv4 API on an IPng host.

Harmful Header Translation. Any transition scenario which requires dynamic header translation between IPv4 and IPng packets will create almost insurmountable practical difficulties:

- IPng functionality will be a superset of IPv4 functionality. However, successful translation between protocols requires that the functionalities of the two protocols which are to be translated are effectively identical. To achieve this, applications will need to know when they are interworking, via the IPng API and a translator somewhere in the network, with an IPv4 host, so as to use only IPv4 functionality. This is an unrealistic constraint.
- Administration of translators will be quite impracticable for large sites, unless the translation mechanism is completely blind and automatic. Specifically, any translation mechanism that requires special tags to be maintained manually for each host in tables (such as DNS tables or router tables) to indicate the need for translation will be impossible to administer. On a site with thousands of hosts running

many versions and releases of several operating systems, hosts move forward and backward between software releases in such a way that continuously tracking the required state of such tags will be impossible. Multiplied across the whole Internet, this will lead to chaos, complex failure modes, and difficult diagnoses. In particular, it will make the identical translation of the IPv4 and IPng functionalities described above impossible to respect.

In practice, the knowledge that translation is needed should never leak out of the site concerned if chaos is to be avoided. Yet, without such knowledge, applications cannot limit themselves to IPv4 functionality when necessary.

To avoid confusion, note that header translation is not the same thing as network address translation (NAT).

Performance issues are not tackled in detail, but clearly another disadvantage of translation is the consequent overhead.

Coexistence. The Internet infrastructure whether global or private must allow coexistence of IPv4 and IPng in the same routers and on the same physical paths.

This coexistence is a necessity, in order that the network infrastructure can be updated to IPng without requiring hosts to be updated in lock step, and without requiring translators.

Note that this requirement does not impose a decision about a common or separate (ships–in–the–night) approach to routing, nor does it exclude encapsulation as a coexistence mechanism.

IPv4 to IPng Address Mapping. People will have to understand what is happening during transition. Although auto–configuration of IPng addresses may be a desirable endpoint, management of the transition will be greatly simplified if there is an optional simple mapping, on a given site, between IPv4 and IPng addresses.

Therefore, the IPng address space should include a mapping for IPv4 addresses, such that (if a site or service provider wants to do this) the IPv4 address of a system can be transformed mechanically into its IPng address, most likely by adding a prefix. The prefix does not have to be the same for every site; it is likely to be at least service–provider specific.

This does not imply that such address mapping will be used for dynamic translation, although it could be, or to embed IPv4 routing within IPng routing, although it also could be. Its main purpose is to simplify transition planning for network operators.

By the way, this address mapping requirement does not actually assume that IPv4 addresses are globally unique.

Neither does it help much in setting up the relationship, if any, between IPv4 and IPng routing domains and hierarchies. There is no reason to suppose these will be in 1:1 correspondence.

Dual–stack Hosts. Stepwise transition without translation is hard to imagine, unless a large portion of hosts are simultaneously capable of running IPng and IPv4. All hosts running IPng must still be able to run IPv4. If A needs to talk to B (an IPng host) and to C (an IPv4 host) then either A or B must be able to run both IPv4 and IPng.

This dual–stack requirement does not imply that IPng hosts really have two completely separate IP implementations (dual stacks and dual APIs), but just that they behave as if they did. Dual–stack hosts are compatible with encapsulation (i.e., one of the two stacks encapsulates packets for the other).

Clearly, management of dual stack hosts will be simplified by address mapping. Only the site prefix has to be configured (manually or dynamically), in addition to the IPv4 address.

In a dual–stack host the IPng API and the IPv4 API will be logically distinguishable even if they are implemented as a single entity. Applications will know from the API whether they are using IPng or IPv4.

Domain Name Service (DNS). The dual–stack requirement implies that DNS has to reply with both an IPv4 and IPng address for IPng hosts, or with a single reply that encodes both.

If a host is attributed an IPng address in DNS, but is not actually running IPng yet, it will appear as a black hole in IPng space.

Smart Dual–stack Code. The dual-stack code may get two addresses back from DNS; which one does it use? During the many years of transition the Internet will contain black holes. For example, somewhere on the way from IPng host A to IPng host B there will sometimes (unpredictably) be IPv4–only routers which discard IPng packets. Also, the state of the DNS does not necessarily correspond to reality; a host for which DNS claims to know an IPng address may in fact not be running IPng at a particular moment. Thus an IPng packet to that host will be discarded on delivery. Knowing that a host has both IPv4 and IPng addresses gives no information about black holes. A solution to this must be proposed and it must not depend on manually maintained information. (If this is not resolved, the dual–stack approach is no better than the packet translation approach.)

Smart Management Tools. A complete set of management tools is going to be needed during the transition. Why is my IPng route different from my IPv4 route? If there is translation, where does it happen? Where are the black holes? Is that host really IPng–capable today? These are only a few of the questions site managers will be asking, and many management tools will be required that can answer them.

Multicasts, High and Low. It is taken for granted that multicast applications must be supported by IPng. One obvious architectural rule is that no multicast packet should ever travel twice over the same wire, whether it is a LAN or WAN wire. Failure to observe this rule would mean that the maximum number of simultaneous multicast transactions would be halved.

A negative feature of IPv4 on LANs is the cavalier use of physical broadcast packets by protocols such as ARP (and various non–IETF copycats). On large LANs this leads to a number of undesirable consequences (often caused by poor products or inexperienced users, not by the protocol design itself). The obvious architectural rule is that physical broadcast should be replaced by unicast (or at worst, multicast) whenever possible.

Asynchronous Transfer Mode (ATM). The networking industry is investing heavily in ATM. No IPng proposal will be plausible, in the sense of gaining management approval, unless it is ATM–compatible, i.e., unless there is a clear model of how it will run over an ATM network. Although a fully detailed document such as RFC-1577 [1] is not needed immediately, it must be shown that the basic model works.(See *Supporting ATM Services in IPng*.) Similar remarks could be made about X.25, Frame Relay, SMDS, etc., but ATM is the case with the highest management hype ratio today.

Policy Routing and Accounting. Unfortunately, policy routing and accounting cannot be ignored, however much one might like to try. Funding agencies want traffic to flow over the lines funded to carry it, and they want to know afterwards how much traffic there was. Accounting information can also be used for network planning and for back–charging.

It is therefore necessary that IPng and its routing procedures allow traffic to be routed in a way that depends on its source and destination in detail. As an example, traffic from the Physics Department of MIT might be required to travel a different route to CERN than traffic from the Math department.

A simple approach to this requirement is to insist that IPng must support provider–based addressing and routing.

Accounting of traffic is required at the same level of detail, or at an even greater level of detail. (For example, how much of the traffic is FTP and how much is World Wide Web?)

Both policy routing and accounting will cost time or money, and may impact more than just the IP layer, but IPng cannot duck them.

Security Considerations. IPng will have to have very good security as a basic function. Corporate network operators, and campus network operators who have been hacked a few times, take this more seriously than many protocol experts. Indeed, many corporate network operators would see improved security as a more compelling argument for transition to IPng than anything else.

Since IPng will presumably be a datagram protocol, limiting what can be done in terms of end–to–end security, IPng must allow more effective firewalls in routers than IPv4. In particular efficient traffic barring, based on source and destination addresses and types of transaction, is needed.

It seems likely that the same features needed to allow policy routing and detailed accounting would be needed for improved firewall security. It is outside the scope of this perspective to discuss these features in detail, but it seems unlikely that they should be limited to implementation details in the border routers. Packets will have to carry some authenticated trace of the (source, destination, transaction) triplet in order to check for unwanted traffic, to allow policy–based source routing, and/or to allow detailed accounting. Presumably any IPng will carry source and destination identifiers in some format in every packet, but identifying the type of transaction, or even the individual transaction, is an extra requirement.

Nimrod IPng
Technical Requirements

J. Noel Chiappa

Overview of Nimrod. Nimrod is a project which aims, in part, to produce a next-generation routing architecture for the Internet; but also, more generally, to try and produce a basic design for routing in a single global-scale communication substrate, a design which will prove sufficiently flexible and powerful to serve into a future as yet unforseeable.

Nimrod does this through the conjunction of two powerful basic mechanisms: distribution of maps, as opposed to distribution of routing tables; and selection of routes by clients of the network, not by the switches in the network.

(This latter approach is sometimes called "source routing," but this term can be a bit misleading, since in Nimrod the route does not have to be chosen by the actual source, but can be the responsibility of an agent working on the source's behalf. The terms "unitary routing" or "explicit routing" have therefore been used to describe this approach. (See *Routing Implications for IPng*). The important thing to realize is that the path is not selected in a fully distributed, hop-by-hop manner, in which each switch has an equal role to play in selecting the path).

The actual operation is fairly simple, in principle. Maps of the network's actual connectivity (maps which will usually include high-level abstractions for large parts of that connectivity, in the same way road maps of an area may not show all the roads, just the "important" ones) are made available to all the entities which need to select paths. Those entities use these maps to compute paths, and those paths are passed to the actual switches, along with the data, as directions on how to forward the data.

The rest of this section discusses how the Nimrod routing and addressing architecture interacts with the rest of the internetwork layer, and what requirements it has upon the internetwork layer protocol's packet format.

The Nimrod Subsystems of the Internetwork Layer. One reason that Nimrod is not simply a monolithic subsystem is that some of the interaction with the other subsystems of the internetwork layer, for instance the resource allocation subsystem, is much clearer and easier to manage if the routing is broken up into several subsystems, with the interaction between them open.

The subsystems which comprise the functionality covered by Nimrod are:

- Routing information distribution (in the case of Nimrod, topology map distribution, along with the attributes (policy, QoS, etc.) of the topology elements)
- Route selection (strictly speaking, not part of the Nimrod system per se, but a local matter, although a necessary one)
- User traffic handling

The first can be defined fairly well without reference to other subsystems, but the second and third (route selection and user traffic handling) are necessarily more involved. For instance, route selection might involve finding out which links have the resources available to handle some required level of service. For user traffic handling, if a particular application needs a resource reservation, getting that resource reservation to the routers is as much a part of getting the routers ready as making sure they have the correct routing information, so here too, routing is tied in with other subsystems.

It is possible to talk about the relationship between the Nimrod subsystems, and the other functional subsystems of the internetwork layer, but until the service model of the internetwork layer is more clearly visible, along with the functional boundaries within that layer, such a discussion is necessarily rather nebulous.

Specific Interaction Issues. Here is an incomplete list of the things that Nimrod would like to see from the internetwork layer as a whole:

- A unified definition of flows in the internetwork layer, and a unified way of identifying, through a separate flow-id field, which packets belong to a given flow (see *IPv6 Technical Overview*).
- A unified mechanism (potentially distributed) for installing state about flows (including multicast flows) in routers.
- A method for getting information about whether a given resource allocation request has failed along a given path; this might be part of the unified flow setup mechanism.

- An interface to (potentially distributed) mechanism for maintaining the membership in a multicast group.
- Support for multiple interfaces; that is, multi-homing. Nimrod does this by decoupling transport level entity ("TLE") identification from interface identification (called "locators" in Nimrod). For example, a packet with any valid destination locator should be accepted by a TCP module, if the destination TLE identifier ("TLEI") is the one assigned to that entity.
- Support for multiple locators per network interface. This is needed for a number of reasons, among them to allow for less painful transitions in the locator abstraction hierarchy as the topology changes.
- Support for multiple TLEIs per TLE. This would definitely include both multiple multicast TLEIs (i.e., TLEIs that refer to a group of TLE's), and at least one unicast TLEI (the need for multiple unicast TLEIs per TLE is not obvious).
- Support for distinction between a multicast group as a named entity, and a multicast flow which may not reach all the members.
- A distributed, replicated, user name translation system (perhaps using the existing Domain Name System - DNS) that maps such user names into (TLEI, locator0, ... locatorN) bindings.

General Principles for Packet Formats. As a general rule, the design philosophy of Nimrod is "maximize the lifetime (and flexibility) of the architecture." Design tradeoffs (i.e., optimizations) that will adversely affect the flexibility, adaptability, and lifetime of the design are not necessarily wise choices; they may cost more than they save. Such optimizations might be the correct choices in a stand-alone system, where the replacement costs are relatively small; in the global communication network, the replacement costs are very much higher.

Providing the Nimrod functionality requires the carrying of certain information in the packets. The design principle noted above has a number of corollaries in specifying the fields to contain that information.

First, the design should be "simple and straightforward," which means that various functions should be handled by completely separate mechanisms, and fields in the packets. It may seem that an opportunity exists to save space by overloading two functions onto one mechanism or field, but general experience is that, over time, this attempt at optimization costs more, by restricting flexibility and adaptability.

Second, fixed field lengths should be specified to be somewhat larger than can conceivably be used; the history of system architecture is replete with examples (processor address size being the most notorious) where fields became too short over the lifetime of the system. Below, for each item, an indication is given as what the smallest reasonable "adequate" lengths are, but this is more of a "critical floor" than a recommendation. A "recommended" length is also given; this is the length which corresponds to the application of the principle above. Note, however, that these "recommended" lengths are not upper bounds; modulo efficiency concerns, fields cannot be "too long," only "too short."

It is important to note that this does not mean that implementations must support the maximum value possible in a field of that size. In practise, system-wide administrative limits would be placed on the maximum values which must be supported. Then, as the need arises, the administrative limit can be increased. This allows an easy, and completely interoperable (with no special mechanisms) path to upgrade the capability of the network. If the maximum supported value of a field needs to be increased from M to N, an announcement is made that this is coming; during the interim period, the system continues to operate with M, but new implementations are deployed; while this is happening, interoperation is automatic, with no transition mechanisms of any kind needed. When things are "ready" (i.e., the proportion of old equipment is small enough), use of the larger value commences.

Packet Format Fields. In considering the packet format, one can distinguish between the host-router part of the packet's path, and the router-router part. It is not absolutely necessary that they be the same (although it is simpler), and if they are different, a format that is good for one may not be best suited to another. In addition, Nimrod has three forwarding modes (flows, datagram, and source-routed packets), and some modes use fields that are not used by other modes.

Bearing these points in mind, what Nimrod would like to see in the internetworking packet is:

- Source and destination TLE identification. There are several possibilities here, such as:

  - "Shortish", fixed-length fields which appear in each packet, in the internetwork header, which contain globally unique, topologically insensitive identifiers for TLEs. For these 48 bits is adequate, but at least 64 bits is recommended.
  - Some shorter field which appears in all packets which contains a value which is not globally unique, but only unique in mapping

tables on each end, tables which map from the small value to a globally unique value, such as a DNS name. For these 8 bits is adequate, but at least 16 bits is recommended.

- Some overall design which does not include any TLE identification in the packet at all, but transfers it at the start of a communication, and from then on infers it. This alternative would have to have some other means of telling which TLE a given packet is for, if there are several TLEs at a given destination. Some coordination on allocation of flow-ids, or higher-level port numbers, etc., might do this.

Any of these will do, but the exact choice of which is a question that includes factors outside the routing, so a specific recommendation cannot be made here.

- Flow identification. There are two basic approaches here, depending on whether flows are aggregated (in intermediate switches) or not. (It should be emphasized at this point that it is not yet known whether flow aggregation will be needed. The only reason to do it is to control the growth of state in intermediate routers, but there is no definite case made that either this growth will be unmanageable, or that aggregating flows will be feasible.)

For the non-aggregated case, a single "flow-id" field will suffice. This *must not* use one of the two previous TLE fields, as in datagram mode the flow-id will be overwritten during transit of the network. It is possible to use non-globally unique flow-ids (which would allow a shorter length to this field), although this would mean that collisions would result, and have to be dealt with. For a non-globally unique flow-id, 24 bits would be adequate, 32 are recommended.

For the aggregated case, three broad classes of mechanism are possible.

- The packet contains a sequence of flow-ids. Whenever aggregation or de-aggregation occurs, the next one along the list is used. This takes the most space, but is otherwise the least work for the routers.
- The packet contains a stack of flow-ids, with the current one on the top. On aggregation, push a new one on; on de-aggregation, take one off. This takes more work, but less space in the packet. Encapsulating packets to do aggregation does basically this, but entire headers are being stacked, not just flow-ids. The clever way to do this flow-id stacking is to find out from flow-setup how deep the

stack will get, and allocate the necessary space in the packet when it's created. That way, all that ever has to happen is adding a new flow-id, or removing one; it is never necessary to modify the header to make room for more flow-ids.

- The packet contains only the "base" flow-id, and the current flow-id. On aggregation, the latter is updated. The tricky part comes on de-aggregation; the correct value must be replaced. To do this, there has to be state in the router at the end of the aggregated flow, which says what the de-aggregated flow for each base flow is. The downside here is obvious: there is no need for individual flow state for each of the constituent flows in all the routers along the path of that aggregated flow, *except* for the last one.

Other than encapsulation, which has significant inefficiency in space overhead fairly quickly, after just a few layers of aggregation, there appears to be no way to do it with just one flow-id in the packet header. Even if there is no modification of the packets, but the aggregation is done by mapping some number of "base" flow-id's to a single aggregated flow in the routers along the path of the aggregated flow, the table that does the mapping is still going to have to have a number of entries directly proportional to the number of base flows going through the switch.

- A looping packet detector. This is any mechanism that will detect a packet which is "stuck" in the network; a timeout value in packets, together with a check in routers, is an example. If this is a hop-count, it has to be more than 8 bits; 12 bits would be adequate, and 16 is recommended (which also makes it easy to update). This is not to say that networks with diameters larger than 256 are good, or that one should design such nets, but limiting the maximum path through the network to 256 hops is likely to provide a very painful limit, later on, just as making "infinity" 16 in RIP did, eventually. When that ceiling is reached, it's going to be very painful, and there won't be an easy fix. Note that path lengths of over 30 hops are already seen in the Internet.

- Optional source and destination "locators." These are structured, variable length items which are topologically sensitive identifiers for the place in the network from which the traffic originates or to which the traffic is destined. The locator will probably contain internal separators which divide up the fields, so that a particular field can be enlarged without creating a great deal of upheaval. An adequate value for maximum length supported would be up to 32 bytes per locator, and longer would be even better; up to 256 bytes per locator is recommended.

- Perhaps (paired with the above), an optional pointer into the locators. This is "forwarding state" (i.e., state in the packet which records something about its progress across the network) which is used in the datagram forwarding mode to help ensure that the packet does not loop. It can also improve the forwarding processing efficiency. It is thus not absolutely essential, but is very desirable from a real-world engineering viewpoint. It needs to be large enough to identify locations in either locator; e.g., if locators can be up to 256 bytes, it would need to be 9 bits.

- An optional source route. This is used to support the "source routed packet" forwarding mode. Although not designed in detail yet, two possible approaches can be discussed.

  - In one, used with "semi-strict" source routing (in which a contiguous series of entities is named, albeit perhaps at a high layer of abstraction), the syntax will likely look much like source routes in PIP;[2] in Nimrod they would be a sequence of Nimrod entity identifiers (i.e., locator elements, not complete locators), along with clues as to the context in which each identifier is to be interpreted (e.g., up, down, across, etc.). Since those identifiers themselves are variable length (although probably most will be two bytes or less, otherwise the routing overhead inside the named object would be excessive), and the hop-count above contemplates the possibility of paths of over 256 hops, it would seem that these might possibly some day exceed 512 bytes, if a lengthy path was specified in terms of the actual physical assets used. An adequate length would be 512 bytes; the recommended length would be 2^{16} bytes (although this length would probably not be supported in practice; rather, the field length would allow it).
  - In the other, used with classical "loose" source routes, the source consists of a number of locators. It is not yet clear if this mode will be supported. If so, the header would need to be able to store a sequence of locators (as described above). Space might be saved by not repeating locator prefixes that match that of the previous locator in the sequence; Nimrod will probably allow use of such "locally useful" locators. It is hard to determine what an adequate length would be for this case; the recommended length would be

2^{16} bytes (with the previous caveat).

- Perhaps (paired with the above), an optional pointer into the source route. This is also optional forwarding state. It needs to be large enough to identify locations anywhere in the source route; e.g., if the source router can be up to 1024 bytes, it would need to be 10 bits.

Addition Methods. It is possible to use Nimrod in a mode where needed information/fields are added by the first-hop router. It is thus useful to ask which of the fields must be present in the host-router header, and which could be added by the router? The only ones which are absolutely necessary in all packets are the TLEIs (provided that some means is available to the routers to map them into locators).

How would additional information/fields be added to the packet, if the packet is emitted from the host in incomplete form? (By this is meant the simple question of how, mechanically, not the more complex issue of where, any needed information comes from. It is assumed here that the packet does not contain empty fields for this information, but rather a format which does not include those fields at all.)

This question is complex, since all the IPng candidates (and in fact, any reasonable inter-networking protocol) are extensible protocols; those extension mechanisms could be used. Also, it would possible to carry some of the required information as user data in the inter-networking packet, with the original user's data encapsulated further inside. Finally, a private inter-router packet format could be defined.

It's not clear which choice is best, but it is possible to discuss which fields the Nimrod routers need access to, and how often; less-used ones could be placed in harder-to-get-to locations (such as in an encapsulated header). The fields to which the routers need access on every hop are the flow-id and the looping packet detector. The locator/pointer fields are only needed at intervals (in what Nimrod's datagram forwarding mode calls "active" routers), as is the source route (the latter on entry to every object which is named in the source route).

Depending on how access control is done, and which forwarding mode is used, the TLEIs and/or locators might be examined for access control purposes, wherever that function is performed.

The Future of Routing. Although this section is specifically about the IPng requirements of the Nimrod routing architecture, there are reasons to believe that any routing architecture for a large, ubiquitous global network will have many of the same basic fundamental principles as the Nimrod architecture, and the requirements that these generate.

While contemporary routing technologies do not yet have the characteristics and capabilities that generate these requirements, they also do not seem to be completely suited to routing in the next-generation Internet. As routing technology moves toward what is needed for the next generation Internet, the underlying fundamental laws and principles of routing will almost inevitably drive the design, and hence the requirements, toward things which look like the material presented here.

Therefore, even if Nimrod is not the routing architecture of the next-generation Internet, the basic routing architecture of that Internet will have requirements that, while differing in detail, will almost inevitably be similar to these. This makes the requirements of Nimrod worth looking at, even if the specific Nimrod design is destined to be nothing more than a historical curiousity.

Routing Implications for IPng

Deborah Estrin
University of Southern California
Tony Li
Yakov Rekhter
Cisco Systems, Inc.

Motivation. The global Internet can be modeled as a collection of hosts interconnected via transmission and switching facilities. Control over this global Internet is not homogeneous, but is distributed among multiple administrative authorities. Resources under control of a single administration form a domain. In order to support each domain's autonomy and heterogeneity, routing consists of two distinct components: intradomain (interior) routing, and inter-domain (exterior) routing. Intradomain routing provides support for communication among hosts where data traverses facilities within a single domain. Interdomain routing provides support for communication where data traverses facilities spanning multiple domains. The entities that forward packets across domain boundaries are called border routers (BRs). The entities responsible for exchanging inter-domain routing information are called route servers (RSs). RSs and BRs may be collocated. As the Internet grows, providing inter-domain routing that can accommodate both increased size and increasingly diverse routing requirements becomes more and more crucial. The number and diversity of routing requirements is increasing due to

- transit restrictions imposed by source, destination, and transit networks;
- different types of services offered and required; and
- the presence of multiple carriers with different charging schemes.

Over the next 5 to 10 years, the types of services available will continue to evolve, and specialized facilities will be employed to provide new services. The combinatorial explosion of mixing and matching these different criteria and capabilities will weigh heavily on the mechanisms provided by conventional hop–by–hop routing architectures. While the number and variety of routes provided by hop–by–hop routing architectures with type of service (ToS) support (i.e., multiple, tagged routes) may be sufficient for a large percentage of traffic, it is important that mechanisms be in place to support efficient routing of specialized traffic types via special routes. Examples of special routes are: (1) a route that travels through one or more transit domains that discriminate according to the source domain, and (2) a route that travels through transit domains that support a service that is not widely or regularly used. We refer to all other routes as generic.

Overview of the Unified Architecture. We want to support special routes. Therefore, we need to exploit aggregation when possible and support special routes for exceptions. Thus, our scalable inter-domain routing architecture consists of two major components: node routing (NR) and explicit routing (ER).[3,4] The NR component in each inter-domain router computes and installs routes that are shared by a significant number of sources. These generic routes are commonly used and warrant wide propagation; consequently, aggregation of routing information is critical.

The ER component computes and installs routes that are not shared by enough sources to justify computation by all inter-domain routers.[5] When a specialized route is needed, it is expressed explicitly in the headers of individual data packets and may be stored in the routers along the path to avoid carrying the explicit route in every data packet. Each inter-domain router is responsible for installing only those explicit routes that pass through it. Routes that are only needed sporadically (i.e., the demand for them is not continuous or otherwise predictable) are also candidates for ER. The potentially large number of different specialized routes, combined with their sparse utilization, make them too costly to support with the NR mechanism.

The NR component uses a path vector protocol because path vector exhibits excellent convergence and overhead properties as network size grows.[6,7] Unlike more traditional distance vector protocols, convergence time does not grow in proportion to the number of nodes in the network; unlike link state routing, route selection and filtering can vary from router to router without causing loops. The particular path vector protocol used supports aggregation of routing information based on topologically assigned addresses.

Moreover, path vectors can provide information about the policy and type of service supported by advertised routes. Policy information is frequently relevant to inter-domain routing decisions, even if the routes are not "specialized," per se. In order to locate routes with special characteristics, the ER component must have the more detailed and complete

information supported by map–based approaches such as link state. Fortunately, explicit routes are only installed when and where they are
needed, and therefore aggregation is less critical. Explicit routing supports both strict and loose routes, and can either use route–setup or carry
routes in all data packet headers.[8]

A useful analogy to this approach is the manufacturing of consumer
products. When predictable patterns of demand exist, firms produce
objects and sell them as "off the shelf" consumer goods. In our architecture NR provides off–the–shelf routes. If demand is not predictable, then
firms accept special orders and produce what is demanded at the time it
is needed. In addition, if a part is so specialized that only a single or small
number of consumers need it, the consumer may repeatedly special order
the part, even if it is needed in a predictable manner, because the consumer does not represent a big enough market for the producer to bother
managing the item as part of its regular production.

ER provides such special–order, on–demand routes. By combining
NR and ER routing, we propose to support inter-domain routing in internets of global scale, while at the same time providing efficient support for
specialized routing requirements. The development of this architecture
does assume that routing requirements will be diverse and that special
routes will be needed.

On the other hand, the architecture does not depend on assumptions
about the particular types of routes demanded or on the distribution of
that demand. Routing will adapt naturally over time to changing traffic
patterns and new services by shifting computation and installation of
particular types of routes between the two components of the hybrid
architecture. Before continuing with our explanation of this architecture,
we wish to state up front that supporting highly specialized routes for all
source–destination pairs in an internet, or even anything close to that
number, is not feasible in any routing architecture that we can foresee.

Hierarchical Routing. Hierarchical routing is used in the Internet as
the primary mechanism to contain the growth of routing information—
without hierarchical routing the Internet routing system would already
have collapsed.[9] Furthermore, hierarchical routing is the only known
mechanism for scaling routing to the current size of the Internet.
Hierarchical routing places certain constraints on address allocation and
management policies. Specifically, hierarchical routing assumes that (a)
addresses have to be unique within an internet if they are to have global
reachability, and (b) addresses need to reflect the topology of the

network. The most typical example of topologically significant addresses is the traditional IP subnet model, where all TCP/IP hosts on a common Data Link subnetwork have the same subnetwork number (address prefix). Consequently, instead of maintaining individual route entries for each host on a subnet, routers can maintain just a single route entry that covers all the hosts on the subnet. Similarly, if an organization connected to the Internet assigns its IP addresses out of a single (contiguous) block of IP addresses, then routers outside of the organization could maintain a single route entry—this entry would be sufficient to provide routing to any destination (host) within the organization.

Additional levels of routing information aggregation could be achieved with "provider–based" addresses. Provider–based addresses means that a provider is assigned (by some addressing authority) a (contiguous) block of IP addresses. Organizations that are subscribers of that provider get their blocks of addresses out of the block assigned to the provider. This way, rather than maintaining individual routing entries for every subscriber of that provider, other providers could maintain a single routing entry that covers all of the destinations in all the subscribers of that provider. Geographically assigned addresses similarly assign addresses based on geographical location.

Summary. In summary, scalable routing for IPng is based on:

1) topologically significant assignment of addresses;
2) separation of inter– and intradomain routing to allow backwards compatability and evolution, simultaneously;
3) a node routing component that scales well as the network grows by exploiting hierarchical address assignment and employing the path vector technique;
4) an explicit routing component to support specialized routes based on policy or ToS requirements (ER avoids burdening the global system of routers with specialized requirements while leaving generic requirements to the more state efficient NR);
5) separation of route computation and packet forwarding for performance enhancement of forwarding and maximization of evolvability of route computation.

Topological Flexibility and Support for Mobility. The following requirements on the IPng should be considered from the perspective of the Unified Routing Architecture.

IPng addressing must provide support for topologically significant address assignment.

Since it is hard to predict how routing information will be aggregated, the IPng addressing structure should impose as few preconditions as possible on the number of levels in the hierarchy. Specifically, the number of levels must be allowed to be different at different parts in the hierarchy. Further, the levels must not be tied to particular parts (fields) statically in the addressing information.

The hop–by–hop forwarding algorithm requires IPng to carry enough information in the Network Layer header to unambiguously determine a particular next hop.

Hierarchical address assignment does not imply strictly hierarchical routing. IPng headers should carry enough information to provide forwarding along both hierarchical and non–hierarchical routes.

IPng should provide a source routing mechanism with the following capabilities, (i.e., flexibility):

- Specification of either individual routers or collections of routers as the entities in the source route.
- The option to indicate that two consecutive entities in a source route must share a common subnet in order for the source route to be valid.
- Specification of the default behavior when the route to the next entry in the source route is unavailable, the packet is discarded, or the source route is ignored and the packet is forwarded based only on the destination address and the packet header will indicate this action.
- A mechanism to verify the feasibility of a source route.

IPng Mobility Considerations

William Allen Simpson

Daydreamer, Independent Consultant

As laptop and hand-held computers, pocket–sized modems, and cellular phones become more prevalent, users desire to take them everywhere, while continuing to use them for remote access to their usual resources as if the user were still at the "home" location. This remote access may be between offices within the same building, or "on the road" for long distances.

The Internet Protocol (IP) is concerned with routing information. Datagrams are currently sent to a node based on location information contained in the node's IP address. Current versions of the Internet Protocol make the assumption that a node's point of attachment remains fixed. If a node moves while keeping its IP address unchanged, its IP network number will not reflect its new point of attachment. The routing protocols will not, therefore, be able to route datagrams to it correctly.

Some movement does not require routing changes. Movement around the same room or within the same area is usually handled by link mechanisms, rather than network routing.

Only when the movement takes the user into a new area does the routing topology need to be updated. This is often called "roaming." The user desires to remain connected during these small changes. This is relatively simple in that each area can "hand off" the user to the next area. The routing changes are local, and maintained locally.

A more complicated scenario occurs when the user does not maintain a continuous connection while moving, and appears to "pop up" in a new location. In this case, the user will need an identity which can be used for both the new "foreign" agent, and to present bonafides to the "home" agent. An entirely new routing path is established to the user, who may now be on the other side of the world.

A number of considerations arise for routing these datagrams to a mobile node: addressing, ownership, topology and topological changes, manufacturer, numbering, configuration, communication, routing updates, path optimization, security, bandwidth, administration, response time, header prediction, and processing.

Terminology. The reader should not be overly concerned with the meaning of acronyms used in this chapter. Many of them have no true expansion, are in a foreign language, or when expanded reflect the usage of a bygone era.

For example, HF once meant "high frequency." Today, that range of frequencies is no longer considered "high," leading to VHF (very), UHF (ultra), and finally the abandonment of the terms altogether. Practitioners in the field no longer use these as anything more than labels for a particular useful range of frequencies.

Another example is CDMA, which ostensibly stands for "Code Division Multiple Access." Actually, it is a clever term which serves to distinguish it from competitors' CDPD and TDMA (expanded as "Cellular Digital Packet Data" and "Time Division Multiple Access," respectively).

None of these terms conveys true meaning to the reader, except as a label for a particular vendor mechanism.

Unique Addressing. Each mobile node should have at least one home address which identifies it to other nodes. The home address should be globally unique.

Address Ownership. The presence of ownership information in the home address would be beneficial. A mobile node will be assigned a home address by the organization that owns the machine, and the mobile node will be able to use that home address regardless of the current point of attachment.

The ownership information should be organized in such a fashion that it will facilitate inverse look–up in the Domain Name Service (DNS) and other similar services that become available.

Ownership information could be used by other nodes to ascertain the current topological location of the mobile node. Ownership information could also be used for generation of accounting records.

Topology. There is no requirement that the home address contain topological information. Indeed, by the very nature of mobility, any such topological information is irrelevant. Topological information in the home address should not hinder mobility, either by preventing relocation or by wasting bandwidth or processing efficiency.

Topological Changes. In order that transport connections be maintained while roaming, topological changes should not affect transport connections. For correspondent nodes which do not implement mobility functions, topological changes should not be communicated to the correspondent. For correspondent nodes which implement mobility functions, the correspondent should be capable of determining topological changes.

Topological change information should be capable of insertion and removal by routers in the datagram path, as well as by the correspondent and mobile nodes.

Manufacturer Information in Address. There is no requirement that the home address contain manufacturer information. As with topological information, manufacturer information in the home address should not hinder mobility, whether by prevention of relocation or by wasting bandwidth or processing efficiency.

Scale. The number of mobile nodes is expected to be constrained by the population of users within the lifetime of the IPng protocol. The maximum worldwide sustainable population is estimated as 16^9, although during the lifetime of IPng the population is not expected to exceed 8^9. Each user is assumed to be mobile, and to have a maximum combined number of personal mobile and home networks on the order of 4^3 nodes. Only 46 bits are needed to densely number all mobile and home nodes. The size of addressing elements is another aspect constrained by bandwidth efficiency and by processing efficiency.

Auto–Configuration and Auto–Registration. Since the typical user is unlikely to be aware of, or willing and able to maintain 4^3 nodes, the assignment of home addresses should be automatically configurable. Registration of the nodes should be dynamic and transparent to the user, both at home and away from home.

Communication. A mobile node should continue to be capable of communicating directly with other nodes which do not implement mobility functions. No protocol enhancements should be required in hosts or routers that are not serving any of the mobility functions. Similarly, no additional protocols should be needed by a router that is not acting as a home agent or a foreign agent to route datagrams to or from a mobile node.

A mobile node using its home address should be able to communicate with other nodes after having been disconnected from the Internet and then reconnected at a different point of attachment. A mobile node using its home address should be able to communicate with other nodes without loss of transport connections while roaming between different points of attachment.

Routing Updates. Because of speed of light considerations in propagating the information around the world, mobile nodes are expected to be able to change their point of attachment no more frequently than once per second. Changes in topology which occur more frequently should be handled at the link layer, and should be transparent to the internetwork layer. It is further noted that engineering margins may require the link layer to handle all changes at a frequency in the neighborhood of ten seconds.

Changes in topology which occur less frequently should be immediately reflected in the mobility updates. As DNS is unable to accomodate this requirement, this may preclude the use of the DNS as the repository of mobility topological information.

Global routing updates do not operate at this frequency. As old topological information may become obsolete faster than global routing updates, access to the repository of mobility topological information should be independent of prior topological information. The mobility–specific repository should use ownership information in the home address for access to the repository.

Path Optimization. Optimization of the path from a correspondent to a mobile node is not required; however, such optimization is desirable. For correspondent nodes which implement mobility functions, the correspondent should be capable of determining the optimal path. The optimization mechanism is also constrained by security, bandwidth efficiency, and processing efficiency.

Mobile Nodes at Home. Mobile nodes do not require special "virtual" home network addresses. Extra addresses or multiple routers are not necessarily available in small networks. Mobile nodes should be able to communicate directly with other nodes on the home subnetwork link without special assistance from routers.

Mobile Nodes Away from Home. When a router is present and the correspondent does not implement mobility functions, the router should be capable of redirecting the correspondent to communicate directly with the mobile node. When no router is present, mobile nodes should be capable of communicating directly with other nodes on the same link.

Security. Mobility should not create an environment which is less secure than the current Internet. Changes in topology should not affect inter–node security mechanisms.

Authentication. Mobility registration messages must be authenticated between the home topological repository and the mobile node. When the correspondent implements mobility functions, redirection or path optimization must be authenticated between the correspondent and mobile nodes.

Anonymity. The capability to attach to a foreign administrative domain without the awareness of the foreign administration should not be prohibited. However, any mobility mechanism should provide the ability to prevent such attachment.

Location Privacy. The capability to attach to a foreign administrative domain without the awareness of correspondents should not be prohibited. However, any such mobility mechanism should provide the ability for the home administration to trace the current path to the point of attachment.

Content Privacy. Security mechanisms which provide content privacy must not obscure or be dependent on the topological location of mobile nodes.

Bandwidth. Mobility must operate in the current link environment, and must not be dependent on bandwidth improvements. The link of the mobile node that is directly attached is likely to be bandwidth–limited.

In particular, radio frequency spectrum is already a scarce commodity. Higher bandwidth links are likely to continue to be scarce in the mobile environment. Current applications of mobility using radio links include HF links which are subject to serious fading and noise constraints, VHF and UHF line-of-sight radio between ships or field sites, and UHF satellite communications links.

The HF radio bandwidth is fixed at 1200 or 2400 bits per second (bps) by international treaty, statute, and custom, and is not likely to change. The European GSM standard for cellular radio is 2400 bps, with expected enhancements to no more than 19,200. The most prevalent deployed analog cellular and land–line modulation used by mobile nodes is 2400.

Current digital cellular deployment (CDPD and TDMA) is 19,200 bps shared among many users. At early installations, under light loads, effective FTP throughput has been observed as low as 200 bps.

Future digital cellular deployment (CDMA) is between 9,600 and 14,400 bps, which is shared between voice and data on a per–user basis. Effective FTP throughput has been measured as low as 7,200 bps.

Future Personal Communications Services (PCS) will also have relatively low bandwidth. In industrialized nations, the bandwidth available to each user is constrained by the density of deployment, and is commensurate with planned digital cellular deployment.

It appears likely that satellite–based PCS will be widely deployed for basic telephony communications in many newly–industrialized and lesser–developed countries. There is already significant PCS interest in East Asia, Southeast Asia, India, and South America.

Van Jacobson–like header prediction [10] is widely used and essential to making the use of such links viable.

Administrative Messages. The mobile node should send and receive as few administrative mobility messages as possible. In order to meet the frequency requirement of changing point of attachment once per second, registration of changes should not require more than a single request and reply.

The size of administrative mobility messages should be as short as possible. In order to meet the frequency requirement of changing point of attachment once per second, the registration messages should not total more than 120 bytes for a complete transaction, including link and internet headers.

Response Time. For most mobile links in current use, the typical TCP over IPv4 datagram overhead of 40 bytes is too large to maintain an acceptable typing response of 200 milliseconds round–trip time.

Therefore, the criterion for IPng mobility is that the response time not be perceptably worse than IPv4. This allows no more than 6 bytes of additional overhead per datagram to be added by IPng.

This was a primary concern in the design of mobility forwarding headers. Larger headers were rejected outright, and negotiation is provided for smaller headers than the default method. Topological headers are removed by the foreign agent prior to datagram transmission over the slower link to the mobile node, which also aids header prediction, as described below.

Header Prediction. Header prediction can be useful in reducing bandwidth usage on multiple related datagrams. It requires a point–to–point peer relationship between nodes so that a header history can be maintained between the peers.

Header prediction is less effective in mobile environments, as the header history is lost each time a mobile node changes its point of attachment. The new Foreign Agent will not have the same history as the previous Agent.

In order for header prediction to operate successfully, changing topological information should be removed from datagram overhead prior to transmission of the datagram on the directly attached link of any final hop. This applies to both the mobile node peering with a foreign agent, and the final link to a correspondent. Otherwise, header prediction cannot be relied upon to improve bandwidth utilization on low–speed mobile and correspondent links.

Since the changing topological information cannot be removed in the forwarding path of the datagram, header prediction will also be affected at any other pair of routers in the datagram path. Each time that a mobile node moves, the topological portion of the header will change, and header history used at those routers will be updated. Unless topological information is limited to as few headers as possible, this may render header prediction ineffective as more mobile nodes are deployed.

Processing. Mobility is required to operate in the current processor environment, and must not be dependent on hardware improvements. Common hardware implementations of mobile nodes include lower-speed processors and highly-integrated components. These are not readily upgradable.

The most prevalent mobile platform is a low speed i86, i286, or i386. The most common ASIC processor is a low speed i186.

Fixed Location. The processing limitations require that datagram header fields which are frequently examined by mobile nodes, or used for datagram forwarding to or from mobile nodes, be in a fixed location and not require lengths and offsets. A varied number of fields is an explicitly bad idea in the design of mobility registration and forwarding headers.

Simple Fields. The processing limitations require that datagram header fields which are frequently examined by mobile nodes, or used for datagram forwarding to or from mobile nodes, be simple and of fixed size. Varied length of fields is an explicitly bad idea in the design of mobility forwarding headers.

Simple Tests. Because the most prevalent processors are "little–endian," while network protocols are in practice "big–endian," the field processing must primarily use simple equality tests, rather than variable shifts and prefix matches.

Type, Length, Value. Fields which are not frequently examined, whether due to infrequent transmission or content that is not relevant in every message, should be of the Type, Length, Value format.

Technical Criteria
for IPng

Part VI

The RFC-1550 [1] white papers, the IPng Area Directorate discussions, and the Big-Internet mailing list discussions were all used by Frank Kastenholz and Craig Partridge in revising their earlier criteria draft to produce "Technical Criteria for Choosing IP The Next Generation (IPng)." Kastenholz and Jon Crowcroft, of University College, London, held a Next Generation Requirements BOF during the March 1994 Seattle IETF meeting to complete review of the draft.

This document is the "clear and concise set of technical requirements and decision criteria for IPng" called for in the charge from the IESG Chair. We used this document as the basic guideline while evaluating the IPng proposals.

The IPng criteria document represents the reasonable set of requirements for an IPng. As described above, the IPng Technical Criteria document was developed in an open manner and was the topic of extensive discussions on a number of mailing lists. We believe that there is a strong consensus that this document accurately reflects the community's set of technical requirements which an IPng should be able to meet.

Technical Criteria for Choosing IP the Next Generation (IPng)

Craig Partridge
BBN Systems and Technologies
Frank Kastenholz
FTP Software, Inc.

By developing a list of criteria for evaluating proposals for the IP Next Generation (IPng), the IETF would make it easier for developers of proposals to prioritize their work and efforts and make reasoned choices as to where they should spend relatively more and less time. Furthermore, a list of criteria could help the IETF community determine which proposals are serious contenders for a next generation IP, and which proposals are insufficient to the task. Note that these criteria are probably not sufficient to make final decisions about which proposal is best. Questions such as whether to trade a little performance (e.g., packets per second routed) for slightly more functionality (e.g., more flexible routing) cannot be easily addressed by a simple list of criteria. However, at minimum, we believe that protocols that meet these criteria are capable of serving as the future IPng.

The criteria presented here were culled from several sources, including "IP Version 7,"[2] "IESG Deliberations on Routing and Addressing,"[3] "Towards the Future Internet Architecture,"[4] the IPng Requirements BOF held at the Washington D.C. IETF Meeting in December of 1992, the IPng Working Group meeting at the Seattle IETF meeting in March 1994, the discussions held on the Big–Internet mailing list, discussions with the IPng Area Directors and Directorate, and the mailing lists devoted to the individual IPng efforts. The decision to develop a set of criteria was motivated by the experience of the IPv4 designers.[5]

There is some speculation in the community that we can extend the life of IPv4 for a significant amount of time by better engineering of, routing protocols, for example, or that we need to develop IPng now. We presume that a new IP–layer protocol is actually desired; we do not address extending IPv4.

This definition of technical criteria for IPng is intended to be informational and not be a standard of IETF, but it does represent a consensus, and as such is being used as a guide to IPng.

Criteria Priority. This set of criteria originally began as an ordered list, with the goal of ranking the importance of various criteria. Eventually, the layout evolved into the current form, where each criterion is presented without weighting, but a time frame was added to the specification, indicating approximately when the criterion should be available.

Vision. We have attempted to state the criteria in the form of goals or requirements, and not demand specific engineering solutions. There has been talk in the community, for example, of making route aggregation a requirement. We believe that route aggregation is not, in and of itself, a requirement, but rather one part of a solution to the real problem of scaling to some very large, complex topology. Therefore, route aggregation is not listed as a requirement; instead, the more general functional goal of having the routing scale is listed instead of the particular mechanism of route aggregation.

In determining the relative timing of the various criteria, we have had two guiding principles. First, IPng must offer an internetwork service akin to that of IPv4, but improve upon IPv4 so that it can handle the well–known and widely understood problems of scaling the Internet architecture to more endpoints and an ever–increasing range of bandwidths. Second, it must be desirable for users and network managers to upgrade their equipment to support IPng. At a minimum, this second point implies that there must be a straightforward way to transition systems from IPv4 to IPng. But it also strongly suggests that IPng should offer features that IPv4 does not; new features provide a motivation to deploy IPng more quickly.

The existing proposals tend to distinguish between endpoint identification of individual hosts, for example, and topological addresses of network attachment points. We do not make that distinction. We use the term address as it is currently used in IPv4; i.e., for both the identification of a particular endpoint or host and as the topological address of a point on the network. We presume that if the endpoint/ address split remains, the proposals will make the proper distinctions with respect to the criteria enumerated below.

Architectural Simplicity.

> In anything at all, perfection is finally attained not when there is no longer anything to add, but when there is no longer anything to take away.
>
> *Antoine de Saint–Exupery*

We believe that many communications functions are more appropriately performed at protocol layers other than the IP layer. We see protocol stacks as hourglass–shaped, with IPng in the middle, or waist, of the hourglass.[6] As such, essentially all higher–layer protocols make use of and rely upon IPng.

Similarly IPng, by virtue of its position in the "protocol hourglass" encompasses a wide variety of lower–layer protocols. When IPng does not perform a particular function or provide a certain service, it should not get in the way of the other elements of the protocol stack which may well wish to perform the function.

One Protocol to Bind Them All. One of the most important aspects of the Internet is that it provides global IP–layer connectivity. The IP layer provides the point of commonality among all nodes on the Internet. In effect, the main goal of the Internet is to provide an IP Connectivity Service to all who wish it.

This does not say that the Internet is a one–protocol internet. The Internet is today, and shall remain in the future, a multi–protocol internet.

Multi–protocol operations are required to allow for continued testing, experimentation, and development and because service providers' customers clearly want to be able to run protocols such as CLNP, DECnet, and Novell IPX over their Internet connections.

Live Long. It is very difficult to change a protocol as central to the workings of the Internet as IP. Even more problematic is changing such a protocol frequently. For example, the SNMP community has had great difficulty moving from SNMPv1 to SNMPv2. Frequent changes in software are hard. On the Internet, frequent changes simply cannot occur.

We believe that it is impossible to expect the community to make significant, non–backward compatible changes to the IP layer more often than once every 10 or 15 years. In order to be conservative, we strongly urge protocol developers to consider what the Internet will look like in 20 years and design their protocols to fit that vision.

Live Long *and* Prosper. Simply allowing for bigger addresses and more efficient routing is not enough of a benefit to encourage vendors, service providers, and users to switch to IPng, with the attendant disruptions of service involved in switching to IPng. These problems can be solved much more simply with faster routers, balkanization of the Internet address space, and other hacks.

Therefore, there must be positive functional or operational benefits to switching to IPng. In other words, IPng must be able to sustain desired usage for a long time and it must allow the Internet to grow to serve new applications and user needs.

Cooperative Anarchy. A major contributor to the Internet's success is the fact that there is no single, centralized, point of control or promulgator of policy for the entire network. This allows individual constituents of the network to tailor their own networks, environments, and policies to suit their own needs. The individual constituents must cooperate only to the degree necessary to ensure that they interoperate.

This decentralized and decoupled nature of the Internet must be preserved. Only a minimum amount of centralization, or forced cooperation, will be tolerated by the community as a whole.

Also, there are some tangible benefits to this decoupled nature:

- It is easier to experiment with new protocols and services, then roll out intermediate and final results in a controlled fashion.
- By eliminating a single point of control, a single point of failure is also eliminated, making it much less likely that the entire network will fail. It allows the administrative tasks for the network to be more widely distributed.

The benefits of this cooperative anarchy can be seen in the Domain Name System (DNS) over the original HOSTS.TXT system.

Criteria. This section enumerates the criteria against which we suggest the IP Next Generation proposals be evaluated. Each criterion is presented in its own section, beginning with a short statement of the criterion, followed by an explanation of the criterion in more detail, a clarification of what it does and does not say, and some indication of its relative importance.

Each criterion also includes a subsection called time frame, intended to give a rough indication of when that particular criterion will become "important." If an element of technology is significant enough to include in this document, we probably understand the technology enough to predict how important that technology will be. In general, these time frames indicate that, within the desired time frame, we should be able to get an understanding of how the feature will be added to a protocol, perhaps after discussions with the engineers doing the development. Time frame is not a deployment schedule since deployment schedules depend on non–technical issues, such as vendors determining whether a market exists, and users fitting new releases into their systems, for example.

Scale. The IPng must scale to allow the identification and addressing of at least 10^{12} end systems (and preferably much more), and the IPng, and its associated routing protocols and architecture must allow for at least 10^9 individual networks (and preferably more). The routing schemes must scale at a rate that is less than the square root of the number of constituent networks.[7]

The initial, motivating, purpose of the IPng effort is to allow the Internet to grow beyond the size constraints imposed by the current IPv4 addressing and routing technologies.

Both aspects of scaling are important: If we can't route, then connecting all these hosts is worthless. But without connected hosts, there's no point in routing, so we must scale in both directions.

In any proposal, particular attention must be paid to describing the routing hierarchy, how the routing and addressing will be organized, how different layers of the routing interact, and the relationship between addressing and routing.

Particular attention must be paid to describing what happens when the size of the network approaches these limits. How are network, forwarding, and routing performance affected? Does performance fall off or does the network simply stop as the limit is neared?

Scaling is the essential problem motivating the transition to IPng. If the proposed protocol does not satisfy this criterion, there is no point in considering it.

One of the white papers solicited for the IPng process indicates that 10^{12} end nodes is a reasonable estimate based on the expected number of homes in the world and adding two orders of magnitude for "safety" (see *A Cable TV Industry View of IPng*). However, this white paper treats each home in the world as an end node of a worldwide Internet. We believe that each home in the world will in fact be a network of the worldwide Internet. Therefore, if we take Mario Vecchi's derivation of 10^{12} as accurate, and change their assumption that a home will be an end node to a home being a network, we may expect that there will be the need to support at least 10^{12} networks, with the possibility of supporting up to 10^{15} end nodes.

Time Frame: Any IPng proposal should be able to show immediately that it has an architecture for the needed routing protocols, addressing schemes, abstraction techniques, algorithms, data structures, and so on that can support growth to the required scales.

Actual development, specification, and deployment of the needed protocols can be deferred until IPng deployment has extended far enough to require such protocols. A proposed IPng should be able to demonstrate ahead of time that it can scale as needed.

Topological Flexibility. The routing architecture and protocols of IPng must allow for many different network topologies. The routing architecture and protocols must not assume that the network's physical structure is a tree.

As the Internet becomes ever more global and ubiquitous, it will develop new and different topologies. We already see cases where the network hierarchy is very broad with many subnetworks, each with only a few hosts, and where it is very narrow, with few subnetworks, each with many hosts. We can expect these and other topological forms in the future. Furthermore, since we expect that IPng will allow for many more levels of hierarchy than are allowed under IPv4, we can expect very "tall" and very "short" topologies in the future.

Constituent organizations of the Internet should be allowed to structure their internal topologies in any manner they see fit. Within reasonable implementation limits, organizations should be allowed to structure their addressing in any manner. We specifically wish to point out that if the network's topology or addressing is hierarchical, constituent organizations should be able to allocate to themselves as many levels of hierarchy as they wish.

It is very possible that the diameter of the Internet will grow to be extremely large; perhaps larger than 256 hops. Furthermore neither the current, nor the future, Internet will be physically structured as a tree, nor can we assume that connectivity can occur only between certain points in the graph. The routing and addressing architectures must allow for multiple connected networks and be able to utilize multiple paths for any reason, including redundancy, load sharing, and type- and quality-of-service differentiation.

Time Frame: Topological flexibility is an inherent element of a protocol and therefore should be immediately demonstrable in an IPng proposal.

Performance. A state of the art, commercial-grade router must be able to process and forward IPng traffic at speeds capable of fully utilizing common, commercially available, high–speed media at the time. Furthermore, at a minimum, a host must be able to achieve data transfer rates with IPng comparable to the rates achieved with IPv4, using similar levels of host resources.

Network media speeds are constantly increasing. It is essential that the Internet's switching elements (routers) be able to keep up with the media speeds. By this we mean commercially available routers and media.

If some network site can obtain a particular media technology "off the shelf," then it should also be able to obtain the needed routing technology "off the shelf." IPng should be routable at a speed sufficient to fully utilize the fastest available media, though that might require specially built, custom, devices. One can always go into some laboratory or research center and find newer, faster technologies for network media and for routing.

More and more services will be available over the Internet. It is not unreasonable, therefore, to expect that the ratio of "local" traffic (i.e., the traffic that stays on one's local network) to "export" traffic (i.e., traffic destined to or sourced from a network other than one's own local network) will change, and the percent of export traffic will increase.

The host performance requirement should not be taken to imply that IPng need only be as good as IPv4. If an IPng candidate can achieve better performance with equivalent resources (or equivalent transfer rates with fewer resources) vis–a–vis IPv4 then so much the better. Many researchers believe that a proper IPng router should be capable of routing IPng traffic over links at speeds that are capable of fully utilizing an ATM switch on the link.

Some developments indicate that the use of very high-speed point–to–point connections may become commonplace. In particular, Vecchi indicates that OC–3 speeds may be widely used in the cable TV industry and there may be many OC–3 speed lines connecting to central switching elements.

Processing of the IPng header, and subsequent headers (such as the transport header), can be made more efficient by aligning fields on their natural boundaries and making header lengths integral multiples of typical word lengths (32, 64, and 128 bits have been suggested) in order to preserve alignment in following headers. We point out that optimizing the header's fields and lengths only to today's processors may not be sufficient for the long term. Word processor and cache–line lengths, and memory widths are constantly increasing. In doing header optimizations, the designer should predict word–widths one or two CPU generations into the future and optimize accordingly. If IPv4 and TCP had been optimized for processors common when they were designed, they would be very efficient for 6502s and Z–80s.

Time Frame: An IPng proposal must provide a plausible argument of how it will scale up in performance. Clearly no one can completely predict the future, but the idea is to illustrate that if current technology trends in processor performance and memory performance continue, and perhaps using techniques like parallelism, there is reason to believe the proposed IPng will scale as technology scales.

Robust Service. The network service and its associated routing and control protocols must be robust.

Murphy's Law applies to networking. Any proposed IPng protocol must be well–behaved in the face of malformed packets, misinformation, and occasional failures of links, routers, and hosts. IPng should perform gracefully in response to management and configuration mistakes (i.e., service outages should be minimized). Putting this requirement another way, IPng must make it possible to continue the Internet tradition of being conservative in what is sent, but liberal in what one is willing to receive.

IPv4 is reasonably robust and any proposed IPng must be at least as robust as IPv4. Hostile attacks on the network layer and Byzantine failure modes must be dealt with in a safe and graceful manner. Robust Service is, in some form, a part of security, and vice–versa.

The detrimental effects of failures, errors, buggy implementations, and misconfigurations must be localized as much as possible. For example, misconfiguring a workstation's IP address should not break the routing protocols. In the event of misconfigurations, IPng must be able to detect and warn, if not work around, any misconfigurations.

Due to its size, complexity, decentralized administration, and error–prone users and administrators, the Internet is a very hostile environment. If a protocol cannot be used in such a hostile environment then it is not suitable for use in the Internet.

Some predictions have been made that, as the Internet grows, and as a greater number of less technically sophisticated sites are connected to it, there will be more failures in the network.

These failures would result from the growth of the network (that is to say, the number of configuration errors will increase as some function of the size of the network) and the resulting reduction in the average experience of the users and operators (that is to say, more innocent and well-meaning mistakes in either the configuration or operation of the Internet will be made).

The IPng protocols should be able to continue operating in an environment that suffers more, total, outages than we are currently used to. Similarly, the protocols must protect the general population from errors either of omission or commission made by individual users and sites.

Time Frame: A proposed architecture for it should be done immediately. Prototype development should be completed in 12–18 months, with final deployment as needed. The elements of Robust Service should be available immediately in the protocol with the following two exceptions: The security aspects of Robust Service are considered a separate criterion and, as such, are described in their own white paper (see *Security Implications for IPng*.) Protection against Byzantine failure modes is not needed immediately.

Transition. The protocol must have a straightforward transition plan from the current IPv4.

A smooth, orderly transition from IPv4 to IPng is needed. If users can't transition to the new protocol, then no matter how wonderful it is, they'll never move to it.

It is not possible to have a "flag–day" form of transition in which all hosts and routers must change over at once. The size, complexity, and distributed administration of the Internet make such a cut-over impossible.

Rather, IPng will need to co–exist with IPv4 for some period of time. There are a number of ways to achieve this co–existence, such as requiring hosts to support two stacks, converting between protocols, or using backward compatible extensions to IPv4. Each scheme has its strengths and weaknesses, which have to be weighed carefully as candidates develop their proposals.

Furthermore, in all probability, there will be IPv4 hosts on the Internet effectively forever. IPng must provide mechanisms to allow these hosts to communicate, even after IPng has become the dominant network layer protocol in the Internet.

The difficulty of running a network that is transitioning from IPv4 to IPng must be minimized. (A good target is that running a mixed IPv4–IPng network should be no more and preferably less difficult than running IPv4 in parallel with existing non–IP protocols).

Furthermore, a network in transition must still be robust. IPng schemes which maximize stability and connectivity in mixed IPv4–IPng networks are preferred.

Finally, IPng is expected to evolve over time and therefore, it must be possible to have multiple versions of IPng, some in production use, some in experimental, developmental, or evaluation use, to co-exist on the network. Transition plans must address this issue.

The transition plan must address the following general areas of the Internet's infrastructure:

- Host protocols and software
- Router protocols and software
- Security and authentication
- Domain Name System (DNS) [8]
- Network management operations tools (e.g., Ping and Traceroute)
- Operations and administration procedures

The impact on protocols which use IP addresses as data (e.g., DNS, distributed file systems, SNMP and FTP) must be specifically addressed. The transition plan should also address the issue of cost distribution. That is, it should identify which tasks are required of the service providers, of the end users, of the backbones, and so on.

Time Frame: A transition plan is required immediately.

Media Independence. The protocol must work across an internetwork of many different LAN, MAN, and WAN media, with individual link speeds ranging from a ones–of–bits per second to hundreds of gigabits per second. Multiple–access and point–to–point media must be supported, as must media supporting both switched and permanent circuits.

The joy of IP is that it works over just about anything. This generality must be preserved. The ease of adding new technologies, and ability to continue operating with old technologies must be maintained.

This range of speed is right for the next twenty years, though terabit performance at the high–end may be advantageous. At a minimum, media running at 500 gigabits–per–second will be commonly available within ten years. The low end of the link–speed range is based on the speed of systems like pagers and ELF (ELF connects to submerged submarines and has a "speed" on the order of less than ten characters per second).

Switched circuits are both "permanent" connections, such as X.25 and Frame Relay services and "temporary" types of dial–up connections similar to today's SLIP and dial–up PPP services, and perhaps, ATM SVCs. The temporary dial–up connection implies that dynamic network access (i.e., the ability to unplug a machine, move it to a different point on the network topology, and plug it back in, possibly with a changed IPng address) is required. This is an aspect of mobility.

Work means a stream of IPng datagrams (whether from one source, or many) that can come close to filling the link at high speeds, but also scales gracefully downward to low speeds.

Many network media are multi-protocol. It is essential that IPng be able to peacefully co-exsist on such media with other protocols. Routers and hosts must be able to discriminate among the protocols that might be present on such a medium. For example, on an Ethernet, a specific IPng Ethernet Type value might be called for; or the old IPv4 Ethernet type is used and the first four (version number in the old IPv4 header) bits would distinguish between IPv4 and IPng.

Different media have different MAC address formats and schemes. It must be possible for a node to dynamically determine the MAC address of a node given that node's IP address. We explicitly prohibit using static, manually configured mappings as the standard approach.

Another aspect of this criterion is that many different MTUs will be found in an IPng internetwork. An IPng must be able to operate in such a multi–MTU environment. It must be able to adapt to the MTUs of the physical media over which it operates. Two possible techniques for dealing with this are path MTU discovery and fragmentation and reassembly; other techniques might certainly be developed.

As of mid–1995, ATM seems to be set to become a major network media technology. Any IPng should be designed to operate over ATM. However, IPng still must be able to operate over other, more "traditional" network media. Furthermore, a host on an ATM network must be able to interoperate with a host on another, non–ATM, medium, with no more difficulty or complexity than hosts on different media can interoperate today using IPv4.

IPng must be able to deal both with "dumb" media, such as we have today, and newer, more intelligent media. In particular, IPng functions must be able to exist harmoniously with lower–layer realizations of the same, or similar, functions. Routing and resource management are two areas where designers should pay particular attention. Some subnetwork technologies may include integral accounting and billing capabilities, and IPng must provide the correct control information to such subnetworks (see *Supporting ATM Services in IPng*).

Time Frame: Specifications for current media encapsulations (i.e., all encapsulations that are currently Proposed Standards, or higher, in the IETF) are required immediately. These specifications must include any auxiliary protocols needed (such as an address resolution mechanism for Ethernet or the link control protocol for PPP). A general "guide" should also be available immediately to help others develop additional media encapsulations. Other, newer encapsulations can be developed as the need becomes apparent.

Datagram Service. The protocol must support an unreliable datagram delivery service. IP's best–effort datagram service has proved popular and very robust and must be supported in IPv6. In particular, the ability, within IPv4, to send an independent datagram, without prearrangement, is extremely valuable (in fact, may be required for some applications such as SNMP) and must be retained.

Furthermore, the design principle that says that we can take any datagram and throw it away with no warning or other action, or take any router and turn it off with no warning, and have datagram traffic still work, is very powerful. This vastly enhances the robustness of the network and vastly eases administration and maintenance of the network. It also vastly simplifies the design and implementation of software (see *Nimrod IPng Technical Requirements*).

The unreliable datagram service should support some minimal level of service; something that is approximately equivalent to IPv4 service. This has two functions; it eases the task of IPv4/IPng translating systems in mapping IPv4 traffic to IPng and vice versa, and it simplifies the task of fitting IPng into small, limited environments such as boot ROMs.

Time Frame: Unreliable datagram service must be available immediately.

Configuration, Administration, and Operation. The protocol must permit easy and largely distributed configuration and operation. Automatic configuration of hosts and routers is required.

People complain that IP is hard to manage. People cannot plug and play. That problem must be fixed. Fully automated configuration, especially for large, complex networks, is still a topic of research. In small and medium-sized, less complex networks the essential knowledge and skills would not be readily available.

In dealing with configuration, administration, and operation, address assignment and delegation procedures and restrictions should be addressed by the proposal. Furthermore, "ownership" of addresses (e.g., user or service provider) has recently become a concern and the issue should be addressed.

We require that a node be able to dynamically obtain all of its operational, IP–level parameters at boot time via a dynamic configuration mechanism.

A host must be able to dynamically discover routers on the host's local network. Ideally, the information which a host learns via this mechanism would also allow the host to make a rational selection of which first–hop router to send any given packet to. IPng must not mandate that users or administrators manually configure first–hop routers into hosts.

Also, a strength of IPv4 has been its ability to be used on isolated subnets. IPng hosts must be able to work on networks without routers present.

Additional elements of this criterion are:

- Ease of address allocation.
- Ease of changing the topology of the network within a particular routing domain.
- Ease of changing network provider.

- Ease of (re)configuring host/endpoint parameters such as addressing and identification.
- Ease of (re)configuring router parameters such as addressing and identification.
- Address allocation and assignment authority must be delegated as far "down" the administrative hierarchy as possible.

The requirements of this section apply only to IPng and its supporting protocols (such as for routing, address resolution, and network–layer control) not to configuration and other elements, such as host parameters and application preferences. Specifically, as far as IPng is concerned, we are concerned only with how routers and hosts get their configuration information.

We note that in general, automatic configuration of hosts is a large and complex problem and getting the network configuration information into hosts and routers is only one, small, piece of the problem. A large amount of additional, non–Internet–layer work is needed in order to be able to do general "plug–and–play" networking. Other aspects of plug–and–play networking include things like: Auto–registration of new nodes with DNS, configuring security service systems (e.g., Kerberos), setting up email relays and mail servers, locating network resources, adding entries to NFS export files, and so on. To a large degree, these capabilities do not have any dependence on the IPng protocol (other than, perhaps, the format of addresses).

We require that any IPng proposal not impede or prevent, in any way, the development of plug–and–play network configuration technologies.

Automatic configuration of network nodes must not prevent users or administrators from also being able to manually configure their systems.

Time Frame: A method for plug–and–play configuration on small subnets is immediately required.

It is an extremely critical area for any IPng. A major complaint of the IP community as a whole has long been the difficulty in administering large IP networks. Furthermore, ease of installation is likely to speed the deployment of IPng.

Secure Operation. IPng must provide a secure network layer.

IPng must not be a network that is a cracker's playground. In order to meet the robustness criterion, some elements of what is commonly shrugged off as "security" are needed; e.g., to prevent a villain from injecting bogus routing packets, and destroying the routing system within the network. This criterion covers those aspects of security that are purely security and not needed to provide the robustness criterion.

Another aspect of security is non–repudiation of origin. In order to adequately support the expected need for simple accounting, we believe that this is a necessary feature. In order to safely support requirements of the commercial world, IPng–level security must have capabilities to prevent eavesdroppers from monitoring traffic and deducing traffic patterns. This is particularly important in multi–access networks such as cable TV networks (see *A Cable TV Industry View of IPng*).

Aspects of security at the IP level to be considered include:

- Denial of service protections (see *High Performance Networking in the Navy*)
- Continuity of operations (*Ibid.*)
- Precedence and preemption (*Ibid.*)
- Ability to allow rule–based access control technologies (*Ibid.*)
- Protection of routing and control–protocol operations [9]
- Authentication of routing information exchanges, packets, data, and sources (e.g., make sure that the routing packet came from a router)(*Ibid.*)
- QoS security (i.e., protection against improper use of network–layer resources, functions, and capabilities)
- Auto–configuration protocol operations in that the host must be assured that it is getting its information from proper sources
- Traffic pattern confidentiality is strongly desired by several communities [10] (see *A Cable TV Industry View of IPng*)

Time Frame: Security should be an integral component of any IPng from the beginning.

Unique Naming. IPng must assign all IP–layer objects in the global, ubiquitous Internet unique names. These names may or may not have any location, topology, or routing significance.

The term name, in this criterion, is synonymous with the term endpoint identifier as used in the Nimrod proposal, or as IP addresses are used to uniquely identify interfaces/hosts in IPv4. These names may or may not carry any routing or topology information.[11]

IPng must provide identifiers which are suitable for use as globally unique, unambiguous, and ubiquitous names for endpoints, nodes, interfaces, and the like. Every datagram must carry the identifier of both its source and its destination (or some method must be available to determine these identifiers, given a datagram). This is required in order to support certain accounting functions.

Other functions and uses of unique names are:

- To uniquely identify endpoints (thus if the unique name and address are not the same, the TCP pseudo–header should include the unique name rather than the address)
- To allow endpoints to change topological location on the network (e.g., migrate) without changing their unique names.
- To give one or more unique names to a node on the network (i.e., one node may have multiple unique names)

An identifier must refer to one and only one object while that object is in existence. Furthermore, after an object ceases to exist, the identifier should be kept unused long enough to ensure that any packets containing the identifier have drained out of the Internet system, and that other references to the identifier have probably been lost. The term existence is as much an administrative issue as a technical one. For example, if a workstation is reassigned, given a new IP address and node name, and attached to a new subnetwork, is it the same object or not? This does argue for a namespace that is relatively large and relatively stable.

Time Frame: Unique naming is a fundamental element of the IP layer and it should be in the protocol from the beginning.

Access. The protocols that define IPng, its associated protocols (similar to ARP and ICMP in IPv4), and the routing protocols (similar to OSPF, BGP, and RIP for IPv4) must be published as standards track RFCs and must satisfy the requirements specified in RFC-1602. [12] These documents should be as freely available and redistributable as the IPv4 and related RFCs. There must be no specification–related licensing fees for implementing or selling IPng software.

An essential aspect of the development of the Internet and its protocols has been the fact that the protocol specifications are freely available to anyone who wishes a copy. Beyond simply minimizing the cost of learning about the technology, the free access to specifications has made it easy for researchers and developers to easily incorporate portions of old protocol specifications in the revised specifications. This type of easy access to the standards documents is required for IPng.

Time Frame: An IPng and its related protocols must meet these standards for openness before an IPng can be approved.

Multicast. The protocol must support both unicast and multicast packet transmission. Part of the multicast capability is a requirement to be able to send to "all IP hosts on a given subnetwork." Dynamic and automatic routing of multicasts is also required.

IPv4 has made heavy use of the ability to multicast requests to all IPv4 hosts on a subnet, especially for auto–configuration. This ability must be retained in IPng. In the past few years, support for wide–area multicast addressing in the internet has begun, and it has proved valuable. This capability must not be lost in the transition to IPng.

Unfortunately, some IPv4 implementations currently use the local media broadcast address to multicast to all IP hosts. This behavior is anti–social in mixed–protocol networks and should be fixed in IPng. There's no good reason for IPng to send to all hosts on a subnet when it only wishes to send to all IPng hosts. The protocol also must make allowances for media that do not support true multicasting.

In the past few years, the Internet community has begun to deploy support for wide–area multicast addressing in the Internet, and it has proved valuable. This capability must not be lost in the transition to IPng.

The ability to restrict the range of a multicast to specific networks is also important. Furthermore, it must be possible to "selectively" multicast packets. That is, it must be possible to send a multicast to a remote, specific portion or area of the Internet (such as a specific network or subnetwork) and then have that multicast limited to just that specific area. Furthermore, any given network or subnetwork should be capable of supporting 2^{16} "local" multicast groups, i.e., groups that are not propagated to other networks. (see *Use of IPng in Combat Simulation.*)

Currently, large–scale multicasts are routed manually through the internet. While this is fine for experiments, a "production" system requires that multicast–routing be dynamic and automatic. Multicast groups must be able to be created and destroyed, hosts must be able to join and leave multicast groups and the network routing infrastructure must be able to locate new multicast groups and destinations and route traffic to those destinations all without manual intervention. Large, topologically dispersed, multicast groups (with up to 10^6 participants) must be supported (see *Use of IPng in Combat Simulation*).

Time Frame: Obviously, address formats, algorithms for processing and interpreting the multicast addresses must be immediately available in IPng. Broadcast and multicast transmission/reception of packets are required immediately. Dynamic routing of multicast packets must be available within 18 months.

Multicast addressing is vital to support future applications such as remote conferencing. It is also used quite heavily in the current internet for things like service location and routing.

Extensibility. The protocol must be extensible; it must be able to evolve to meet the future service needs of the internet. This evolution must be achievable without requiring network–wide software upgrades. IPng is expected to evolve over time. As it evolves, it must be able to allow different versions to co-exist on the same network.

Today, all of the things that people will want the Internet to be able to do 10 years from now are not known. At the same time, it is not reasonable to ask users to transition to a new protocol with each passing decade. Thus, it must be possible to extend IPng to support new services and facilities. Furthermore, it is essential that any extensions can be incrementally deployed to only those systems which desire to use them. Systems upgraded in this fashion must still be able to communicate with systems which have not been upgraded.

There are several aspects to extensibility:

Algorithms. The algorithms used in processing IPng information should be decoupled from the protocol itself. It should be possible to change these algorithms without necessarily requiring protocol, data structure, or header changes.

Headers. The content of packet headers should be extensible. As more features and functions are required of IPng, it may be necessary to add more information to the IPng headers. The community should keep in mind that the IPv4 option handling has proved inefficient, thus discouraging the use of options. IPv6 should try to find a less expensive way to be extensible.

Data Structures. The fundamental data structures of IPng should not be bound with the other elements of the protocol. For example, things like address formats should not be intimately tied with the routing and forwarding algorithms in the way that the IPv4 address class mechanism was tied to IPv4 routing and forwarding.

Packets. It should be possible to add additional packet–types to IPng. For example, these could be for new control and/or monitoring operations.

Everything else being equal, having larger, oversized number spaces is preferable to having number spaces that are "just large enough." Larger spaces afford more flexibility on the part of network designers and operators and allow for further experimentation on the part of the scientists, engineers, and developers (see *The Advantages of Many Addresses per Host*).

Time Frame: A framework showing mechanisms for extending the protocol must be provided immediately.

Network Service. The protocol must allow the network (routers, intelligent media, hosts, and so on) to associate packets with particular service classes and provide them with the services specified by those classes.

For many reasons, such as accounting, security, and multimedia, it is desirable to treat different packets differently in the network. For example, multimedia is now on our desktop and will be an essential part of future networking. Ways to support it must be found; and a failure to support it may mean users choose to use protocols other than IPng.

The distribution of audio and video of the IETF meetings over the Internet has shown that we can currently support multimedia over internetworks with some hitches. If the network can be guaranteed to provide the necessary service levels for this traffic, we will dramatically increase its success.

This criterion includes features such as policy–based routing, flows, resource reservation, network service technologies, type–of–service and quality–of–service and so on.

In order to properly support commercial provision and use of internetwork service, and account for the use of these services (i.e., support the economic principle of "value paid for value received") it must be possible to obtain guarantees of service levels. Similarly, if the network cannot support a previously guaranteed service level, it must report this to those to whom it guaranteed the service.

Network service provisions must be secure. The network–layer security must generally prevent one host from surreptitiously obtaining or disrupting the use of resources which another host has validly acquired. (Some security failures are acceptable, but the failure rate must be quantifiable and acceptable to those using the service.)

One of the parameters of network service that may be requested must be one of cost to a given network service. As far as possible, given the limitations of underlying media and IP's model of a robust internet datagram service, real–time, mission–critical applications must be supported by IPng (see *High Performance Networking in the Navy*). Users must be able to confirm that they are, in fact, getting the services that they have requested.

Time Frame: This should be available within 24 months of IPng's implementation.

Support for Mobility. The protocol must support mobile hosts, networks, and internetworks. Again, mobility is becoming increasingly important. Look at the portables that everyone is carrying. Note the strength of the Apple commercial showing someone automatically connecting up her Powerbook to her computer back in the office. There have been a number of pilot projects showing ways to support mobility in IPv4. All have some drawbacks. But like network service grades, if IPng can support mobility, it will have features that will encourage transition.

An encompassing definition of "mobility" is used here. Mobility typically means one of two things to people: 1) Hosts that physically move and remain connected (via some wireless datalink) with sessions and transport–layer connections remaining "open" or "active" and 2) Disconnecting a host from one spot in the network, connecting it back in another arbitrary spot and continuing to work. Both forms are required.

In *High Performance Networking in the Navy*, the HPN Working Group discusses possible future use of IP–based networks in the U.S. Navy's ships, planes, and shore installations. Their basic model is that each ship, plane and shore installation represents at least one IP network. The ship– and plane–based networks, obviously, are mobile as these craft move around the world. Furthermore, most, if not all, Naval surface combatants carry some aircraft (at a minimum, a helicopter or two). So, not only must there be mobile networks (the ships that move around), but there must be mobile internetworks: the ships carrying the aircraft where each aircraft has its own network, which is connected to the ship's network and the whole thing is moving.

There is also the requirement for dynamic mobility; a plane might take off from aircraft carrier A and land on carrier B so it obviously would want to "connect" to B's network. This situation might be even more complex since the plane might wish to retain connectivity to its "home" network; that is, the plane might remain connected to the ship–borne networks of both aircraft carriers, A and B.

These requirements are not limited to just the Navy. They apply to the civilian and commercial worlds as well. For example, in civil airliners, commercial cargo and passenger ships, trains, cars, and so on.

Time Frame: The mobility algorithms are stabilizing and we would hope to see an IPng mobility framework within a year.

Control Protocol. The protocol must include elementary support for testing and debugging networks.

An important feature of IPv4 is the ICMP and its debugging, support, and control features. Specific ICMP messages that have proven extraordinarily useful within IPv4 are Echo Request/Reply (A.K.A. Ping), Destination Unreachable, and Redirect. Functions similar to these should be in IPng.

This criterion explicitly does not concern itself with configuration-related messages of ICMP. We believe that these are adequately covered by the configuration criterion in this memo.

One limitation of today's ICMP that should be fixed in IPng's control protocol is that more than just the IPng header plus 64 bits of a failed datagram should be returned in the error message. In some situations, this is too little to carry all the critical protocol information that indicates why a datagram failed. At minimum, any IPng control protocol should return the entire IPng and transport headers (including options or nested headers).

Time Frame: Support for testing and debugging is required immediately.

Private Networks. IPng must allow users to build private internetworks on top of the basic Internet infrastructure. Both private IP–based internetworks and private non–IP–based (e.g., CLNP or AppleTalk) internetworks must be supported.

In the current Internet, these capabilities are used by the research community to develop new IP services and capabilities (e.g., the MBone) and by users to interconnect non–IP islands over the Internet (e.g., CLNP and DECnet use in the UK). The capability of building networks on top of the Internet have been shown to be useful. Private networks allow the Internet to be extended and modified in ways that 1) were not foreseen by the original builders and 2) do not disrupt the day–to–day operations of other users.

Today in the IPv4 Internet, tunneling is widely used to provide these capabilities. Finally, there might not be any features that specifically need to be added to IPng in order to support the desired functions (i.e., one might treat a private network protocol simply as another IP client protocol, just like TCP or UDP). If this is the case, then IPng must not prevent these functions from being performed.

Time Frame: Some of these capabilities may be required to support other criteria (e.g., transition) and as such, the timing of the specifications is governed by the other criteria (e.g., immediately in the case of transition). Others may be produced as desired.

Things We Chose Not to Require. This section contains items which should not impact the choice of an IPng. Listing an item here does not mean that a protocol must not do it; it means that it is not mandatory that the feature be in the protocol. If a protocol includes one of the items listed here, that's cool. If it doesn't; that's cool too. A feature might be necessary in order to meet some other criterion. The point is merely that the feature need not be *required* for its own sake.

Fragmentation. The technology exists for path MTU discovery. Presumably, IPng will continue to provide this technology. Therefore, IPng fragmentation and reassembly, as provided in IPv4, is not necessary. Fragmentation has been shown to be detrimental to network performance and it is strongly recommended that it be avoided.

IP Header Checksum. There has been discussion indicating that the IP checksum does not provide enough error protection to warrant its performance impact. The argument states that there is almost always a stronger datalink level CRC, and that end–to–end protection is provided by the TCP checksum. Therefore an IPng checksum is not required per se.

Firewalls. Some experts have requested that IPng include support for firewalls. Firewalls are one particular solution to the problem of security, and therefore not a valid "technical requirement" for IPng. (At the same time, no IPng should be hostile to firewalls without offering some equivalent security solution.) (see *Security Implications for IPng*).

Network Management. Network management is a task that should be properly carried out by additional protocols and standards, such as

SNMP and its MIBs. Network management, per se, is not an attribute of the IPng protocol. Furthermore, network management is viewed as a support, or service, function. Network management should be developed to fit IPng and not the other way around.

Accounting. Accounting, like network management, must be designed to fit the IPng protocol, and not the other way around. Therefore, accounting, in and of itself, is not a requirement of IPng. However, there are some facets of the protocol that have been specified to make accounting easier, such as non–repudiation of origin under Secure Operation, and the Unique Naming criterion for sorting datagrams into classes. Note that a parameter of Network Service that IPng must support is cost.

Routing. Routing is a very critical part of the Internet. In fact, the Internet Engineering Task Force has a separate area which is chartered to deal only with routing issues. This area is separate from the more general Internet area.

Routing is also a critical component of IPng. There are several criteria, such as Scale, Unique Naming, and Network Services, which are intimately entwined with routing. In order to stress the critical nature and importance of routing, a separate section has been specifically devoted to enumerating some of the requirements and issues that IPng routing must address. All of these issues fall out of the general criteria presented in the previous section.

Scale. First and foremost, the routing architecture must scale to support a very large internet. Current expectations are for an internet of about 10^9 to 10^{12} networks. The routing architecture must be able to deal with networks of this size. Furthermore, the routing architecture must be able to deal with this size without requiring massive, global databases and algorithms. Such databases or algorithms would, in effect, be single points of failure in the architecture (which is not robust), and because of the nature of internet administration (cooperative anarchy), it would be impossible to maintain the needed consistency.

Policy. Networks (both transit and non–transit) must be able to set their own policies for the types of traffic that they will admit. The routing architecture must make these policies available to the network as a whole. Furthermore, nodes must be able to select routes for their traffic based on the advertised policies.

Quality of Service (QoS). A key element of the network service criteria is that differing applications wish to acquire differing grades of network service. It is essential that this service information be propagated around the network.

Feedback. As users select specific routes over which to send their traffic, they must be provided feedback from the routing architecture. This feedback should allow the user to determine whether the desired routes are actually available or not, whether the desired services are being provided, and so forth. This would allow users to modify their service requirements or even change their routes, as needed.

Stability. With the addition of data into the routing system (i.e., routes are based not only on connectivity, as in IPv4, but also on policies, service grades, and so on), the stability of the routes may suffer. We offer as evidence the early ARPANET which experimented with load–based routing. Routes would remain in flux, changing from one saturated link, to another unused link. This must not be allowed to happen. If anything, routes should be even more stable under IPng's routing architecture than under the current architecture.

Multicast. Multicast will be more important in IPng than it is today in IPv4. Multicast groups may be very large and very distributed. Membership in multicast groups will be very dynamic. The routing architecture must be able to cope with this. Furthermore, the routing architecture must be able to build multicast routes dynamically, based on factors such as group membership, member location, requested and available qualities of service, and so on.

IETF IPng Proposals

Part VII

The Proposals

By the time that the IPng Area was formed, the IETF had already aimed a considerable amount of effort at solving the Internet's addressing and routing problems. Several proposals had been made, and some of these reached the level of having a working group chartered. A number of these groups subsequently merged forming groups with a larger consensus.

By February 1992, the Internet community had developed four separate proposals for IPng, [1] "CNAT," "IP Encaps," "Nimrod," and "Simple CLNP." By December 1992, three more proposals followed; "The P Internet Protocol" (PIP), "The Simple Internet Protocol" (SIP), and "TP/IX." After the March 1992 San Diego IETF meeting "Simple CLNP" evolved into "TCP and UDP with Bigger Addresses" (TUBA), and "IP Encaps" evolved into "IP Address Encapsulation" (IPAE).

By November 1993, IPAE had merged with SIP while still maintaining the name SIP. This group then merged with PIP and the resulting working group called themselves "Simple Internet Protocol Plus" (SIPP). At the same time the TP/IX Working Group changed its name to "Common Architecture for the Internet" (CATNIP).

The IPng Area evaluated the three remaining IPng proposals as they were described in their RFC-1550 [2] white papers: CATNIP,[3] SIPP,[4] and TUBA.[5] (The IESG viewed Nimrod as too much of a research project for consideration as a full-fledged IPng candidate.) None of these proposals were wrong nor were others right. They all represented different views on the issues which confronted the Internet and they all sought to optimize different aspects of the possible solutions. All of the proposals would work in some ways to provide a path to overcome the obstacles the Internet faced as it expanded. The task of the IPng Area was to ensure that the IETF understood the offered proposals, and learned from them, and then to provide a recommendation on which path best resolved the current issues while providing the best foundation upon which to build for the future. What follows is a brief description of each of these proposals, highlighting their most significant features.

Common Architecture for the Internet (CATNIP). The objective of CATNIP was to provide common ground between the Internet, ISO, and the Novell protocols, as well as to advance the Internet technology to the scale and performance of the next generation of internetwork technology.

CATNIP was conceived of as a convergence protocol, integrating CLNP, IP, and IPX. The CATNIP design enables any of the transport layer protocols in use-for example TP4, CLTP, TCP, UDP, IPX and SPX-to run over any of the network layer protocol formats: CLNP, IP (version 4), IPX, and CATNIP. With some attention paid to details, CATNIP would make it possible for a transport layer protocol (such as TCP) to operate properly with one end system using one network layer (e.g., IPv4) and the other using a different network protocol, such as CLNP.

CATNIP supports ISO Network Service Access Point (NSAP) format addresses. It also uses cache handles to provide both rapid identification of the next hop in high-performance routing as well as abbreviation of the network header by permitting the omission of addresses when a valid cache handle was available. The fixed part of the network layer header carries the cache handles.

TCP/UDP over CLNP-Addressed Networks (TUBA). The TUBA proposal seeks to minimize the risk associated with migration to a new IP address space while allowing the Internet to scale, promoting the use of Internet applications in a very large ubiquitous worldwide Internet. Therefore, in the TUBA proposal, the existing Internet transport and application protocols continue to operate unchanged, except for the replacement of 32-bit IP addresses with larger addresses. Although based on CLNP, TUBA does not mean having to move over to ISO completely, only replacing IP with CLNP. TCP, UDP, and the traditional TCP/IP applications would run on top of CLNP.

The TUBA effort would expand the Internet's ability to route packets by using addresses that support more levels of hierarchy than the current IP address space. TUBA specifies the continued use of Internet transport protocols, in particular TCP and UDP, but specifies their encapsulation in ISO 8473 (CLNP) packets. This structure would allow the continued use of Internet application protocols such as FTP, SMTP, Telnet, etc. TUBA also seeks to upgrade the current system by a transition from the use of IPv4 to ISO's CLNP and the corresponding large Network Service Access Point (NSAP) address space.

The TUBA proposal makes use of a simple long-term migration strategy based on a gradual update of Internet Hosts (to run Internet applications over CLNP) and DNS servers (to return larger addresses). This proposal requires routers to be updated to support forwarding of CLNP in addition to IP. However, this proposal does not require encapsulation, translation of packets, or address mapping. IP and NSAP addresses may be assigned and used independently during the migration period. Routing and forwarding of IP and CLNP packets may be done independently.

Simple Internet Protocol Plus (SIPP). A new version of IP, SIPP was designed to be an evolutionary step and a natural increment from IPv4 rather than a radical step away from the current Internet Protocol. Functions that worked in IPv4 were kept in SIPP and those that didn't were removed. SIPP can be installed as a normal software upgrade in internet devices and is interoperable with the current IPv4. Its deployment strategy was designed not to have any "flag" days. SIPP is designed to run well on high-performance networks (e.g., ATM) while at the same time remaining efficient for low bandwidth networks (e.g., wireless). In addition, it provides a platform for new internet functionality that will be required in the near future.

SIPP increases the IP address size from 32 bits to 64 bits to support more levels of addressing hierarchy and a much greater number of addressable nodes. SIPP addressing can be further extended, in units of 64 bits, by a facility equivalent to IPv4's Loose Source and Record Route option, in combination with a new address type called "anycast addresses," which identify topological regions rather than individual nodes.

The changes made to the way in which IP header options are encoded under SIPP allows for more efficient forwarding, less stringent limits on the length of options, and greater flexibility for introducing new options in the future. A new capability has been added to allow the labeling of packets belonging to particular traffic flows for which the sender requests special handling, such as non-default quality of service or "real-time" service.

Proposal Reviews. The IPng Directorate discussed and reviewed the candidate proposals during its biweekly teleconferences and through its mailing list. In addition, members of the Big-Internet mailing list discussed many of the aspects of the proposals, particularly when the Area Directors posted several specific questions to stimulate discussion.

Each Directorate member was requested to evaluate the proposals in preparation for a two-day retreat held near Chicago in May 1994. The retreat opened with a roundtable airing the views of each of the participants, including the Area Directors, the Directorate, and a number of guests invited by the working group chairs for each for the proposals.

The following table summarizes each of the three proposals reviewed against the requirements in the IPng Criteria document. "Yes" means the reviewers mainly felt the proposal met the specific criterion. "No" means the reviewers mainly felt the proposal did not meet the criterion. "Mixed" means that the reviewers had mixed reviews with none dominating. "Unknown" means that the reviewers felt that the documentation did not address the criterion.

	CATNIP	SIPP	TUBA
complete specification	no	yes	mostly
simplicity	no	no	no
scale	yes	yes	yes
topological flexibility	yes	yes	yes
performance	mixed	mixed	mixed
robust service	mixed	mixed	yes
transition	mixed	no	mixed
media independent	yes	yes	yes
datagram	yes	yes	yes
configuration ease	unknown	mixed	mixed
security	unknown	yes	mixed
unique names	mixed	mixed	mixed
access to standards	yes	yes	mixed
multicast	unknown	yes	mixed
extensibility	unknown	mixed	mixed
service classes	unknown	yes	mixed
mobility	unknown	mixed	mixed
control protocol	unknown	yes	mixed
tunneling	unknown	yes	mixed

CATNIP Reviews. In general, all the reviewers felt that CATNIP was not fully specified. However, some of the reviewers felt that the CATNIP proposal contained the most innovative ideas and displayed the best vision of all of the proposals. In particular, the use of the ISO's Network Service Attachment Point Addresses (NSAPs) was well thought out, and the routing handles were innovative.

However, while the goal of uniting three major protocol families, IP, ISO's CLNP and Novell IPX, was laudable, the reviewers generally agreed that the developers had not provided detailed enough plans to realize that goal. The plans that were specified suffered from excess complexity resulting from the attempt at uniting a number of existing network protocols. Some reviewers felt that CATNIP basically mapped IPv4,

IPX, and SIPP addresses into NSAPs and, as such, did not deal with the routing problems of the current and future Internet.

Additionally, the reviewers felt that CATNIP had poor support for multicasting and mobility and did not specifically deal with such important topics as security and autoconfiguration.

TUBA Reviews. The reviewers agreed that the most important feature TUBA had to offer was its foundation on ISO's CLNP (Connectionless Network Protocol). This CLNP foundation offered the advantages of a significant installed base of CLNP-capable routers throughout the Internet (although the number of CLNP-capable hosts or actual networks running CLNP is questionable) and the potential for convergence of ISO and IETF networking standards.

However, a number of aspects of CLNP were considered to be problematic, including inefficiencies introduced by the lack of any particular word alignment of the header fields, the CLNP source route, the lack of a flow ID field, the lack of a protocol ID field, and the use of CLNP error messages. The CLNP packet format or procedures would have to be modified to resolve at least some of these issues.

It was this need to alter CLNP that caused the greatest source of conflict for the reviewers. First of all, as a number of reviewers pointed out, if TUBA were to be based on an altered CLNP, then the advantage of an existing CLNP infrastructure would be lost, and the ISO/IETF convergence potential would be reduced. Second, there was a question about the right of the IETF to modify the ISO CLNP standard. While many reviewers and even some of the CLNP document authors were adamant that the IETF could make whatever modifications to the base standards it wished, many others were just as adamant that the standards could be changed only through the ISO standards process. The IETF firmly believed that it must "own" the standards on which its future was based and must maintain the right to modify them as needed. Therefore, this disagreement within the TUBA community was extremely disquieting.

There was also disagreement over the advisability of using NSAPs for routing given the wide variety of NSAP allocation plans. The Internet would have to restrict the use of NSAPs to those that were allocated with the actual underlying network topology in mind, if the required degree of aggregation of routing information was to be achieved.

Therefore, for a number of reasons, unfortunately including prejudice in a few cases, the reviews of the TUBA proposals were much more mixed than they were for SIPP or CATNIP. Clearly TUBA met the requirements for the ability to scale to large numbers of hosts, supported flexible topologies, was media independent, and was a datagram protocol. To the reviewers, it was less clear that TUBA met the other IPng requirements and these views varied widely.

SIPP Reviews. Most of the reviewers, including those predisposed to other proposals, felt, as one reviewer put it, that SIPP was an "aesthetically beautiful protocol well-tailored to compactly satisfy today's known network requirements." The SIPP Working Group had been the most dynamic, producing myriad documentation detailing almost all of the aspects necessary to produce a complete protocol description.

However, the reviewers had some negative comments on a number of issues. The biggest problem was with IPAE, SIPP's transition plan. The overwhelming feeling was that IPAE was fatally flawed and could not be made to work reliably in an operational Internet.

There was significant disagreement about the adequacy of SIPP's 64-bit address size. Although 64 bits can theoretically enumerate 10^{15} end nodes, reviewers had different views about how much inefficiency real-world routing plans would introduce. (See *Address Assignment Efficiency*.) The majority of reviewers felt that-whether or not a 64-bit address size was adequate to meet the present demands of the Internet-it was most likely inadequate for the hierarchy required to meet the needs of the future Internet. In addition, since no one had any experience with extended addressing and routing concepts of the type proposed in SIPP, the reviewers generally felt quite uncomfortable with this methodology. The reviewers also felt that the extended address design introduced some significant security issues.

A number of reviewers also felt that SIPP did not address the routing issue in any useful way. In particular, the SIPP proposal made no serious attempt to develop ways to abstract topology information or to aggregate information about areas of the network.

Finally, most of the reviewers questioned the high-level of complexity in the SIPP autoconfiguration plans, as well as in SIPP's overall structure, except for the structure of the header itself.

Summary of Proposal Reviews. As the reviews indicate, significant problems were seen in all three of the proposals. Reviewers felt that, to one degree or another, both SIPP and TUBA could work in the Internet context but that each exhibited its own problems, some of which would have to be rectified immediately before either one would be ready to replace IPv4, much less be the vehicle to carry the Internet into the future. Other problems could be addressed over time. CATNIP was felt to be too incomplete to be considered.

A Revised Proposal. During the May 1994 retreat with the IPng Area Directorate and invited guests, there was considerable discussion of the strengths and weaknesses of the various IPng proposals. In response to the reviewers' comments, the co-chairs of the SIPP Working Group, Steve Deering and Paul Francis, proposed a number of changes to SIPP. These changes addressed the reviewers' two major concerns: 1) the complexity, manageability, and feasibility of IPAE; and 2) the adequacy, correctness, and limitations of SIPP's addressing and routing model, especially the use of loose source-routing to accomplish extended addressing.

In response to these concerns, the SIPP Working Group chairs proposed modifying SIPP as follows: [6]

- The address size be increased from 64 bits to 128 bits (fixed-length).
- Optional use of serverless autoconfiguration of the 128-bit address be specified by using IEEE 802 address as the low-order ("node ID") part.
- Higher-layer protocols that used internet-layer addresses as part of connection identifiers (e.g., TCP), be required to use the entire 16-byte addresses.
- Use of the Route Header for extended addressing be eliminated.

After considerable discussion on the SIPP and Big-Internet mailing lists about these proposed changes, the SIPP Working Group submitted a revised version of SIPP [7] with the above changes, and a new addressing architecture, and a simplified transition mechanism. This proposal represented a synthesis of multiple IETF efforts, with much of the basic protocol coming from the SIPP effort, the autoconfiguration and transition portions influenced by TUBA, the addressing structure based on the CIDR work, and the routing header evolving out of the SDRP deliberations.

The Question of Address Size. One of the most hotly discussed aspects of the IPng design possibilities was address size and format. During the IPng process four distinct views were expressed about these issues:

- The view that a 64-bit address size is enough to meet the current and future needs of the Internet (squaring the size of the current IP address space). More bits would waste bandwidth, promote inefficient assignment, and cause problems in some networks (such as mobiles and other low-speed links).
- The view that a 128-bit address size is just about right. That length supports easy autoconfiguration as well as organizations with complex internal routing topologies in conjunction with the global routing topology now and well into the future.
- The view that 160-bit ISO NSAP addresses should be used in the interests of global harmonization.
- The view that variable length addresses, which might be smaller or larger than 128 bits, should be used to embrace all the above options and more, so that the size of the address could be adjusted to the demands of the particular environment, and to ensure the ability to meet any future networking requirements.

Good technical and engineering arguments were made for and against all of these views. Unanimity was not achieved, but a clear majority view emerged that the use of 128-bit fixed length addresses was the best compromise between efficiency, functionality, flexibility, and global applicability. [8]

Some indication of the complexity of the engineering tradeoffs, and some additional perspective for understanding the address size decision that was made, are found in the following sections about the nature of addressing by J. Noel Chiappa and Christian Huitema.

Address Length in Global Networks

J. Noel Chiappa

The term "address," in internetworking, usually indicates an identifier with "topological significance." In other words, the address has some structure in it which helps you identify ist location in the internetwork's "topology," which is the network's connectivity structure. Such addresses are in contrast to "flat" addresses, where each address is a unique quantity, and is assigned with no particular relationship to its location.

The structure in topologically significant addresses is usually a hierarchy of larger and larger topological units, much like a person's street address, which provides a geographic address using a hierarchy of larger and larger geographic units: the house, street, city, region/province, country, etc. This hierarchy results in a sequence of elements in the address, those elements being the name of each unit, be it geographical or topological.

This has all sorts of useful consequences. For instance, looking at two hierarchical topologically significant addresses will usually tell you something about how close the places identified by the two of them are, by how much of their address they have in common. In the exact same way, looking at two geographically significant addresses will tell you something about how geographically close they are. However, this is not the most important consequence.

The real reason addresses must have both hierarchy and topological significance is that, in a very large network like the Internet, the absence of such properties would make the cost of finding paths through the network (from a given source, to a given destination with which it wishes to communicate) rise to the point where it is infeasible. The reason why this is so is not a matter of poor engineering, but is implicit in the underlying mathematics used in finding paths through networks, and cannot be avoided by clever design.

Recent internetworking designs have attempted to carry such hierarchical, topologically significant addresses in fixed length fields in places such as internetwork protocol packet headers. This is a non-functional design choice in a network which is intended to be global in size.

The "address abstraction hierarchy" is what we call the organization of hierarchical topological units that are used in topological addresses. To give you a simple analogy to this concept, the geographic address abstraction hierarchy is the set of hierarchical geographical units— countries, states/provinces, cities, etc.—organized in a way which shows the relationships between them. Obviously, not all of these boundaries are of equal importance; a given set of state/province boundaries are in one country, etc., and have a more local meaning and utility.

You can draw a diagram of the "tree" of the geographic boundary hierarchy (much like the diagrams of tree-structured file systems you may be familiar with), in which all the states/provinces which are part of one country are depicted underneath that country, connected to it, but "hanging" from it, and so on. The diagram starts from a base, the "root," under which are all the highest level entities; countries in this case. The ends of the lowest level branches, the "leaves," are individual geographic street addresses. The full hierarchical geographic address is given by concatenating the names of the geographic entities along the path from the root to the individual leaf.

To make this more concrete, imagine drawing a map of the network (or at least a part of it) on a piece of paper. (Obviously, to draw a map of the whole network would take a very, very large piece of paper!) First, draw (probably in a separate color, to make it clearer) non-overlapping circles around small pieces of the network; these are the lowest level entities. Now, draw circles (again, in a different color) which include groups of the circles you drew previously. You have drawn a hierarchy of topological boundaries, just as state boundaries enclose groups of counties, etc.

In a typical hierarchical file system, some filenames have more elements in them than others; in some places one will have a top-level directory with a relatively large number of layers of sub-directories underneath it; in other places, a top-level directory may have no layers of sub-directories beneath it.

In a very large-scale network, the length of the address (i.e., the number of elements along the path from the root of the abstraction hierarchy to a given leaf) will vary, since the structure of the abstraction hierarchy is not uniform, i.e., it is not controlled by some centralized authority to ensure that this happens. Moreover, not only is it not uniform, but it is constantly changing as the network grows, which it will continue to do for decades to come.

The geographic address abstraction hierarchy does not show this kind of behavior, but then again, geography is not as flexible as network topology. Also, many geographic boundaries are based on political arrangements, which again tend to change slowly. The situation in the network is completely different, and much, much more dynamic.

We can now see why a hierarchical address is inherently of variable length: a hierarchical address is just the list of the topological entities in the address abstraction hierarchy, along the path from the root to the individual leaf, and the number of entries here can vary.

Clearly, it is chancy to try to store such an inherently variable length item in a fixed-length field, as has been tried in many recent internetworking architectures, especially for a a network which is intended to be global in size. Certainly, one can allocate a fixed-length field, and for some time, at least, the inherently variable-length data item can be stored in it without problems. Inevitably, though, will come instances when the desired length address is too large for the fixed-length field, and the users will be prevented from doing what they want, although they may be able to find some alternative which is functional, if not preferable. From that point on, the fixed-length field will be more and more of a problem; eventually, cripplingly so.

Surely one can estimate the maximum size needed, though? Not really. A global network, with consequent massive infrastructural investment, must of necessity be intended to last for many years. Exactly what the network will look like toward the end of that lifespan is anyone's guess. Any choice of a fixed field size is thus a risky bet.

This variability in the abstraction hierarchy is allowed in a large network because there is no global control over the structure of the abstraction hierarchy. There is no need for it; it would be extremely difficult to do in any case, and such a global control would unduly restrict the flexibility of address assignment.

For example, the world telephone system does not have a central control over what phone numbers in all the individual countries look like: how long they are, or how many segments they are split up into. Individual countries may decide to change the way their phone numbers look, perhaps because they run out of phone numbers, but this change is a local change in the telephone number abstraction hierarchy, and is not controlled by any worldwide organization; such an organization would be a practical impossibility.

As to why this kind of variability in the address abstraction hierarchy happens, it happens because it is useful. Each section of the tree is organized according to what seems most useful for that section. The reasons why differing organizational principles are used in different parts of the abstraction hierarchy are many.

For example, a single site may grow so large that it may decide it needs an extra layer of hierarchy to organize its addressing. Growth of an order of magnitude in any entity at a given layer can probably be handled without adding another layer of hierarchy, but growth beyond that point requires the addition of another layer; and one thing the history of the deployment of computers shows us is that the number of computers has been increasing exponentially for some time, and shows no signs of slowing down anytime soon.

Another reason for increasing the number of layers in the hierarchy is somewhat arcane at the moment, but will very probably come to be more common soon. That is the need for what is called "policy routing," by which it is meant that the user wishes to exert some control over where their traffic goes. To use a simple example, when someone gets into their car, they make numerous decisions about which path to take to their destination, taking into account such factors as whether they wish to pay a toll fee, etc. The network is going to need to provide this same flexibilty to the users of the network, to chose service providers, etc.

To do this, the network needs to be able to provide ways of naming the transmission facilities used. To use our road example again, a road which charges a toll is usually given a special name (and color) on roadmaps, so that people can recognize it as a distinct entity when they are deciding what path to take. In the same way, the network will need to be able to name regions of the topology about which statements concerning the kind of service, etc., they offer can be made. This also will increase the numbers of layers of hierarchy needed.

So, there are many reasons why a lot of local variability in the address abstraction hierarchy is needed, and this local variability makes the length of addresses (which are, remember, derived from this abstraction hierarchy) inherently variable. Storing such an inherently variable-length item in a fixed-length field is a chancy business.

Address Assignment Efficiency

Christian Huitema
INRIA

Efficiency of Address Assignment. A substantial portion of the IPng debate has been devoted to the question of optimal address size. A key factor in the choice of address size is the concept of "assignment efficiency"—the ratio of the effective number of systems in the network to the theoretical maximum. For example, the 32-bit IPv4 address size can in theory enumerate over seven billion systems; however, as of today we have about 3.5 million addresses reported in the DNS, translating into an efficiency of 0.05%.

But this classic evaluation is misleading, as it does not take into account the effect of the number of hierarchical elements contained in IP addresses. IPv4 addresses, for example, have at least three degrees of hierarchy: network, subnet, and host. This hierarchical address structure reduces the number of individual addresses that can be enumerated by a set number of bits, because not all possible combinations of bits constitute usable addresses; address values are assigned to sites that don't need so many and can't be used by other sites that do need them. Therefore, in order to obtain a more accurate sense of the address space that can be accommodated by a given address size, I have developed an efficiency ratio based on a logarithmic scale that reduces the effect of hierarchical structure on the efficiency ratio. This ratio is represented by H, where:

$$H = \frac{\log (number\ of\ objects)}{available\ bits}$$

This H ratio is not nearly as dependent on the number of hierarchical levels as a direct proportion (number of objects/available bits) would be. For example, let us compare the H ratio of two different address structures, one with two levels encoded on 8 bits each, and the other with a single level encoded on 16 bits. We will obtain the same efficiency ratio for both if we allocate an average of 100 elements at each 8-bit level, or simply 10,000 elements in the single 16-bit level.

Note that base 10 logs are used in what follows, because this is the standard convention. It follows from this choice of units that H varies between 0 and a theoretical maximum of 0.30103 (log base 10 of 2).

Estimating Reasonable Values for the H Ratio. Indeed, no one expects to achieve a ratio of 0.30 in practice. What we need to do is to determine the values which can reasonably be expected. One way to do this is to study existing numbering plans and, in particular, examine the point at which the plans broke (i.e., when they were forced to add digits or bits to accommodate any more users). Here are a number of instructive examples.

The French telephone system was forced to add one digit, moving from 8 digits to 9, when the number of telephone numbers reached a threshold of 10^7. The log value is 7, the number of bits is about 27 (1 decimal digit uses approximately 3.3 bits). Therefore, the H ratio is 0.26.

The U.S. telephone system expanded the number of area codes, making it effectively 10 digits long, when the level of 10^8 subscribers was reached. Here, the log value is 8, the number of bits is 33, and the resulting H ratio is about 0.24.

SITA expanded the size of its 7-character address with approximately 64,000 addressed points in their network, scattered in 1200 cities in 180 countries. An upper case character takes up about 5 bits of addressing, resulting in an H efficiency ratio of 0.14. However, SITA represents an extreme case because it uses fixed length tokens in its hierarchy.

The globally-connected physics/space science DECnet (Phase IV) stopped growing at about 15,000 nodes. DECnet's 16-bit address size yields a ratio of 0.26.

There are about 200 million IEEE 802 nodes in a 46-bit space, representing a ratio of 0.18. That number space, however, is clearly not yet saturated.

From this empirical evidence, we can estimate that the saturation point is usually reached at an H efficiency ratio of between 0.14 and 0.26.

The H Ratio for the Present Internet. There are currently about 3 million hosts on the Internet, with an address size of 32 bits. The log of 3×10^6 is about 6.5, yielding an H efficiency ratio of only 0.20. This ratio suggests that the Internet has not yet reached the saturation point with its 32-bit address size. Indeed, we believe that 32 bits will still be enough for some years. Even if we were to increase the number of hosts by a factor of ten, the H ratio would climb to only 0.23.

Evaluating Proposed Address Plans for IPng. Reversing the process of computing the H ratio, we can use given H ratios to determine expected maximum population counts in the network at various address sizes.

Address size	Maximum number of addresses at a pessimistic H ratio (0.14)	Maximum number of addresses at an optimistic H ratio (0.26)
32 bits	3.0×10^4 (!)	2.0×10^8
64 bits	9.0×10^8	4.0×10^{16}
80 bits	1.6×10^{11}	2.6×10^{27}
128 bits	8.0×10^{17}	2.0×10^{33}

This chart indicates why some IPng developers feel that 64 bits is not enough while others feel it is sufficient by a large margin: depending on the given H efficiency ratio, 64 bits yields population counts either well below the 10^{15} target or well above. In my view, however, there is no question that 128 bits provides more than enough address space. Even if we presume the lowest efficiency, 128 bits still yields an address space well above the hyperbolic estimate of 10^{15} Internet hosts.

It is also interesting to note that if we devote 80 bits of a 128-bit address to the "network" and use 48 bits for "stateless autoconfiguration," we can still number more that 10^{11} networks, even in the pessimistic case. In fact, it would only take an H efficiency ratio of 0.15 to reach the 10^{12} networks hyperbole.

Therefore, a 128-bit address size appears entirely safe for the next 30 years. The level of constraints that will have to be incorporated into address assignment policies appears very much in line with what we know how to do today.

The IPng Recommendation

The Timing of the Recommendation. A prime topic of discussion within the Internet community was the timing of the IPng recommendation—whether it should be made now or further down the road. Our reading of the consensus of the Internet community—taken from opinions expressed on the Big-Internet mailing list, the open IPng Directorate meeting in Seattle, the ipdecide BOF in Amsterdam, and in some of the RFC-1550 papers—was that the most appropriate time to make a recommendation was now, and that, from this point on, the IETF should proceed with a single IPng effort.

Although some people felt that additional research would help resolve some of the technical issues that were currently unresolved, many others argued that selecting a single protocol to work on now would clarify the picture for the community and focus the resources of the IETF on finalizing its details. Furthermore, since the argument could be made that there would be open research items at any point in time, there might never be a "right" time.

In fact, there was no particular reason to think that the basic recommendation would be significantly different if we waited for another six months or a year. Clearly some details that were unresolved could be filled in if the recommendation were delayed, but the fragmentation of the IETF's energies would limit the efficiency of this type of detailed resolution. Concentrating the resources of the IETF behind a single effort seemed to us to be a more efficient way to proceed.

Addressing Architecture Issues. One of the original problems that led to the initiation of the IPng effort in the IETF was the too rapid increase in the size of the routing tables in the routers that support the Internet backbones. The use of strict hierarchical addressing, as defined in CIDR [9], where the structure of the address reflects the structure of the underlying network topology, did slow the growth rate for a while. The rate of growth has recently increased again and is, at the time of this writing, growing faster than it was growing at any time during the IPng process. The reasons for the accelerated growth in routing table requirements seem to be many, but a major contributing factor is the difficulty of renumbering existing IPv4 networks when their position in the global networking architecture changes. A corporation should renumber their network when they change IP providers but it is hard to do.

We feel that developing an ability to easily renumber hosts is a key to reducing the rate of growth in the routing tables. There are many other parts of a network that must also reflect any change in network addresses but if changing the host addresses can be facilitated, the problem gets much simpler. Thus we emphasized autoconfiguration in our evaluation of the IPng proposals.

Address autoconfiguration is not the only answer to the routing issues that face the Internet. New address architectures, different routing protocols, new internetworking technologies, all will affect this issue. (See *Evolutionary Possibilities for the Internetwork Layer* and *Nimrod IPng Technical Requirements*.) More research is required before we can know if any of these will be a significant help in resolving the issues involved in scaling the routing infrastructure.

IPng Recommendation. After a great deal of discussion in many forums and with the consensus of the IPng Directorate, the IPng Area Directors recommended that the protocol described in the revised document *Simple Internet Protocol Plus (SIPP)* [10] be adopted as the basis for IPng, the next generation of the Internet Protocol.

This revised SIPP proposal resolved most of the perceived problems, particularly in the areas of addressing, routing, transition and address autoconfiguration. It included the broad base of the SIPP proposal effort, flexible address autoconfiguration features, and a merged transition strategy. It clearly met the requirements outlined in the IPng Technical Criteria Document and provided the framework to fully meet the needs of the greater Internet community for the foreseeable future. The Internet Assigned Number Authority (IANA) assigned version number 6 to IPng, and the protocol itself is now referred to as IPv6.

IPng Criteria Document and IPv6. The following list demonstrates the extent to which IPv6 is responsive to the IPng Technical Criteria Document.

Complete Specification. The base specifications for IPv6 are complete but address autoconfiguration remains to be finalized.

Architectural Simplicity. The protocol is simple, easy to explain, and uses well-established paradigms.

Scale. An address size of 128 bits easily meets the need to address 10^9 networks even in the face of the inherent inefficiency of address allocation for efficient routing.

Topological Flexibility. The IPv6 design places no constraints on network topology except for the limit of 255 hops.

Performance. The simplicity of processing, the alignment of the fields in the headers, and the elimination of the header checksum will allow for high performance handling of data streams.

Robust Service. IPv6 includes no inhibitors to robust service and the addition of packet-level authentication allows the securing of control and routing protocols without the need for separate procedures.

Transition. The IPv6 transition plan is simple and realistically covers the transition methods that will be present in the marketplace.

Media Independence. IPv6 retains IPv4's media independence, and it may be possible to make use of IPv6's Flow Label in some connection-oriented media such as ATM.

Datagram Service. IPv6 preserves datagram service as its basic operational mode, although it is possible that the use of path MTU discovery will complicate the use of datagrams in some cases.

Configuration Ease. IPv6 will have easy and flexible address autoconfiguration which will support a wide variety of environments from nodes on an isolated network to nodes deep in a complex internet.

Security. IPv6 includes specific mechanisms for authentication and encryption at the internetwork layer; however, the security features rely on the presence of a yet to be defined key management system.

Unique Names. IPv6 addresses may be used as globally unique names although they do have topological significance.

Access to Standards. All of the IPv6-related standards will be published as RFCs with unlimited distribution.

Multicast Support. IPv6 specifically includes multicast support.

Extensibility. The use of extension headers and an expandable header option feature will allow the introduction of new features into IPv6 when needed in a way that minimizes the disruption of the existing network.

Service Classes. The IPv6 header includes a Flow Label which may be used to differentiate requested service classes.

Mobility. The definition of IPv6 mobility is still under development, but will be completed within the year the criteria recommends.

Control Protocol. IPv6 includes the familiar IPv4 control protocol features.

Tunneling Support. Encapsulation of IPv6 or other protocols within IPv6 is a basic capability described in the IPng specifications.

IPv6

Part VIII

This section includes overviews of IPv6 itself, IPv6 address autoconfiguration, and the IPv4 to IPv6 transition mechanisms. These are meant to be general descriptions of the technologies involved. These printed words will remain static whereas the protocols will change over time as we acquire implementation and deployment experience. Please refer to the RFCs for the up-to-date definitive details.

IPv6 Technical Overview

Robert M. Hinden
Ipsilon Networks
Stephen E. Deering
Xerox Corporation

Introduction. This document presents an overview of the Internet Protocol Next Generation which was recommended by the IPng Area Directors of the Internet Engineering Task Force at the Toronto IETF meeting on July 25, 1994, and documented in RFC-1752, "The Recommendation for the IP Next Generation Protocol." [1] The recommendation was approved by the Internet Engineering Steering Group on November 17, 1994 and made a Proposed Standard. The formal name of this protocol is IPv6.

IPv6 is a new version of IP designed as an evolutionary step and a natural increment from IPv4. It can be installed as a normal software upgrade in internet devices and is interoperable with the current IPv4. Its deployment strategy was designed so that no "flag days"—during which users would have to upgrade all systems—would be necessary. IPv6 is designed to run well on high-performance networks (e.g., ATM) while at the same time remaining efficient for low bandwidth networks (e.g., wireless). In addition, it provides a platform for new internet functionality that will be required in the near future.

Summary of Capabilities. IPv6 resolves many of the problems inherent in IPv4 and incorporates numerous enhancements. It solves the Internet scaling problem, provides a flexible transition mechanism, and meets the needs of such new markets as nomadic personal computing devices, networked entertainment, and device control. It does this in an evolutionary way which reduces the risk of architectural problems.

Ease of transition is a key point in the design of IPv6 rather than being tacked on as an afterthought. IPv6 was designed to interoperate with IPv4. Specific mechanisms (embedded IPv4 addresses, pseudo-checksum rules, etc.) have been built into IPv6 to support transition and compatibility with IPv4. These mechanisms permit a gradual and piecemeal deployment with a minimum of dependencies.

IPv6 supports large hierarchical addresses and new routing capabilities which will allow the Internet to continue to grow. Its new "anycast" address type can be used for policy route selection, and its scoped multicast address provides improved scalability over the IPv4 multicast address. IPv6 also includes local use addresses whose mechanisms provide the ability for "plug and play" installation.

The address structure of IPv6 was also designed to support other internet protocol suites' addresses, such as Novell IPX and OSI NSAP addresses, facilitating the eventual migration of these other internet protocols to IPv6.

Responding to the needs of the Internet and broader communications industry, IPv6 provides a platform for new Internet functionality, including support for real-time flows, provider selection, host mobility, end-to-end security, autoconfiguration, and autoreconfiguration.

Overview of Features. IPv6 is a new version of the Internet Protocol, designed as a successor to IPv4. It was not a design goal to take a radical step away from IPv4. Therefore, functions which work in IPv4 have been kept in IPv6 and functions that didn't were removed. Some of the changes incorporated into IPv6, while not revolutionary, introduce fundamental improvements in function and architecture:

Header Format Simplification. Some IPv4 header fields have been dropped or made optional to reduce the common-case processing cost of packet handling and to keep the bandwidth cost of the IPv6 header as low as possible-despite the increased size of the addresses. Also, even though IPv6 addresses are four times longer than IPv4 addresses, the IPv6 header is only twice the size of the IPv4 header.

Improved Support for Options Using Extension Headers. Changes in the way IP header options are encoded allow for more efficient forwarding, less stringent limits on the length of options, and greater flexibility for introducing new options in the future.

Expanded Routing and Addressing Capabilities. IPv6 increases the IP address length from 32 bits to 128 bits in order to support more levels of addressing hierarchy, a much greater number of addressable nodes, and simpler autoconfiguration of addresses.

A new type of address called an "anycast address" is defined. An anycast address identifies a set of multiple nodes for which incoming packets are delivered to just one of the nodes. The use of anycast addresses in the IPv6 source route allows nodes to control the path through which their traffic flows.

The scalability of multicast routing is improved by adding a "scope" field to multicast addresses.

Quality-of-Service Capabilities. A new capability has been added to enable the labeling of packets belonging to particular traffic "flows" for which the sender requests special handling, such as non-default quality of service or "real-time" service.

Expanded Security Capabilities. IPv6 incorporates extensions that support authentication, data integrity, and confidentiality. These features are a basic element of IPv6 and will be included in all implementations.

Header Format. The IPv6 protocol consists of two parts, the basic IPv6 header and IPv6 extension headers. The basic IPv6 header is shown in Figure 2.

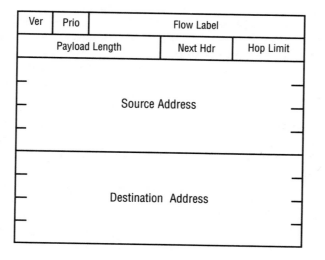

Figure 2. IPv6 Header

Version. 4-bit Internet Protocol version number = 6.

Prio. 4-bit Priority value. See *IPv6 Priority section.*

Flow Label. 24-bit field. See *IPv6 Quality of Service.*

Payload Length. 16-bit unsigned integer. Length of payload, i.e., the rest of the packet following the IPv6 header, in octets.

Next Header. 8-bit selector. Identifies the type of header immediately following the IPv6 header. Uses the same values as the IPv4 Protocol field. [2]

Hop Limit. 8-bit unsigned integer. Decremented by 1 by each node that forwards the packet. The packet is discarded if Hop Limit is decremented to zero.

Source Address. 128 bits. The address of the initial sender of the packet. [3]

Destination Address. 128 bits. The address of the intended recipient of the packet (possibly not the ultimate recipient, if an optional Routing Header is present).

Extension Headers. IPv6 includes an improved option mechanism over IPv4. IPv6 options are placed in separate extension headers that are located between the IPv6 header and the transport-layer header in a packet. Most IPv6 extension headers are not examined or processed by any router along a packet's delivery path until it arrives at its final destination, facilitating a major improvement in router performance for packets containing options. In contrast, the presence of any options in IPv4 requires the router to examine all options. The other improvement is that, unlike IPv4 options, IPv6 extension headers can be of arbitrary length, and the total number of options carried in a packet is not limited to 40 bytes. As a result of these two improvements, IPv6 options can be used for functions that were not practical in IPv4. A good example of this is the IPv6 Authentication and Security Encapsulation options.

In order to improve the performance when handling subsequent option headers and the transport protocol which follows, IPv6 options are always an integer multiple of 8 octets long, a length which retains the alignment for subsequent headers.

The IPv6 extension headers which are currently defined are:

Option	Function
Routing	Extended Routing (like IPv4 source route)

Fragmentation	Fragmentation and Reassembly
Authentication	Integrity and Authentication
Security Encapsulation	Confidentiality
Hop-by-Hop Option	Special options which require processing at every node
Destination Options	Optional information to be examined by the destination node only

Addressing. IPv6 addresses are 128-bits long and identify individual interfaces and sets of interfaces. It is important to note that IPv6 addresses are assigned to interfaces, not nodes. Since each interface belongs to a single node, any of that node's interfaces' unicast addresses may be used as an identifier for the node. A single interface may be assigned multiple IPv6 addresses.

There are three types of IPv6 addresses: unicast, anycast, and multicast. Unicast addresses identify a single interface. Anycast addresses identify a set of interfaces such that a packet sent to an anycast address will be delivered to only one member of the set. Multicast addresses identify a group of interfaces, such that a packet sent to a multicast address is delivered to all of the interfaces in the group. IPv6's multicast address type supersedes the broadcast address in IPv4.

IPv6 supports addresses that are four times the number of bits as IPv4 addresses (128 vs. 32). This creates an address space that is 4 billion times 4 billion (2^{96}) times the size of the IPv4 address space (2^{32}). The IPv6 address space works out to be:

340,282,366,920,938,463,463,374,607,431,768,211,456.

This is an extremely large address space. In a theoretical sense this is approximately   665,570,793,348,866,943,898,599 addresses per square meter of the surface of the planet Earth (assuming the earth surface is 511,263,971,197,990 square meters).

In more practical terms, the assignment and routing of addresses requires the creation of hierarchies that reduce the efficiency of the address space usage. In Christian Huitema's analysis [see *Address Assignment Efficiency*], he evaluated the efficiency of other addressing architectures (including the French telephone system, U.S. telephone systems, the current Internet using IPv4, and IEEE 802 nodes). He concluded that 128-bit IPv6 addresses could accommodate between 8×10^{17} to 2×10^{33} nodes assuming efficiency in the same ranges as these other addressing architectures. Even according to his most pessimistic estimate, 128-bit addresses would provide 1,564 addresses for each square meter of the surface of the planet Earth. The optimistic estimate would allow for 3,911,873,538,269,506,102 addresses for each square meter of the surface of the planet Earth.

The specific type of IPv6 address is indicated by the leading bits in the address. The variable-length field comprising these leading bits is called the Format Prefix (FP). The initial allocation of these prefixes is as follows:

Initial IPv6 Prefix Allocation

Allocation	Prefix (binary)	Fraction of Address Space
Reserved	0000 0000	1/256
Unassigned	0000 0001	1/256
Reserved for NSAP Allocation	0000 001	1/128
Reserved for IPX Allocation	0000 010	1/128
Unassigned	0000 011	1/128
Unassigned	0000 1	1/32
Unassigned	0001	1/16
Unassigned	001	1/8
Provider-based Unicast Address	010	1/8
Unassigned	011	1/8
Reserved for Geographic Unicast Addresses	100	1/8
Unassigned	101	1/8
Unassigned	110	1/8
Unassigned	1110	1/16
Unassigned	1111 0	1/32
Unassigned	1111 10	1/64
Unassigned	1111 110	1/128
Unassigned	1111 1110 0	1/512
Link Local Use Addresses	1111 1110 10	1/1024
Site Local Use Addresses	1111 1110 11	1/1024
Multicast Addresses	1111 1111	1/256

This allocation supports the direct allocation of provider addresses, local use addresses, and multicast addresses. Space is reserved for NSAP addresses, IPX addresses, and geographic addresses. The remainder of the address space is unassigned for future use. This can be used for expansion of existing use (e.g., additional provider addresses, etc.) or new uses (e.g., separate locators and identifiers).

Approximately fifteen percent of the address space is initially allocated. The remaining 85% is reserved for future use.

Anycast addresses are not shown because they are a usage of unicast format addresses.

Unicast Addresses. There are several forms of unicast address assignments in IPv6: the global provider-based unicast address, the site-local-use address, the link-local-use address, and the IPv4-capable host address. In addition, IPv6 provides for such other address types as the geographic unicast address, the NSAP address, and the IPX hierarchical address. Additional address types can be defined in the future.

Provider-Based Unicast Addresses. Provider-based unicast addresses are used for global communication. They are similar in function to IPv4 addresses under CIDR. The initial assignment plan formats for these unicast addresses are: [4, 5] The format of IPv6 provider-based unicast addresses is shown in Figure 3.

3	n	m bits	o bits	p bits	125-n-m-o-p
010	REG ID	PROVD ID	SUBSC ID	SUBNET ID	INTF ID

Figure 3. IPv6 Provider-based Unicast Address

The first 3 bits identify the address as a provider-oriented unicast address. The next field (REGISTRY ID) identifies the internet address registry which assigns provider identifiers (PROVIDER ID) to internet service providers, which then assign portions of the address space to subscribers. This usage is similar to assignment of IP addresses under CIDR. The SUBSCRIBER ID distinguishes among multiple subscribers attached to the internet service provider identified by the PROVIDER ID. The SUBNET ID identifies a specific physical link. There can be multiple subnets on the same physical link, but a specific subnet cannot span multiple physical links. The INTERFACE ID identifies a single interface among the group of interfaces identified by the subnet prefix.

Local-Use Addresses. A local-use address is a unicast address that has only local routability scope (within the subnet or within a subscriber network), and may have local or global uniqueness scope. It is intended for use inside of a site for "plug and play" local communication and for bootstrapping up to use of a global address. It fulfills the goals of RFC-1597, but by using a pre-allocated address format, there can be no risk of accidentally connecting IPv6 local-use addresses to the global Internet.

There are two types of local-use unicast addresses defined: Link-Local-Use (for use on a single link) and Site-Local-Use (for use in a single site). The format of IPv6 Link-Local-Use addresses is shown in Figure 4.

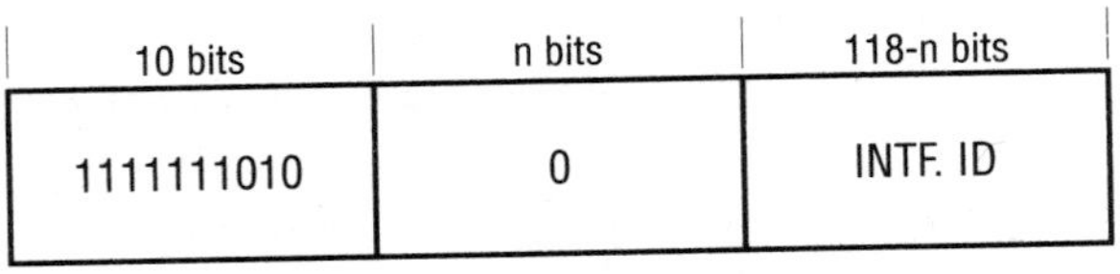

10 bits	n bits	118-n bits
1111111010	0	INTF. ID

Figure 4. IPv6 Link-local Addresses

Link-Local-Use addresses are designed to be used for addressing on a single link for purposes such as auto-address configuration.

The format for IPv6 Site-Local-Use addresses is shown in Figure 5.

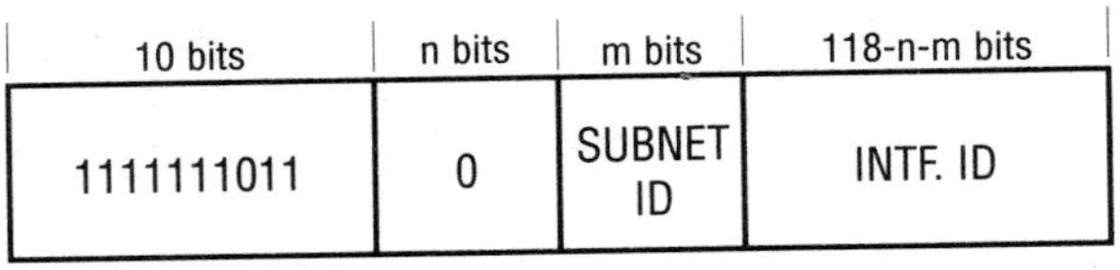

10 bits	n bits	m bits	118-n-m bits
1111111011	0	SUBNET ID	INTF. ID

Figure 5. IPv6 Site-local Addresses

For both types of local-use addresses the INTERFACE ID is an identifier that must be unique in the domain in which it is being used. In most cases these interfaces will use a node's IEEE-802 48-bit address. The SUBNET ID identifies a specific subnet in a site. The combination of the SUBNET ID and the INTERFACE ID form a local use address which allows a large private internet to be constructed without any other address allocation.

Local-use addresses allow organizations that are not (yet) connected to the global Internet to operate without having to request an address prefix from the global Internet address space. Local-use addresses can be used instead. If the organization later connects to the global Internet, it can use its SUBNET ID and INTERFACE ID in combination with its global prefix (e.g., REGISTRY ID + PROVIDER ID + SUBSCRIBER ID) to create a global address.

Addresses with Embedded IPv4 Addresses. The IPv6 transition mechanisms include a technique for hosts and routers to dynamically tunnel IPv6 packets over IPv4 routing infrastructure. IPv6 nodes that utilize this technique are assigned special IPv6 unicast addresses that carry an IPv4 address in the low-order 32-bits. This type of address is termed an "IPv4-compatible IPv6 address" and has the format shown in Figure 6.

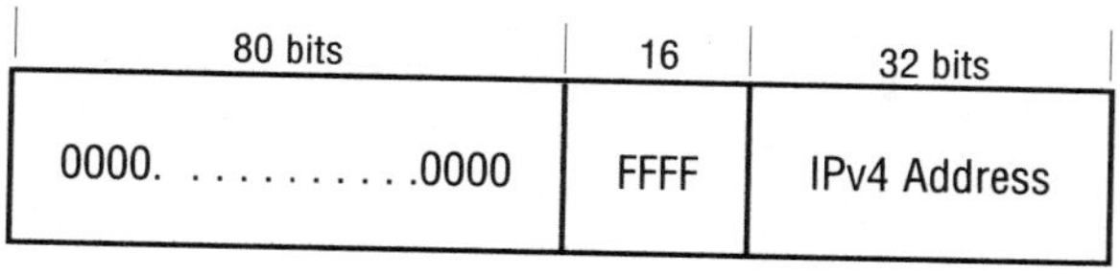

80 bits	16	32 bits
0000. 0000	FFFF	IPv4 Address

Figure 6. IPv6 Compatible Addresses

A second type of IPv6 address that holds an embedded IPv4 address is also defined. This address is used to represent the addresses of IPv4-only nodes (those that do not support IPv6) as IPv6 addresses. This type of address is termed an "IPv4-mapped IPv6 address" and has the format shown in Figure 7.

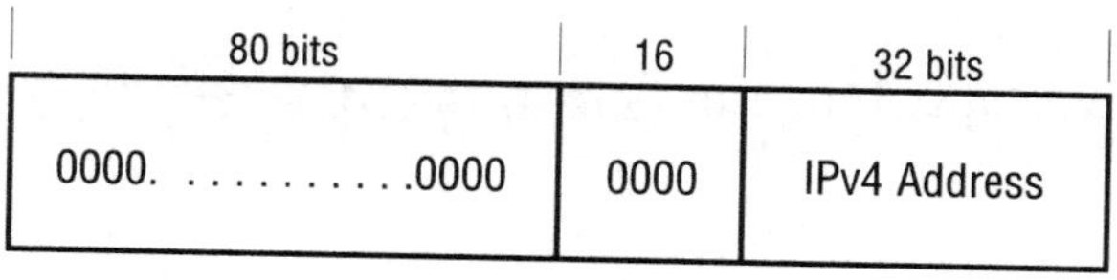

80 bits	16	32 bits
0000. 0000	0000	IPv4 Address

Figure 7. IPv4-mapped Addresses

These addresses may be used in specialized systems that may do automatic translation between IPv4 and IPv6.

Anycast Addresses. An IPv6 anycast address is an address that is assigned to more than one interface (typically belonging to different nodes), with the property that a packet sent to an anycast address is routed to the "nearest" interface having that address, according to the routing protocols' measure of distance.

An anycast address, when used as part of a route sequence, permits a node to select which of several internet service providers it wants to carry its traffic. This capability is sometimes called "source selected policies." It can be implemented by configuring anycast addresses to identify the set of routers belonging to internet service providers (e.g., one anycast address per internet service provider). These anycast addresses can be used as intermediate addresses in an IPv6 routing header, so that a packet will be delivered via a particular provider or sequence of providers. Other possible uses of anycast addresses are to identify the set of routers attached to a particular subnet, or the set of routers providing entry into a particular routing domain.

Anycast addresses are allocated from the unicast address space, using any of the defined unicast address formats. Thus, anycast addresses are syntactically indistinguishable from unicast addresses. When a unicast address is assigned to more than one interface, thereby transforming it into an anycast address, the nodes to which the address is assigned must be explicitly configured to recognize its anycast nature.

Multicast Addresses. A multicast address is an identifier for a group of interfaces. An interface may belong to any number of multicast groups. The format of IPv6 multicast addresses is shown in Figure 8.

8 bits	4	4	112 bits
11111111	flags	scop	Group ID

Figure 8. IPv6 Multicast Address

The value 11111111 at the start of the address identifies the address as being a multicast address.

Figure 9. IPv6 Multicast Flags

IPv6 multicast flags: (shown in Figure 9)

The high-order 3 flags are reserved, and must be initialized to 0.

T = 0 indicates a permanently-assigned ("well-known") multicast address, assigned by the global internet numbering authority.

T = 1 indicates a non-permanently-assigned ("transient") multicast address.

The SCOP field is a 4-bit multicast scope value used to limit the scope of the multicast group. The values are:

0	reserved
1	node-local scope
2	link-local scope
3	(unassigned)
4	(unassigned)
5	site-local scope
6	(unassigned)
7	(unassigned)
8	organization-local scope
9	(unassigned)
A	(unassigned)
B	(unassigned)
C	(unassigned)
D	(unassigned)
E	global scope
F	reserved

The GROUP ID field identifies the multicast group, either permanent or transient, within the given scope.

Routing. Routing in IPv6 is almost identical to IPv4 routing under CIDR except for the effect of 128-bit address size. With very straightforward extensions, all of IPv4's routing algorithms (OSPF, RIP, IDRP, ISIS, etc.) can be used to route IPv6.

IPv6 also includes simple routing extensions which support powerful new routing functionality. These capabilities include:

- Provider Selection (based on policy, performance, cost, etc.)
- Host Mobility (route to current location)
- Auto-Readdressing (route to new address)

The new routing functionality is obtained by creating sequences of IPv6 addresses using the IPv6 routing option. The routing option is used by an IPv6 source to list one or more intermediate nodes (or topological groups) to be "visited" on the way to a packet's destination. This function is very similar in function to IPv4's Loose Source and Record Route option.

In order to make address sequences a general function, an IPv6 host is required in most cases to reverse routes in a packet it receives containing address sequences (if the packet was successfully authenticated using the Auth Header information) in order to return the packet to its originator. This approach is taken to make IPv6 host implementations support the handling and reversal of source routes from the start. This process is essential for allowing them to work with hosts that implement such new features as provider selection or extended addresses.

The following three examples demonstrate how the address sequences can be used. In these examples, address sequences are shown by a list of individual addresses separated by commas. For example:

SRC, I1, I2, I3, DST

Where the first address is the source address, the last address is the destination address, and the middle addresses are intermediate addresses.

For these examples assume that two hosts, H1 and H2 wish to communicate. Assume that H1 and H2's sites are both connected to providers P1 and P2. A third wireless provider, PR, is connected to both providers P1 and P2. (See Figure 10.)

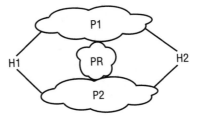

Figure 10. Sample Data Network

The simplest case (no use of address sequences) is when H1 wants to send a packet to H2 containing the addresses:

H1, H2

When H2 replies, it reverses the addresses and constructs a packet containing the addresses:

H2, H1

In this example either provider could be used, and H1 and H2 would not be able to select how the provider traffic would be routed.

If H1 decides that it wants to enforce a policy that all communication to and from H2 can only use provider P1, it would construct a packet containing the address sequence:

H1, P1, H2

This address sequence ensures that when H2 replies to H1, it will reverse the route, and the reply will also travel over P1. The addresses in H2's reply looks like:

H2, P1, H1

There could be a circumstance in which H2 must go to P1 in all cases via P2 and that H2 has a reason to specify this in its address sequence. In this case, H2 may choose to use its own address sequence-H2, P2, P1, H1-because of its local requirements, but this sequence would not occur by default.

If H1 becomes mobile and moves to provider PR, it can maintain communication with H2 (not breaking any transport connections) by sending packets that contain the address sequence:

H1, PR, P1, H2

This sequence ensures that when H2 replies, it enforces H1's policy of exclusive use of provider P1 and sends the packet to H1's new location on provider PR. The reversed address sequence would be:

H2, P1, PR, H1

As one can see from these examples, IPv6's address sequence facility can be used for provider selection, mobility, and re-addressing. It is a simple but powerful capability.

Quality-of-Service Capabilities. The Flow Label and Priority fields in the IPv6 header may be used to identify those packets for which a host specifies special handling by IPv6 routers, such as non-default quality of service, "real-time" service, or relative priority. This capability is particularly important in order for IPv6 to support multimedia, "real-time," and other applications that require some degree of consistent throughput, delay, and/or jitter.

Flow Labels. A flow is a sequence of packets sent from a particular source to a particular (unicast or multicast) destination for which a source desires special handling such as non-default quality of service or real-time service. The 24-bit Flow Label field in the IPv6 header may be used for this purpose.

A flow is uniquely identified by the combination of a source address and a non-zero flow label. Packets that do not belong to a flow carry a flow label of zero. The exact nature of the special handling is conveyed to the intervening routers by a control protocol, such as a resource reservation protocol, or by information within the flow's packets themselves, e.g., in a hop-by-hop option.

A flow label is assigned to a flow by the source node. New flow labels must be chosen (pseudo)-randomly and uniformly from the range 1 to FFFFFF hex. The purpose of the random allocation is to make any set of bits within the Flow Label field suitable for use as a hash key by routers, for looking up the state associated with the flow.

There may be multiple active flows from a source to a destination, as well as traffic that is not associated with any flow. All packets belonging to the same flow must be sent with the same source address, same destination address, and same non-zero flow label. If any of those packets include a Hop-by-Hop Options header, then they all must be originated with the same Hop-by-Hop Options header contents (excluding the Next Header field of the Hop-by-Hop Options header). If any of those packets include a Routing header, then they all must be originated with the same contents in all extension headers up to and including the Routing header (excluding the Next Header field in the Routing header). The routers or destinations are permitted, but not required, to verify that these conditions are satisfied. If a violation is detected, it is reported to the source by an ICMP Parameter Problem message, Code 0, pointing to the high-order octet of the Flow Label field (i.e., offset 1 within the IPv6 packet).

Routers are free to "opportunistically" set up a flow-handling state for any flow, even when no explicit flow establishment information has been provided to them via a control protocol, a hop-by-hop option, or other means. For example, upon receiving a packet from a particular source with an unknown, non-zero flow label, a router may process its IPv6 header and any necessary extension headers as if the flow label were zero. That processing would include determining the next-hop interface, and possibly other actions, such as updating a hop-by-hop option, advancing the pointer and addresses in a Routing header, or deciding on how to queue the packet based on its Priority field. The router may then choose to "remember" the results of those processing steps and cache that information, using the source address plus the flow label as the cache key. Subsequent packets with the same source address and flow label may then be handled by referring to the cached information rather than examining all those fields that, according to the requirements of the previous paragraph, can be assumed unchanged from the first packet seen in the flow.

The flow label function is, at the time of writing, still experimental and subject to change as the requirements for flow support in the Internet become clearer. Hosts or routers that do not support the functions of the Flow Label field are required to set the field to zero when originating a packet, pass the field on unchanged when forwarding a packet, and ignore the field when receiving a packet. Even though some routers may never support this capability, flow functions may still be effective, as long as the routers that implement the functions are key ones.

Priority. The 4-bit Priority field in the IPv6 header enables a source to identify the desired delivery priority of its packets, relative to other packets from the same source. The Priority values are divided into two ranges: Values 0 through 7 are used to specify the priority of traffic for which the source is providing congestion control, i.e., traffic that "backs off" in response to congestion, such as TCP traffic. Values 8 through 15 are used to specify the priority of traffic that does not back off in response to congestion, e.g., "real-time" packets being sent at a constant rate.

For congestion-controlled traffic, the following Priority values are recommended for particular application categories:

0 - uncharacterized traffic
1 - "filler" traffic (e.g., netnews)
2 - unattended data transfer (e.g., email)
3 - (reserved)
4 - attended bulk transfer (e.g., FTP, NFS, HTTP)
5 - (reserved)
6 - interactive traffic (e.g., Telnet, X)
7 - internet control traffic (e.g., routing protocols, SNMP)

Please note, however, that NFS and HTTP may not do congestion control-for separate reasons-NFS, because of lack of windows; and HTTP, because the connections are too short to get feedback.

For non-congestion-controlled traffic, the lowest Priority value (8) should be used for those packets that the sender is most willing to have discarded under conditions of congestion (e.g., high-fidelity video traffic), and the highest value (15) should be used for those packets that the sender is least willing to have discarded (e.g., low-fidelity audio traffic).

There is no relative ordering implied between the congestion-controlled priorities and the non-congestion-controlled priorities.

Security. The current Internet has a number of security problems and lacks effective privacy and authentication mechanisms below the application layer. IPv6 remedies these shortcomings by offering two integrated options that provide security services. These two options may be used singly or together to provide differing levels of security to different users. This capability is very important because different user communities have different security needs.

The first mechanism, called the "IPv6 Authentication Header," is an extension header that provides authentication and integrity (without confidentiality) to IPv6 datagrams. While the extension is algorithm-independent and supports many different authentication techniques, the use of keyed MD5 is proposed to help ensure interoperability within the worldwide Internet. The IPv6 Authentication Header can be used to eliminate a significant class of network attacks, including host masquerading attacks. Its use is particularly important with source-routing, a well-known security risk. Its placement at the internet layer can help provide host origin authentication to those upper layer protocols and services that currently lack meaningful protections. This mechanism should be exportable by vendors in the United States and other countries with similar export restrictions because it provides only authentication and integrity, and specifically does not provide confidentiality. The exportability of the IPv6 Authentication Header encourages its widespread deployment and use.

IPv6's second security extension, the "IPv6 Encapsulating Security Header," provides integrity and confidentiality to IPv6 datagrams. It is simpler than some similar security protocols (e.g., SP3D, ISO NLSP) but remains flexible and algorithm-independent. To achieve interoperability within the global Internet, the use of DES CBC is being used as the standard algorithm for use with the IPv6 Encapsulating Security Header.

Address Autoconfiguration

Susan Thomson
Bellcore

Address autoconfiguration is a feature that enables a host to configure one or more addresses per interface automatically. The aim of autoconfiguration is to enable a host to operate in "plug-and-play" mode, that is, to enable a machine to be connected to the network and immediately ready for use without any manual intervention. Autoconfiguration is an important element in the scalability of the Internet since it facilitates the process of bringing on new users. It is certainly impractical for each and every host to require system administration before it can be used. Furthermore, most Internet users do not have the knowledge or desire to perform system administration tasks every time they switch on their machine. In addition, manual configuration tends to be extremely error-prone.

Addresses need to be configured each time an interface is initialized, and may also need to be reconfigured at other times for a number of reasons. One reason is that a host may be moved to a different link (with a different corresponding subnet prefix), due, for example, to an office move. Indeed, with the advent of portable laptop computers, host relocation is becoming increasingly commonplace. Another reason for a host to change addresses has to do with provider-based address assignment. If addresses are assigned using a provider-based scheme, it is critical for route scaling that a host change addresses when its site switches to a new Internet service provider.

To be useful in a wide range of network environments, address autoconfiguration needs to meet the following requirements:

- It should support simple, routerless, serverless networks as well as more complex topologies.
- It should support varying levels of system administrative control. In particular, address autoconfiguration should not always rely on the presence of routers on a link.

Also, while supporting plug-and-play behavior, address autoconfiguration should not preclude administrative control over address assignment. In some environments, system administrators need to have control over which hosts can attach to a link at the site in addition to the precise addresses assigned. In such a case, system administrators may want to avoid the overhead of manually configuring each host, but do want control over a centralized database that hosts can query to configure themselves. In other environments, system administrative control is neither necessary nor feasible. For example, there is little reason for users at home to have to configure a database before switching on a personal computer. Also, controlling address configuration may not be feasible in public environments where there are many different users who log in for relatively short periods of time.

In IPv4, hosts have traditionally been manually configured. However, there are two mechanisms that have been specified in IPv4 to partially automate address configuration: the Bootstrap Protocol (BOOTP) and its successor, the Dynamic Host Configuration Protocol (DHCP). Both of these protocols provide access to a server that maintains a database of address bindings per host interface. In BOOTP, the database is statically and manually configured on a per host basis. Thus, BOOTP supports a minimal form of autoconfiguration that eliminates the need for individual host configuration, but requires preconfiguration of a database on a per host basis. Also, BOOTP does not support reconfiguration; once configured an address cannot be changed dynamically. DHCP can be operated in the same mode as BOOTP, but in addition provides support for dynamic reconfiguration. In DHCP, a specific lifetime is associated with an address, after which the address becomes invalid and can no longer be used. The protocol allows a host to renew an address, if the address is needed for longer than its originally specified lifetime. Also, DHCP reduces the amount of database preconfiguration required by means of a mechanism that, given the subnet prefix of the link, enables the server to generate an identifier for a host interface (interface ID) to form an address on demand.

The above IPv4 mechanisms provide support for environments in which system administrative control of a database is feasible, e.g., in large corporate networks, or desirable, e.g., for security reasons. However, these mechanisms do not support the needs of all environments since they do not supply a way to autoconfigure an address in the absence of a router or a BOOTP/DHCP server on a link, nor do they allow for a host to autoconfigure an address without preconfiguration of some database.

In IPv6, the address autoconfiguration requirements listed above are fully met by means of two separate configuration mechanisms, one that supports very simple networks and requires minimal special system administration, and the other that supports greater system administrative control in a manner similar to that of DHCP. The mechanism used to support the former set of requirements is referred to as the "stateless" mechanism, since it does not require a special-purpose database. In contrast, the DHCP-like mechanism is referred to as the "stateful" mechanism.

IPv6 stateless address autoconfiguration requires that a host be preconfigured with a token for every individual interface. A token must be suitable for use as the interface ID portion of an IPv6 address and also must be unique per link. The definition of a token is link-dependent and might typically be the link-layer address. For example, link-layers that use IEEE 802 addressing always use a 48-bit IEEE 802 address as a token.

In the routerless/serverless topology, it is sufficient for a node to form a link-local address autonomously, without any help from a router or server. A link-local address consists of a well-known prefix and an interface ID. On initialization of an interface, a node configures a link-local address by appending the interface token to the well-known prefix. Note that there is no need for a link-local address to change dynamically since the prefix is fixed, and the interface token is expected to remain constant (except possibly on interface reinitialization).

In networks that have routers, stateless address autoconfiguration works in a similar way to the formation of a link-local address, with two major exceptions:

- Hosts need a mechanism to determine current subnet prefixes associated with the link in order to form global or site-local addresses
- the addresses must be reconfigurable. The mechanism used to determine prefixes is through router advertisements. Routers are preconfigured with the prefixes of the link and advertise these prefixes periodically, or when solicited by a host.

A host maintains a list of addresses per interface. On hearing a prefix advertisement, the host checks to determine whether an address with that prefix is already present in the list. If not, the host creates an address by concatenating the network prefix with the interface token.

To enable the address list to change dynamically, routers advertise two lifetime values along with the prefix. One of these values indicates how long the address formed from that prefix is valid. Whenever the prefix is readvertised, the lifetime of the address is reset to the new value, allowing its lifetime to be renewed periodically or possibly cut short. When the prefix is no longer advertised, the address will expire after the last advertised lifetime runs out.

The second lifetime value indicates when the address formed from the prefix will be deprecated. Although still valid, a deprecated address is one that is about to become invalid. The purpose of this deprecation value is to indicate to software initiating new communications when to stop choosing that address as a source address for new sessions and choose another non-deprecated address of appropriate scope (if any) instead. Since there is no current support in upper networking layers such as TCP or UDP for address change during a communication session (e.g., a TCP connection or a UDP request-response where the address is expected to remain the same), the deprecation lifetime is an important new feature. (Strictly speaking, applications can change source address in UDP exchanges, but this practice is not recommended). It enables a host to choose an address that is likely to last for the duration of the communication, rather than one that is likely to become invalid, causing the communication to break.

Because there are two address autoconfiguration mechanisms available to IPv6 hosts-the stateless and the stateful-hosts need to be told which one to use (if not both). Routers advertise this information periodically along with the prefix information.

The stateless autoconfiguration features in AppleTalk and Novell Netware are a popular and worthwhile addition to their internetwork suites. The same features have long been needed in IP. IPv6 stateless autoconfiguration, along with DHCPng, will provide an even richer set of functions to help contain the level of complexity as the use of TCP/IP and of the Internet continues to expand rapidly.

IPv6 Transition Mechanisms Overview

Robert E. Gilligan
Sun Microsystems, Inc.
Ross Callon
Bay Networks, Inc.

Introduction to Transition. The IETF has invested considerable energy in the design of transition mechanisms that will ensure a straight-forward, graceful evolution from IPv4 to IPv6. If not managed carefully, the cost, complexity, and hassle of transitioning to IPv6 could easily deter users from upgrading to the new protocol. To avoid these pitfalls, the transition mechanisms are intended to make the adoption of IPv6 as unin-trusive as possible for both end users and administrators, allowing the benefits of the new IPv6 features to become a motivating factor in IPv6 adoption while alleviating potential downsides.

One of the transition mechanism designers' primary goals was to allow as much flexibility as reasonably possible. Because different user communities will have different transition requirements, a wide variety of transition scenarios are supported, as well as the capability for meas-ured, incremental deployment. If sites were required to upgrade a group of machines in concert (e.g., they must upgrade all machines on a subnet at the same time), the difficulty of coordinating the work might discourage them. Instead, users should be able to deploy IPv6 one host or router at a time.

As much as possible, the transition strategy avoids dependencies between the various elements of a network during the upgrade process. If a user must wait for some other machine to be upgraded to IPv6 before his or her own machine can be upgraded (e.g., if routers must be upgraded before hosts can be), the transition may be delayed. To combat this difficulty, IPv6 can be introduced in hosts first, in routers first, or in both, on an as-needed basis. Wherever possible, the transition model creates no prerequisites for upgrading any specific host or router to IPv6 before the upgrade process can proceed.

Existing IPv4 infrastructures have been built up over a long period of time and at great expense. Consequently, users will not recklessly discard these assets in order to deploy IPv6. (See *IPng and Corporate Resistance to*

Change.) To leverage the installed base and minimize start-up costs, the transition strategy lets IPv6 nodes exploit in-place IPv4 resources to whatever degree is appropriate for each site.

To accommodate the full range of potential IPv6 adopters, the IPv6 transition mechanisms include two major elements that work independently or in a synergistic fashion:

- Dual-IP layers in hosts and routers: Name servers and routers provide support for both IPv4 and IPv6 throughout the transition period. Hosts are gradually upgraded over a period of time. This allows upgraded nodes to interoperate with both IPv4 and IPv6 nodes using their native protocol.
- Tunneling IPv6 over IPv4: Hosts (and optionally routers) can tunnel IPv6 traffic through IPv4 routing topologies by encapsulation. This capability leverages the existing installed IPv4 routing system and allows IPv6 operation to get started early.

With these two mechanisms, network designers have the freedom to decide for themselves how transition is achieved. Some sites will upgrade a number of hosts first and take advantage of IPv6's ability to tunnel through an IPv4 routing fabric. Other sites will upgrade some or all routers first to dual-IP layers, laying a foundation for any IPv6 hosts that come on line as transition proceeds. Still other sites may use a combination of these approaches.

In most cases, pockets of an enterprise will convert to IPv6 first, while other areas will remain with IPv4 for an extended period of time. With the tunneling and dual-IP features, IPv6 does not require that all the nodes in an IP area or even a subnet be converted all at once, so some sub-areas may contain both protocols.

Beyond the basic mechanics of dual-IP nodes and IPv6 tunneling, the IETF transition work addresses the implications of routing in highly heterogeneous IPv4/IPv6 networks, encompassing the various ways that topology structures and routing protocols (e.g., OSPF, RIP) operate in mixed environments. This section contains basic overviews of dual-IP-layer nodes and tunneling, and concludes with a look at routing operation in the presence of tunnels.

Overview of Dual-IP Layer Networks. One of the important features of the IPng transition is that it allows IPv6 support to be added to the network over a period of time, without disrupting the existing IPv4 infrastructure. This is accomplished via a "dual-IP layer" transition scheme that allows IPv6 to be added to hosts, DNS servers, and routers, without any change or disruption in the existing IPv4 support.

The IPng transition therefore makes use of a simple long-term transition model that allows gradual update of Internet Hosts to run internet applications over IPv6, while, in parallel, name-to-address lookup resources (such as DNS) are updated so they are able to return IPv6 addresses. The basic model outlined in this section assumes that routers will be updated to support forwarding of IPv6 (in addition to IPv4) before IPv6 is introduced into hosts. However, the following section describes tunneling techniques which can be used to eliminate the dependency on early router updates.

The basic dual-IP layer transition method allows existing Internet transport and application protocols to continue to operate unchanged, except for the replacement of 32-bit IPv4 addresses with 128-bit IPv6 addresses. This will have some effect on applications and associated APIs.

In a dual-IP layer transition, hosts are updated to be able to use either IPv4 or IPv6 depending upon the capability of the corresponding host that they are contacting. Major servers and other hosts can run dual-IP layers indefinitely (until they are converted solely to IPv6, after completion of an extended transition period). Hosts with dual-IP layers can talk directly to IPv4 or IPv6 partners and they can use either IPv6 or IPv4 routes to communicate.

Figure 11 illustrates the basic operation of a dual-IP layer (IPv4 and IPv6) network. The figure shows a single Internet Routing Domain, which is also interconnected to Internet backbones and/or regionals. Nodes include two dual-IP layer hosts, N1 and N2, as well as two IPv4-only hosts H1 and H2, plus a Domain Name System (DNS) server and two border routers. It is assumed that the routers internal to the routing domain are capable of forwarding both IPv4 and IPv6 traffic. Typically this would be accomplished by using multi-protocol routers which can forward both protocol suites (although it would be possible to use a different set of routers for each suite).

Dual hosts talk to IPv4 hosts using IPv4 unchanged. Dual hosts talk to other dual hosts using IPv6. This implies that dual hosts are able to send and receive either traditional packets (using IPv4), or new style packets (using IPv6). Which type of packet to send is determined via the normal name-to-address lookup. In the IPv6 and dual-IP layer environments, DNS servers are upgraded to accommodate a new record type that handles the 128-bit addresses of IPv6. In some cases, this function will alternatively be provided by 128-bit local host tables.

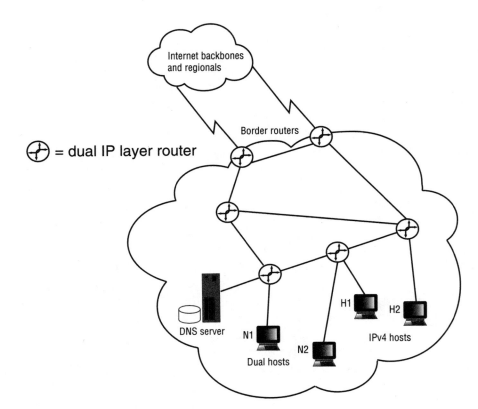

Figure 11. Overview of a Dual-IP network

Suppose that host N1 wants to communicate with host H1. N1 asks its local DNS server for the address associated with H1. In this case, since H1 is not updated, the address available for H1 is an IPv4 address, and thus the DNS response returned to N1 specifies a conventional 32-bit IP address, letting N1 know that it needs to send an IPv4 packet to H1.

Now suppose that host N1 wants to communicate with host N2. Again, N1 contacts the DNS server. If the DNS record type for N2 has not been updated, then the DNS server will respond with an IPv4 address, and the communication between N1 and N2 will use IPv4. In this case, however, assuming that the DNS server has been updated to be able to return 128-bit addresses (and that the appropriate resource records have been configured into the DNS server), the DNS server will respond to N1 with the IPv6 address for N2. This allows N1 to know to use IPv6 instead of IPv4 for communication with N2 (more on the DNS below).

Addressing in a Dual-IP Layer Network. A major aspect of the IPv6 transition plan is the assignment of IPv6 addresses to hosts and routers. As in traditional IPv4 environments, IPv6 routers will typically receive address assignment manually as part of the topology definition process. Address assignments for IPv6 hosts can be manual or can take advantage of the full range of automatic assignment mechanisms which are being defined for IPv6, including the new stateless autoconfiguration services.

Dual IPv6/IPv4 nodes need to be configured with both IPv4 and IPv6 addresses. Although the two addresses may be related to each other, this is not required. It is permissible for IPv4 and IPv6 address assignments to be completely independent. For example, there are some environments in which IPv4 hosts have been assigned local addresses (i.e., addresses which are not globally unique). This is typically done in situations where the IPv4 host does not require global Internet access, or where sufficient addresses were not available.

If it were later determined that a host with an IPv4 address required global Internet access using IPv6, then it would be perfectly reasonable to assign the host a global IPv6 address even though its IPv4 address is local. Note that the use of globally significant addresses may be desirable even for systems which do not require Internet access for two reasons: one, because it eliminates one possible source of confusion in network management; and two, because it allows consistent addressing based on a single prefix for all systems on a network, while simultaneously allowing for the possibility that some of these systems may require Internet access.

For sites that require global Internet access, it is desirable to assign IPv6 addresses in a manner that facilitates global Internet routing. The best way to do this is a topic of current research and debate. At the time of writing, the best-known method for address assignment that facilitates routing makes use of topologically significant addresses based on provider administration of the addresses. This has become known as "CIDR" (Classless Inter-Domain Routing). (See *Pv4 Address Lifetime Expectations.*)

Updating the Domain Name System. The Domain Name System (DNS) is used in both IPv4 and IPv6 to map host names into IP addresses. A new DNS resource record type named "AAAA" has been defined for IPv6 addresses. The IPv4 DNS records are referred to as type "A," (for address record). IPv6 records are AAAA or "quad A" because IPv6 addresses are four times larger than the 32-bit IPv4 addresses. Since dual-IP layer hosts need to be able to resolve host names (e.g.,

241

"ds.internic.net") into either IPv4 or IPv6 addresses, they must be capable of dealing with both record types.

Before a DNS server can service IPv6 and dual-IP layer clients, it must be upgraded to handle the new AAAA record type. DNS servers are typically hard-coded for certain record types, so AAAA support will be provided by system software vendors and other TCP/IP utility sources. Fortunately, DNS software may well be one of the first things that vendors will offer because IPv6 support is a relatively easy change.

Note that, since the queries for IPv6 addresses from dual-IP layer clients can utilize IPv4, the DNS servers that provide AAAA record support need not necessarily themselves be upgraded to make use of IPv6 for data transfer between DNS servers.

For sites that have not yet upgraded their DNS, IPv6 nodes may resolve network names to addresses by using manually defined local host tables. These are files that reside on hosts that map names to IP addresses. Use of host tables may be particularly useful in the very early stages of transition before the DNS infrastructure has been converted to support AAAA records. The local host table mechanism does not scale very well, however, so its use is not recommended for large sites. This is because local tables only work if the network administrator manually enters the names and addresses of all the hosts that the host needs to communicate with.

Application Issues. With the dual-IP layer approach to transition, traditional IPv4 applications can run indefinitely over the IPv4 routing infrastructure without any modifications whatsoever. New applications can be written to IPv6 exclusively, or to both protocols, with minimal overhead. Although IPv4-based applications can continue to operate for the foreseeable future, at some point, as IPv6 takes hold and IPv4 addresses run out, it is likely that IPv4 applications will be limited to a scope that is local within individual companies (that is, IPv4 may continue to be suitable for certain applications that typically do not require global connectivity, such as printing).

In the IPv6 transition process, no enhancements need be made to non-network applications or to applications that indirectly access the network via resident network services such as FTP, SMTP, Telnet, etc. Applications that directly access the IPv6 stack will of course have to be upgraded before they can use the network. This includes FTP, SMTP, Telnet, and rlogin utilities, as well as network-aware database and office automation applications.

At a minimum, network applications will have to be enhanced to request AAAA records from the DNS and to pass the 128-bit addresses to the local TCP/IP socket or similar interface. An upgrade to handle the new address space will require as little as a few lines of code change. Applications that take advantage of IPv6's advanced features (security, flow control, encryption, etc.) will require more extensive changes.

An extension to the standard TCP/IP sockets interface has been written and introduced into the public domain. This specification helps developers write applications that use TCP and UDP over IPv6. [6]

Routing and Dual-IP Layer Networks. The dual-IP layer transition allows IPv4 and IPv6 to be routed independently. Much of the flexibility of the IPv6 transition strategy stems from the fact that routers already deal with multiple protocols. It is common in today's networks to find routers that support IPv4, IPX, DECnet, SNA, AppleTalk, and other protocols simultaneously. Usually each protocol is supported by a separate routing protocol using independent addressing structures. Hence, an additional protocol (IPv6) is not a major change.

The addition of IPv6 for routers can be somewhat simplified (relative to the addition of other protocol suites) in that IPv6 can use the same routing protocol (RIP or OSPF) as IPv4. Similarly, IPv6 can be managed using the same management protocol (SNMP), as well as using the same name service (DNS). Thus, there is a considerable administrative overlap with the in-place IPv4 infrastructure, and the "learning curve" required to add IPv6 support is minimized.

One possible minor enhancement entails the use of a single instance of an integrated routing protocol to support routing for both IPv4 and IPv6. At the time of writing there is no protocol that has yet been enhanced to support this feature. But if such a protocol is developed, it would not change the basic dual-IP layer nature of the transition.

When completely independent routing functions are employed, forwarding of IPv4 packets is based on routes learned through running IPv4-specific routing protocols, while forwarding of IPv6 packets is based on routes learned through running IPv6-specific routing protocols. This structure implies that separate instances of routing protocols are used for IPv4 and for IPv6, although it could consist of two instances of OSPF and/or two instances of RIP (since both OSPF and RIP are capable of supporting both IPv4 and IPv6 routing).

Structuring Dual-IP Networks. With a pure dual-stack transition strategy, the architectures of the IPv6 and IPv4 networks can be logically decoupled, even though they are running on the same physical infrastructure. In this case, existing IPv4 functions remain independent and unaffected, including such aspects as the feeding of route information between routing domains and local address assignments. In effect, the IPv6 topology is built from scratch.

Although some network designers may want to think of the new IPv6 architecture as entirely independent, there are some advantages to aligning the structures of the two logical networks. In many cases the IPv4 and IPv6 domain boundaries may be the same, so the enterprise's backbone and organizational structure can be retained. This involves using the same domain boundaries and the same area boundaries for partitioning the topology.

There are many efficiencies to this approach, but as long as the new IPv6 network uses true dual-IP layer and true IPv6 addresses, it can be considered an independent architecture that can evolve in its own direction. If for instance, the current IPv4 addressing is not ideal (e.g., designers fail to use CIDR-based addressing) or if IPv4 has an awkward area structure, these problems could be fixed in an independent IPv6 network with minimal effort.

Overview of Tunneling. In most deployment scenarios, the IPv6 routing infrastructure will be built up over time. Tunneling provides a way to use an existing IPv4 routing infrastructure to carry IPv6 traffic for as long as there are no native IPv6 resources to exploit. While IPv6 is being deployed, the existing IPv4 routing infrastructure can remain functional and can be used to carry IPv6 traffic. IPv6/IPv4 hosts and routers tunnel IPv6 datagrams over regions of IPv4 routing topology by encapsulating them within IPv4 packets. Tunneling can simplify the transition process for users as well as providing a number of other advantages:

Tunneling leverages the existing IPv4 routing system to build the IPv6 routing system. In cases where the initial IPv6 topology represents a small portion of the total network, it may be significantly more efficient to tunnel IPv6, rather than build a completely new IPv6 topology.

Tunneling helps activate a global IPv6 service early on in the transition. Early adopters of IPv6, who may be geographically dispersed, can use tunneling to provide global IPv6 connectivity without waiting for the entire Internet to be converted to IPv6.

Tunneling supports a transition strategy in which the IPv6 routing infrastructure can be built incrementally over time. It allows the IPv6 infrastructure to be brought to the sites where it is needed when it is needed.

Although there are a variety of tunneling methods, most of the underlying mechanisms are the same. To send a packet into a tunnel, a node first creates and prepends an encapsulating IPv4 header, and then transmits the encapsulated packet, as shown in Figure 12.

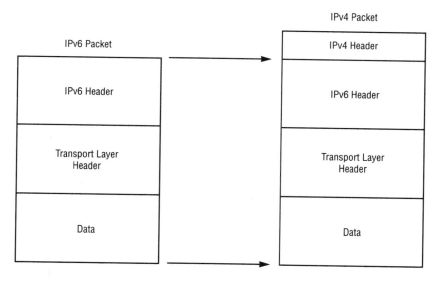

Figure 12. Encapsulating IPv6 in IPv4

The destination address of the encapsulating IPv4 packet specifies the tunnel endpoint-the node that receives the encapsulated packet strips off the encapsulating IPv4 header, updates the IPv6 header, and then processes the enclosed IPv6 packet as it would any other received packet.

Automatic versus Configured Tunneling. Two major tunneling methods are available: configured tunneling and automatic tunneling. Configured tunneling employs traditional tunneling methods in which individual logical "tunnel links" are configured between two nodes, typically routers, that are separated by an arbitrary IPv4 topology. These logical, layer-3 links are treated by tunneling nodes as virtual point-to-point connections. Each tunnel link is configured manually by assigning IP addresses to one or both tunnel endpoints (see Figure 13).

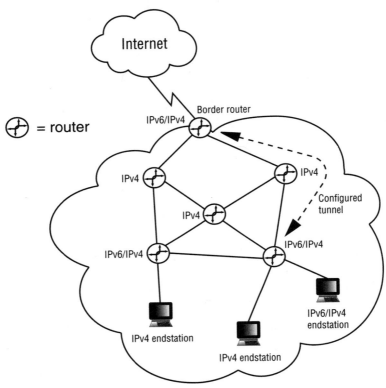

Figure 13. Configured Tunneling

Automatic tunneling uses the same underlying mechanisms as configured tunneling, but eliminates the need to configure each tunnel individually. A special IPv6 address format is defined—the IPv4-compatible address—which holds an IPv4 address in the low-order 32-bits. An IPv4-compatible address is identified by an all-zeros 96-bit prefix, and holds an IPv4 address in the low-order 32 bits. IPv4-compatible addresses are structured as shown in Figure 14.

80 bits	16	32 bits
0000. 0000	0000	IPv4 Address

Figure 14. IPv4-Compatible IPv6 Address Format

An IPv4-compatible address can be viewed as a single address that serves both as IPv6 and IPv4 addresses. The entire 128-bit IPv4-compatible IPv6 address is used as the node's IPv6 address, while the IPv4 address embedded in low-order 32 bits serves as the node's IPv4 address. The embedded IPv4 address is assigned according to the IPv4 addressing plan. Nodes that already have an IPv4 address assignment can use that address in an IPv4-compatible address.

Hosts that engage in automatic tunneling are assigned IPv6 addresses of this form. When an IPv6 node wishes to deliver an IPv6 packet that is addressed to an IPv4-compatible IPv6 address, it can tunnel that packet through the IPv4 routing fabric to the end destination by using the IPv4 address embedded in the IPv6 destination address. Since the tunnel end-point address is implicit in the compatible destination address of the packet, this form of tunneling is only used when sending packets to their final end destination. So automatic tunneling is typically used to send packets to hosts, not for links between routers (see Figure 15).

IPv6/IPv4 nodes that perform automatic tunneling may use IPv4 address configuration protocols such as DHCP, BOOTP or RARP to learn their IPv4-compatible IPv6 addresses. They do this by simply pre-pending the 96-bit all-zeros prefix 0:0:0:0:0:0: to the IPv4 address that they acquire via the IPv4 configuration protocol. This mode of configuration allows IPv6/IPv4 nodes to "leverage" the installed base of IPv4 address configuration servers. It can be particularly useful in environments where IPv6 routers and address configuration servers have not yet been deployed.

Applied Tunneling. Because both hosts and routers can play the tunnel endpoint role, there are a number of feasible configurations for tunneling. Some of these configurations lend themselves to automatic tunneling while others require the configured tunneling method.

- Router-to-Router. IPv6/IPv4 routers interconnected by an IPv4 infrastructure can tunnel IPv6 packets between themselves. In this case, the tunnel spans one segment of the end-to-end path that the IPv6 packet takes.
- Host-to-Router. IPv6/IPv4 hosts can tunnel IPv6 packets to an intermediary IPv6/IPv4 router that is reachable via an IPv4 infrastructure. This type of tunnel spans the first segment of the packet's end-to-end path.

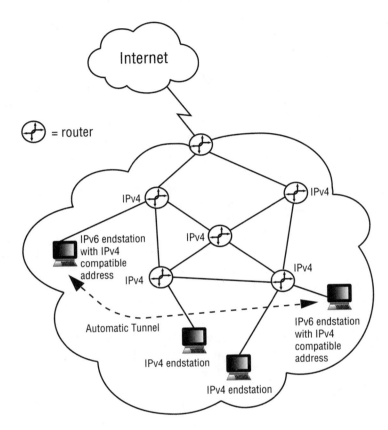

Figure 15. Automatic Tunneling

- Host-to-Host. IPv6/IPv4 hosts that are interconnected by an IPv4 infrastructure can tunnel IPv6 packets between themselves. In this case, the tunnel spans the entire end-to-end path that the packet takes.
- Router-to-Host. IPv6/IPv4 routers can tunnel IPv6 packets to their final destination IPv6/IPv4 host. This tunnel spans only the last segment of the end-to-end path.

In the first two tunneling methods listed above—router-to-router and host-to-router—the IPv6 packet is being tunneled to a router. These configurations typically use configured tunneling. The tunnel endpoint is most likely an intermediary router which must decapsulate the IPv6 packet and forward it on to its final destination. When tunneling to a router, the endpoint of the tunnel is different from the ultimate destination so the addresses in the IPv6 packets being tunneled do not provide the IPv4 address of the tunnel endpoint. Instead, the tunnel endpoint address must be determined from configuration information on the node performing the tunneling.

For each configured tunnel, the encapsulating node must store the tunnel endpoint address. When an IPv6 packet is transmitted over a tunnel, the tunnel endpoint address is used as the destination address for the encapsulating IPv4 header. The determination of which packets to tunnel is usually made by routing information on the encapsulating node. This is usually done via a routing table, which directs packets based on their destination address using the prefix mask and match technique.

Default Configured Tunnel. IPv6 or dual nodes that are connected to IPv4 routing infrastructures may use a configured tunnel to reach an IPv6 "backbone." If the IPv4 address of an IPv6/IPv4 router bordering the backbone is known, a tunnel can be configured to that router. This tunnel can be configured into the routing table as a "default route." That is, all IPv6 destination addresses will match the route and could potentially traverse the tunnel. Since the "mask length" of such default route is zero, it will be used only if there are no other routes with a longer mask that match the destination.

The tunnel endpoint address of such a default tunnel could be the IPv4 address of one IPv6/IPv4 router at the border of the IPv6 backbone. Alternatively, the tunnel endpoint could be an IPv4 "anycast address." With this approach, multiple IPv6/IPv4 routers at the border advertise IPv4 reachability to the same IPv4 address. All of these routers accept packets to this address as their own, and will decapsulate IPv6 packets tunneled to this address. When an IPv6/IPv4 node sends an encapsulated packet to this address, it will be delivered to only one of the border routers, but the sending node will not know which one. The IPv4 routing system will generally carry the traffic to the closest router.

Using a default tunnel to an IPv4 "anycast address" provides a high degree of robustness since multiple border routers can be provided, and, using the normal fallback mechanisms of IPv4 routing, traffic will automatically switch to another router when one goes down.

Automatic Tunneling. When a host is the target endpoint (in host-to-host and router-to-host tunneling), IPv6 packets are tunneled all the way to the final destination. These configurations typically use automatic tunneling. In this case, the tunnel endpoint is the node to which the IPv6 packet is addressed. Since the endpoint of the tunnel is the ultimate destination of the IPv6 packet, the tunnel endpoint can be determined from the destination IPv6 address of that packet: If that address is IPv4-compatible, then the low-order 32 bits hold the IPv4 address of the destination node, and that can be used as the tunnel endpoint address. Hence automatic tunneling avoids the need to explicitly configure the tunnel endpoint address. IPv6 packets that are not addressed to an IPv4-compatible address cannot use automatic tunneling.

IPv6/IPv4 nodes need to determine which IPv6 packets can be sent via automatic tunneling. One technique is to use the IPv6 routing table to direct automatic tunneling. An implementation can have a special static routing table entry for the prefix 0:0:0:0:0:0/96 (that is, a route to the all-zeros prefix with a 96-bit mask). Packets that match this prefix are sent to a pseudo-interface driver which performs automatic tunneling. Since all IPv4-compatible IPv6 addresses will match this prefix, all packets to those destinations will be auto-tunneled (unless a better match route is available).

Tunneling and DNS. When an IPv4-compatible IPv6 address is assigned to an IPv6/IPv4 host that supports automatic tunneling, the corresponding A and AAAA records can be listed in the DNS. The AAAA record holds the full IPv4-compatible IPv6 address, while the A record holds the low-order 32 bits of that address. The AAAA record will be located by queries from IPv6 hosts, while the A record will be found by queries from IPv4-only hosts.

The decision to store an AAAA record holding an IPv4-compatible address in the DNS for an IPv6 host can be used as a policy control for traffic to that host. If an IPv4-compatible address is listed, then other hosts will originate tunneled traffic to that host. If only an A record is listed, then the host will "appear" to others to be an IPv4-only host, and only IPv4 traffic will be sent.

When a query from an IPv6/IPv4 host locates an AAAA record holding an IPv4-compatible IPv6 address, as well as an A record holding the corresponding IPv4 address, the resolver library need not necessarily return both addresses to the application. It has three options:

- Return only the IPv6 address to the application.
- Return only the IPv4 address to the application.
- Return both addresses to the application.

The determination of which address to return can be used as a policy switch on the host to control the type of traffic originated from that host. If the system administrator wishes to prevent that host from originating tunneled traffic, he or she can configure the resolver library to return only IPv4 addresses to the application. If tunneled traffic is permissible, then the administrator can allow IPv6 addresses (and hence IPv4-compatible addresses) to be returned to applications.

Tunneling Implementation Issues. Nodes that perform tunneling need to deal with a few implementation issues, which are common to both automatic and configured tunneling. Many of these issues relate to the fact that the topology and routing operations of an IPv4 tunnel is largely transparent to the IPv6 nodes using it.

- Tunnel MTU and fragmentation. It is technically feasible for an encapsulating node to treat a tunnel as a virtual IPv6 link with a large MTU, relying on IPv4 layer fragmentation and re-assembly to deliver IPv6 packets that are larger than the MTU of the underlying links of the path between the encapsulating and decapsulating node. But this would result in fragmentation inside the tunnel, which is inefficient. A better approach is for the encapsulating node to perform IPv4 path MTU discovery of the tunnel path, and then use the IPv6 path MTU discovery to report the MTU of the tunnel back to the originating host.
- Maintaining tunnel state information. If the encapsulating node performs IPv4 path MTU discovery on its tunnels, it will need to maintain state information for each tunnel. Since the number of tunnels that a node may be using may grow to be quite large, this node should employ a scheme to cache the state information it needs, and periodically discard state information that is not being used.
- IPv6 hop limit and IPv4 TTL. IPv6 tunnels over IPv4 are treated as "single hop" links from the IPv6 perspective. That is, the IPv6 hop limit is decremented by one when an IPv6 packet traverses a tunnel. But the encapsulating node must use a TTL value in the encapsulating IPv4 header that is large enough to guarantee that the encapsulated packet will not expire in the tunnel, enroute to the decapsulating node.
- IPv4 ICMP error messages and tunneling. Tunneled packets may fail to be delivered to the tunnel endpoint because the tunnel endpoint is unreachable, the IPv4 TTL is not large enough, or the packet is too

big. These failures will elicit IPv4 ICMP error messages, directed back to the tunnel entry point, from IPv4 routers along the tunnel path. Some of these ICMP error messages may not contain enough of the original IPv6 packet to identify its source, since many IPv4 routers return only 8 bytes of data beyond the IPv4 header of the packet in error. Other IPv4 routers return much more data. If possible, the encapsulating node should attempt to recover the original IPv6 packet, and generate the appropriate IPv6 ICMP error message back to the originating node.

Tunneling and Routing in Depth. During an extended IPv4-to-IPv6 transition period, both IPv4 and IPv6 routing infrastructure will be present. Earlier we discussed how in the basic pure dual-IP layer operation, routing within the IPv4 infrastructure may be essentially independent of routing within the IPv6 infrastructure. However, at least initially, IPv6-capable domains might not be globally interconnected via IPv6-capable Internet infrastructure and therefore may need to communicate by using tunneling across IPv4-only backbone networks.

In order to achieve dynamic routing in such a mixed environment, there need to be mechanisms to globally distribute IPv6 network-layer reachability information to routing nodes in dispersed IPv6 domains. (Alternatively, some of the same techniques might be used in later stages of the transition to route IPv4 packets between isolated IPv4-only networks over IPv6 backbones.)

Use of tunneling requires consistency of routes between IPv4 and IPv6. For example, consider a packet which starts off as an IPv6 packet, but then passes through an IPv4 tunnel (i.e., is encapsulated in an IPv4 packet) in the middle of its path from source to destination. This packet must be routed (using IPv6 routing) to the correct initial tunnel endpoint, traverse the tunnel as an IPv4 packet, and then traverse the remainder of the path again as an IPv6 packet. Clearly this packet has to follow a consistent route for the entire path from source to destination. The implications of this process on routing are discussed separately for router-to-router tunnels, host-to-host tunnels, host-to-router tunnels, and router-to-host tunnels.

Router-to-Router Tunnels. Router-to-router tunnels are based on manual configuration of both ends of the tunnel. Specifically, the router at each end of the tunnel must be manually configured to know the addresses associated with the other end of the link. Such tunnels are also referred to as "fully manually configured" tunnels, since both ends of the link must be configured.

In router-to-router tunnels handling IPv6 over IPv4, routers treat the link as they would any other normal point-to-point link. For example, dynamic routing protocols such as OSPF or BGP/IDRP may send reachability information over this link as they would over any other type of link. The decision to forward a packet over a manually-configured router-to-router tunnel is therefore made in the same manner as the decision to forward a packet over any other type of link. Specifically, packets are forwarded based on the routes computed by standard routing protocols. These routes may use normal links and tunneled links in any combination.

Use of router-to-router manually configured tunnels has the advantage that the underlying infrastructure is transparent to the protocols that are forwarded over the tunnel. For example, if IPv6 is tunneled over IPv4, then the IPv4 infrastructure is used for forwarding IPv6, but the internal details of the IPv4 infrastructure is of no concern to IPv6 routers and IPv6 routing protocols. Also, all types of IPv6 addresses without exception can be advertised in IPv6 routing and tunneled over IPv4 networks. Since IPv6 packets are encapsulated only when they travel over network segments that do not support IPv6, and are forwarded according to their native headers elsewhere, this method does not constrain the types of policy routing which may be employed over the IPv6 portion of the data path.

However, a router-to-router manually configured tunnel differs from a normal link in one important aspect: in many cases it is likely to have lower performance, such as lower throughput or greater delay. The use of a routing protocol such as RIP, which treats each link as being equal, could lead to sub-optimal routes. However, this is not a problem with more flexible routing protocols such as OSPF, which allows a wide dynamic range in the metrics assigned to each link. Specifically with OSPF, the tunneled link could be given a higher cost when compared to other links.

Beyond router-to-router configured tunnels, tunnels in which both ends of the link are manually configured can, in principle, also be used from host to router or from host to host. However, when a number of hosts are involved as endpoints, the requirement that each end of the tunnel be configured makes "fully manual" tunnels less useful than it is for routers.

Host-to-Host Automatic Tunneling. If both source and destination hosts make use of IPv4-compatible IPv6 addresses, then it is possible for automatic tunneling to be used for the entire path from the source host to the destination host. In this case, the IPv6 packet is encapsulated in an IPv4 packet by the source host, and is forwarded by routers as an IPv4 packet all the way to the destination host. As discussed earlier, this feature allows initial deployment of IPv6-capable hosts before any routers are updated.

A source host may make use of host-to-host automatic tunneling provided that ALL of the following are true:

- The source address is an IPv4-compatible IPv6 address.
- The destination address is an IPv4-compatible IPv6 address.
- The source host doesn't know of any neighboring IPv6-capable router.
- The source host does know of one or more neighboring IPv4-capable routers.

If all of these requirements are true, then the source host may encapsulate the IPv6 packet in an IPv4 packet, using a source IPv4 address extracted from the associated source IPv6 address, and a destination IPv4 address extracted from the associated destination IPv6 address. Where host-to-host automatic tunneling is used, the packet is forwarded as a normal IPv4 packet for its entire path, and is decapsulated (i.e., the IPv4 header is removed) only by the destination host. Host-to-host automatic tunneling requires that normal IPv4 routing be operational, but makes no requirements whatsoever on IPv6 routing.

Host-to-Router Tunnels. In some cases a dual-IP layer host may need to transmit an IPv6 packet, but may have no local IPv6-capable router that it can use for this purpose. Instead, the host may use tunneling to an IPv6-capable router. This capability allows the host to transmit packets through an arbitrary number of IPv4 nodes to an IPv6-capable backbone, which will then in turn transmit the packets using normal IPv6 forwarding. Host-to-router tunnels may be accomplished by manually configuring the dual-IP layer host with an IPv4 address that it can use to reach the IPv6 backbone.

For the conversation to work in both directions it is necessary for a router-to-host tunnel to have a return path. This requires either that both ends of the tunnel be manually configured, or that automatic tunneling be used in the backward (router-to-host) direction. This latter type of tunnel may be referred to as a "half manually configured" tunnel (see Figure 16), since manual configuration is used in one direction, but automatic tunneling is used in the other.

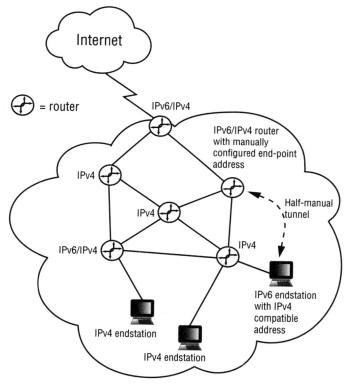

Figure 16. Half-manual Tunnel

A half-manually configured tunnel occurs when the host is configured to know how to find the router, but the router is not configured with any specific knowledge of the host and will use automatic tunneling to find it. This, of course, requires that the host have an IPv4-compatible IPv6 address and that the host be configured with an IPv4 address to use for tunneling to the IPv6-capable router.

A source host may make use of host-to-router half-manually configured tunneling provided that ALL of the following are true:

- The source address is an IPv4-compatible IPv6 address.
- The source host does not know of any neighboring IPv6-capable router.

- The source host does know of one or more neighboring IPv4-capable routers.
- The source host is configured with an IPv4 address of a router which can serve as the tunnel endpoint.
- The destination address is NOT IPv4-compatible (if the destination address is IPv4-compatible, then host-to-host automatic tunneling may be used instead).

If all of these requirements are true, then the source host may encapsulate the IPv6 packet in an IPv4 packet, using a source IPv4 address that is extracted from the associated source IPv6 address, and a destination IP address that corresponds to the configured address of the dual router which is serving as the tunnel endpoint.

Reachability for Host-to-Router Tunnels. The dual router which is serving as the end point of the half-manual tunnel must advertise reachability into IPv4 routing sufficient to cause the encapsulated packet to be forwarded to it. The simplest approach is for a single IPv4 address to be assigned to the router for use as a tunnel endpoint. A tunneling dual router with connectivity to the IPv6 backbone can advertise a host route to this address (into the IPv4-only network). Each dual host in the associated IPv4-only network is configured with the address of this tunnel endpoint.

In some cases there may be multiple dual routers which can serve as endpoints for automatic tunneling to hosts from any one IPv4-only network. In this case, again, each host may be configured with a single address representing the tunnel endpoint. However, all dual routers with connectivity to the IPv6 backbone that are capable of serving as endpoints for the automatic tunnels from this region may advertise a host route to the associated IPv4 address. This allows encapsulating packets using host-to-router tunneling to be forwarded to the tunnel endpoint that is selected by the local routing policy (in general this will be the nearest dual router). In this case the one IPv4 address is operating as an "anycast" address, since it allows the tunneled packets to be delivered to any one of the multiple dual routers.

Finally, in some cases there may be some reason for specific hosts to prefer one of several tunnel endpoints, while allowing all potential tunnel endpoints to serve as backups in case the preferred endpoint is not reachable. In this case, each dual router with IPv6 backbone connectivity that is serving as a potential tunnel endpoint is given a unique IPv4 address taken from a single IPv4 address block. (For example, if there are less than 255 such dual routers, a single class C IPv4 network number may be used). Each dual router then advertises two routes into the IPv4 network: a host route corresponding to the tunnel endpoint address specifically assigned to it, and also a network route to the associated IPv4 address block (e.g., to the class C network in the normal case).

Each dual host in the IPv4-only region is configured with an IPv4 address corresponding to the preferred tunnel endpoint. If the associated dual router is operating, then the packet will be delivered to it based upon the associated host route. However, if the associated dual router is down, but some other dual router serving as potential tunnel endpoint is operating, then the packet will be delivered to the nearest operating tunnel endpoint.

Router-to-Host Automatic Tunneling. Clearly if tunneling is used from a host to a backbone IPv6 router, it is also necessary to be able to use tunneling from the router to the host. In this case (provided that the destination host has an IPv4-compatible IPv6 address) normal IPv6 forwarding may be used for part of the packet's path, and router-to-host automatic tunneling may be used to get the packet from an encapsulating dual router to the destination host.

Normal packet forwarding is straightforward in this case: the encapsulating router creates the encapsulating IPv4 header using an IPv4 address assigned to itself as the source IPv4 address, and using a destination IPv4 address extracted from the destination IPv4-compatible IPv6 address. The encapsulated packet is forwarded from the encapsulating router to the destination host using normal IPv4 routing.

In this case, the challenging part is the IPv6 routing required to deliver the IPv6 packet from the source host to the encapsulating router. For this to happen, the encapsulating router has to advertise reachability for the appropriate IPv4-compatible IPv6 addresses into the IPv6 network.

Router-to-host tunneling typically occurs when one or more dual-IP layer routers are sitting on the boundary between an IPv4-only network and a dual-IP layer network. In this case, these "border routers" need to advertise into IPv6 routing (in the dual network) that they can reach certain IPv4-compatible IPv6 addresses corresponding to the addresses that exist in the IPv4 network. In general this requires manual configuration of the border routers. However, in most cases it may require only one or a small number of address prefixes be advertised for the entire local IPv4 network. This is, therefore, likely to represent much less configuration than individually configuring router-to-host links.

Security Considerations

Part IX

Network Security and IPv6

Security on the Internet. The security of the Internet has long been questioned. It has been the topic of much press coverage, many conferences, and numerous workshops. Almost all of this attention has been negative, pointing out the many places where the level of available security is far less than that deemed necessary for the current and future uses of the Internet.

Many of the papers in Parts 4 and 5 strongly emphasize the need to improve the level of available security as does *Realizing the Information Future.* [1]

An improvement in the basic level of security in the Internet is vital to its continued success. Users must be able to assume that their exchanges are safe from tampering, diversion, and exposure. Organizations that wish to use the Internet to conduct business must be able to have a high level of confidence in the identity of their correspondents and in the security of their communications. The goal must be to provide strong protection as a matter of course throughout the Internet.

IAB Security Workshop. In February of 1994, the IAB convened a workshop on security in the Internet architecture. The report of this workshop [2] included an exploration of many of the security problem areas and made a number of recommendations to improve the level of security that the Internet offers its users. The retreat focused on four major areas:

- end-to-end security
- end-system security
- secure QoS
- secure network infrastructure

End-to-end Security. The most obvious area where security is required in the network is in the exchange of end-to-end information. A customer, using a web browser to order a T-shirt over the net and providing a credit card number, should be able to assume that the card number is safe from exposure. A warehouse, receiving an email message containing an electronic order for more T-shirts, wants to be able to rely on the identity of the sender of the order. A manufacturer getting an electronic bill for the

261

cloth to make additional T-shirts wants to be able to know that the bill has not been altered since it was sent.

There are many reasons in addition to the commerce-related ones, that the Internet requires good end-to-end security. As the Internet becomes a more integral part of societal interaction it is starting to be used in place of venues of exchange. Electronic support groups for people with emotional problems or specific diseases are becoming quite common. There are now calls by some to be able to interact with medical or clinical personnel over the net. Clearly, all such exchanges must be able to be kept confidential and, in some cases, anonymous.

End-system Security. At this time, the majority of security problems observed within the Internet are traceable to poor security on an end system. In addition to the many security exposures that come from bugs in system software, poor system administration can provide a easy target for would-be intruders. The acceptance of shared or poor passwords, the use of access methods which transmit passwords in clear text across the Internet, and the assumption that the installation of external firewalls ensures that the access of all potential intruders is blocked (forgetting the many network users within the firewall), are examples of the type of problems that can lead to compromised end systems.

Secure QoS. The pending addition of Quality-of-Service features to the Internet will bring a new set of security issues. The controls of the devices which will provision the services must be protected to ensure that users cannot utilize more resources than they are authorized to or deny services to users who have legitimate uses. The users of the services must be authenticated to ensure that the services are being consumed by the users for which they are intended.

Secure Network Infrastructure. The network itself must be protected. The validity of the routing and control messages must be assured in order for the net to function reliably. The exchange of routing information between logically adjacent routers must be authenticated in order to prevent false information from being inserted into the routing tables and disrupting traffic. The source of routing information itself must also be authenticated for the same reason. In addition, the protocols which are used to monitor and control the routers, servers, and other network devices must be secured for authentication, integrity, and confidentiality.

The actual network structure or the location of one end of an electronic conversation may need to be kept confidential. A person traveling with a laptop computer may not want anyone to know where she is, or even that she is not at her normal place of work. This might be because she is acting as a liaison to an unannounced business partner or because she fears being tracked and stalked. A service provider may not want their competitors to know that they are restructuring their network until it is too late for the competitor to counter the move.

Authentication and Encryption. Support for authentication—in which a host is able to confirm the identity of another host—and support for encryption—in which the actual communication is secure—are two separate security functions that Internet users should be able to use independently. There are some applications in which authentication of a correspondent is sufficient and others where the data exchanged must be kept private.

Security in the Internetworking Layer. The IAB report also pointed out that many of the tools necessary to support the types of security needed, although not a function of the internetworking layer of the protocol, could make use of strong security features in the internetworking layer if such functions were present. While there will most likely be a number of special high-level security packages available for specific Internet constituencies, support for basic packet-level authentication and encryption would make possible the adoption of a much needed, widespread, security infrastructure throughout the Internet.

Security in IPv6. In light of the recommendations from the IAB workshop and with the support of the IPng Directorate we recommended that the basic building blocks of network security be part of the set of IPv6 functions for which a vendor must include support in order to be able to state that the implementation is compliant with the IPv6 standards. This does not mean that the use of authentication or encryption is required. Only support for authentication and encryption is required. If an application wants to request the use of encryption to a remote site, and if the remote site supports encryption, the local IPv6 implementation must be able to support the encrypted communication. The IESG approved our recommendation.

Thus IPv6 will support packet authentication and confidentiality as basic and required functions. Applications must be able to rely on support for this feature in every IPv6 implementation. Support for the authentication header, the MD5 authentication algorithm, the Privacy Header, and the DES-CBC privacy authentication algorithm are required in IPv6 implementations if they wish to claim compliance with the standards. [3,4,5,6,7]

The work on defining the security features for IPv6 started in the IPng Working Group with a parallel activity in the IPSEC working group within the IETF Security Area, which was charged with developing standards for security in the existing IPv4 world. Many of the same people were active in both groups and it became clear, after a while, that a common solution might be found for both IPv4 and IPv6. We transferred the IPv6 security development work to the IPSEC working group in order to facilitate a common solution. The result of the combined effort is a set of documents which may be used with IPv4 or IPv6. Implementation of the security additions is optional for IPv4 and mandatory for IPv6.

The architecture of both the authentication and encryption functions supports the specification of algorithms in addition to the required ones. Support for additional authentication or encryption algorithms is optional.

Problems Resulting from Supporting Security. Although the use of authentication and encryption may add to the cost and impact the performance of internet systems, the assured availability of security functions for end-use and infrastructure protection is worth the penalty. Moreover, whatever negative repercussions result should decrease in time with improved software and hardware assistance.

Key Management. Clearly, a key management infrastructure is required in order to facilitate the use of the authentication and encryption headers. Although defining such an infrastructure is outside the scope of the IPv6 effort, there are on-going IETF activities in this area with which the IPv6 transition working groups are coordinated.

Controls on Encryption Technology. The adoption of any form of secure encryption technology as a part of the mandatory set of functions in an Internet standard has export control and usage implications. The export of most good encryption technology is restricted by a number of governments, including the U.S. government. The use of encryption technology by people not in the military or banking industry is restricted in other countries. These facts led to a long and spirited discussion within the

IETF when we proposed to recommend mandatory encryption support as part of the IPv6 recommendation. [8] A number of normally non-IETF organizations and people joined in the discussion.

The basic argument was that, since a vendor could not export the type of encryption technology we were requiring they would have to produce products which they could not claim were IPv6 standards compliant for export. Many companies refuse, as a business practice, to produce separate versions of software for domestic and export use. Together, this might mean that IPv6 security—and even IPv6 itself—would be held back by making the support for confidentiality mandatory.

The basic counter argument was that, unless the support was mandatory, vendors could ship products that the users thought supported the security features of IPv6, since the products claimed compliance to the standards, only to find out that the support for confidentiality was missing. Thus, the only way to meet the goal stated above of ensuring that the Internet be able to provide strong protection as a matter of course was to make the support mandatory.

The issue was discussed in the IPng Area Directorate meetings, on the IETF mailing list, and during IETF working group and plenary meetings. After considerable discussion it was clear that there was a strong consensus within the IETF that the support be made part of the basic, required functionality of IPv6.

Firewalls. The IAB workshop spent quite a bit of time discussing firewalls. The use of firewalls is increasing on the Internet. The presence of the authentication and privacy features in IPv6 may reduce the need for firewalls, but they will continue to be used for the foreseeable future. In this light, clear guidance should be given to firewall developers on the best ways to design and configure them for the IPv6 environment.

A guideline for IPv6 firewall design and configuration needs to be developed, including an examination of the ways in which the Authentication Header can be used to strengthen firewall technology. The details of how the IPv6 packet should be analyzed by a firewall must be specified as part of the guidelines.

Other Security Issues. Some aspects of security require additional study. For example, it has been pointed out (See *A Cable TV Industry View of IPng*) that, even in non-military situations, there are instances in which procedures to thwart traffic analysis are required. These security measures could be accomplished by the use of encrypted encapsulation.

However, this and other similar requirements must be addressed on an on-going basis by the Security Area of the IETF. The design of IPv6 must be flexible enough to support the later addition of such security features.

Summary. We believe that IPv6, with its inherent security features, will provide the foundation upon which the Internet can continue to expand its functionality and user base.

The Ongoing Process

Part X

The Ongoing IETF Process

With a working proposal in hand, the IETF's focus has shifted to the process of working out the details and procedures to complete the definition of IPv6. A number of working groups have been established for the purpose of completing IPv6 specifications for autoconfiguration, transition, address structure, and the impact of IPv6 on the IETF and other standards.

Address Autoconfiguration. As data networks become more complex, the need to be able to bypass at least some of the complexity and move toward "plug-and-play" becomes ever more acute. The user cannot be expected to understand the details of the network architecture or know how to configure the network software in their host. In the ideal case, a user should be able to unpack a new computer, plug it into the local network, and "just have it work" without needing to enter any special information.

The basic requirement of plug-and-play operation is autoconfiguration—the feature that enables a host to acquire an address dynamically, either when attaching to a network for the first time or when re-addressing is required because the host moved or because the identity of the network changed. Although security concerns may restrict the ability to offer a high level of transparent address autoconfiguration in some environments, the mechanisms must be in place to support whatever level of automation the local environment feels comfortable with.

The address configuration protocol must be suitable for a wide range of network topologies, from a simple isolated network to a sophisticated globally connected network. It should also allow for varying levels of administrative control, from completely automated operation to very tight oversight. In addition, the address autoconfiguration protocol—together with IPv6 system discovery—will provide the minimal bootstrapping information necessary to enable hosts to acquire further configuration information (such as that provided by DHCP in IPv4). The scope does not include router configuration or any other host configuration functions.

There are many other functions required to support a full "plug-and-play" environment. [1] Most of these must be addressed outside of the

IPv6 Area, but a focused effort to define a host address autoconfiguration protocol is, and should be, part of the IPv6 process.

Transition. The transition of the Internet from IPv4 to IPv6 must meet two separate needs: a short-term need to define the specific technologies and methods to transition IPv4 networks-including the Internet-into IPv6 networks and an IPv6 Internet; and a long-term need to do broad-based operational planning for transition-developing strategies and methods for decentralized migration, understanding the ramifications of a long period of coexistence, and developing an understanding of the architectural and interoperability testing that will be required to ensure a reliable and manageable Internet in the future.

Transition—Short-Term Concerns. Any IPng transition plan must take into account the realities of the types of devices vendors will build and network managers will deploy. The IPng transition plan must define the procedures required to successfully implement those functions which vendors will be likely to include in their devices. This is the case even if there are good arguments to recommend against a particular function, for example, header translation. If the products exist, it is better to have them interoperate than not.

The IPng Transition Working Group (ngtrans) has been formed to design the mechanisms and procedures to support the transition of the Internet from IPv4 to IPv6 and recommend the most effective procedures and techniques. Using the *Simple SIPP Transition (SST)* [2] overview document as a starting point, the group explained the mechanisms to be employed in the transition; exactly how the transition will work; the assumptions about infrastructure deployment inherent in the operation of these mechanisms; and the functionality that applications developers will be able to assume as the protocol mix changes over time. (See *IPv6 Transition Mechanisms Overview.*)

In addition, the Working Group has specified the mandatory and optional mechanisms that vendors should implement in hosts, routers, and other components of the Internet in order for the transition to be carried out. Dual-stack, encapsulation, and header translation mechanisms must all be defined, as well as the interaction between hosts using different combinations of these mechanisms. The Working Group will also articulate a concrete operational plan for the transition from IPv4 to IPv6 that network operators and Internet subscribers can execute.

Transition—Long-Term Concerns. Beyond defining the specific IPv4 to IPv6 mechanisms and their deployment, operation, and interaction, a number of more general transition-related topics need to be addressed. The ramifications and procedures of migrating to a new technology or to a new version of an existing technology must be fully understood.

The Transition and Coexistence Including Testing (TACIT) Working Group will explore some of the basic issues associated with deploying new technologies into an established Internet. Because enhancements to IPv6 will eventually be developed and need to be incorporated, the group will not limit itself to the upcoming IPv4 to IPv6 transition, but will focus on the more generic issues of transition, continuing its work well beyond the actual IPv6 transition. The TACIT Working Group will explore such issues as:

- Making the transition from a currently-deployed protocol to a new protocol while accommodating heterogeneity and decentralized management
- The characteristics and operation of a long period of coexistence between a new protocol and the existing protocol
- Testing IPv6 and future upgrades.

The process of testing is particularly important for IPv6 and future upgrades. The Internet must now be considered a utility and is far removed from the days when a new technology would actually be deployed to see if it would work in large-scale situations. Rigorous architectural and interoperability testing must be part of the predeployment phase of any proposed software for the Internet. Testing the scaling-up behaviors and robustness of a new protocol will offer particular challenges. The Working Group will look at the deployment of OSPF, BGP4, and CIDR, the AppleTalk 1 to 2 transition, DECnet Phase 4 to Phase 5 planning and transition, among others, to see if there are important lessons to be learned.

Based on the results of their investigation, the TACIT Working Group will provide detailed descriptions of problem areas in transition and coexistence, both predicted and observed, as the IPv6 transition progresses. In addition, the group will recommend specific procedures for testing, handling coexistence operations, and smoothing a decentralized transition process. [3]

Other Address Families. There are many environments in which one or more network protocols have already been established, or where a significant and comprehensive network addressing plan already exists. In such cases there may be a desire to integrate IPv6 into the environment by using the existing addressing plan to define all or part of the IPv6 addresses. This strategy has two major advantages. It permits unified management of address space among multiple protocol families, and the use of common addresses can facilitate the transition from other protocols to IPv6.

If the existing addresses are globally unique and assigned with regard to network topology, this may be a reasonable idea. The IETF should work with other organizations to develop algorithms for mapping addresses between IPv6 and other environments, possibly including Novell IPX, some types of ISO NSAPs, E164 addresses, and SNA addresses. Each of these possibilities must be carefully examined to ensure that any mapping algorithm provides an unambiguous one-to-one map between individual addresses, and that it solves more problems than it creates. In some cases it may be better to recommend either that a native IPng addressing plan be developed instead, or that an IPv6 address be used within the non-IP environment. [4]

Impact on Other IETF Standards. Many current IETF standards are affected by IPv6. At least 27 of the current 51 full Internet Standards must be revised for IPv6, along with at least 6 of the 20 Draft Standards and at least 25 of the 130 Proposed Standards. [5]

In some cases, the revisions consist of simple changes to the text. For example, in a number of RFCs an IP address is referred to in passing as a "32-bit IP address." Obviously these references must be updated to reflect IPv6's 128-bit address size, even though the IP address format is not an essential element in the protocol being defined. All of the standards track documents will have to be checked so that all such references can be updated.

In other cases, revisions to the actual protocols, including packet formats, will be required. In many of these cases, the address is simply being carried as a data element, so that the revised format with a larger address field will have no effect on the functional paradigm. However, in a few remaining cases-for example, the security and source route mechanisms-some facet of the protocol's operation is fundamentally changed as a result of IPv6. Those protocols and applications that rely on IPv4 functionality will have to be redesigned or rethought so that an equivalent function can be used in IPv6.

Lastly, in a few cases, the IETF should take the opportunity to determine if some of the RFCs should be moved to Historic, for example, EGP [6] and IP over ARCNET. [7]

In addition to the standards track RFCs, there are many Informational and Experimental RFCs that will be affected, as well as numerous Internet Drafts.

A number of working groups will be needed to make these changes. The base IPng Working Group will be responsible for defining new versions of ICMP, ARP/RARP, and UDP. It will also review RFC-1639, *FTP Operation Over Big Address Records (FOOBAR)* [8] and RFC-1191 *Path MTU Discovery.* [9]

Existing working groups will examine revisions for some of the routing protocols: RIPv2, IS-IS, IDRP, and SDRP. A new working group may be required for OSPF. The existing DHCP Working Group will revise DHCP and examine BOOTP.

A number of new working groups will be formed to deal with standards such as SNMP, DNS, NTP, NETbios, OSI over TCP, Host Requirements, and Kerberos as well as reviewing most of the RFCs that define IP usage over various media.

Impact on Non-IETF Standards and on Products. Many products and user applications that rely on the size or structure of IPv4 addresses will need to be modified to work with IPv6. While the IETF can facilitate an investigation of the impact of IPv6 on non-IETF standards and products, the primary responsibility for doing so resides with the other standards bodies and the vendors.

Examples of non-IETF standards that are affected by IPv6 include the POSIX standards, Open Software Foundation's DCE and DME, X-Open, Sun ONC, the Andrew File System and MIT's Kerberos. Most products that provide specialized network security, including firewall-type devices, are among those that must be extended to support IPv6.

Application Program Interfaces (APIs). It is traditional to state that the IETF does not *do* APIs. While there are many reasons for this, the one most commonly referred to is the fact that there are too many different environments, operating systems, programming languages, and platforms in which TCP/IP is used. The feeling is that the IETF should not get involved in attempting to define a language and operating system-independent interface in the face of such complexity.

However, in the case of IPv6, it may be time for the IETF to reexamine its historical tendency to avoid dealing with APIs. In a few specific cases, the prevalence of a particular type of API is such that a single common solution for the modifications made necessary by IPv6 should be documented.

Afterword

It is now just about two years since Phill Gross tapped us for this task. It has been quite an experience, both harder and easier than we thought when we agreed.

During these two years the Internet has quintupled in size, and is projected to continue its rate of growth, or even to accelerate it, as companies such as Microsoft start providing Internet connectivity as part of the default applications package that comes with just about every PC. The routing and addressing for the Internet remain manageable now, but we feel there is a strong impetus to begin initial assignments of IPv6 addresses and to begin the work on transition and coexistences as early as possible.

In 1993, the U.S. government was still mandating the use of GOSIP, and many observers felt it was only a matter of time until the full suite of OSI protocols would sweep the marketplace. In the intervening years, the Federal Internetworking Requirements Panel (FIRP) reexamined the GOSIP requirement and concluded that the TCP/IP protocol suite should be accepted on a part with the OSI suite, as a result of which many of the same observers now predict that TCP/IP will retain its hold on the marketplace.

TCP/IP has moved from being just one of many protocols in use in the local and wide area networks, with a penetration of about 25%, to being in use in about a third of all data networks and being part of almost all data network manager's future plans. Current projections estimate that over half of all data traffic will be TCP/IP by 1998.

The biggest change has been in the money involved. It was only a few years ago that the work of the IETF, while important to a few router vendors, was uninteresting to many of the big technology companies, since they felt their futures lay elsewhere. This is no longer the case. Very large investments now ride on the deliberations of all too many working groups. Unfortunately, this complication of our working groups will only get worse.

Thus, the effort we were engaged in has turned out to be potentially more important at the end of the process than we could have imagined when we started.

The process has been very exciting. Many of the most innovative and visionary of today's technologists have been involved in discussions which have brought us to this point. The discussions were occasionally more exciting than we might have hoped for, but the people involved have always had as their main goal to produce the best networking technology possible.

It is now up to the implementers, a number of whom have recently demonstrated interoperable early versions of their software.

The IPng Area will pass into history in the next month or two, and we will be able to go back to our normal lives and our duties as area directors in other IETF areas. We will continue to be involved in the development and deployment of IPv6; as we both have more than a bit of pride of parenthood. The IETF process will return to its original organization, with the continuing development of IPv6 (and the work on all of the IETF protocols affected by IPv6) being done in their normal areas.

While not all of our community feels that the result of the IPng process met all of their goals, we strongly believe that the technology described in this book will take the Internet far into the future, and will help create the global information infrastructure that will help enlighten us while, at the same time, helping to redefine how society can interact.

Appendices

IPng Proposal Overviews

Ford, P., and M. Knopper, *TUBA as IPng: A White Paper*, Work in Progress, LANL, AADS, August 1994.

Hinden, R., *Simple Internet Protocol Plus White Paper*, RFC-1710, Sun Microsystems, October 1994.

McGovern, M., and R. Ullmann, *CATNIP: Common Architecture for the Internet*, RFC-1707, Sunspot Graphics, Lotus Development Corp., October 1994.

RFC-1550 White Papers

Adamson, B., *Tactical Radio Frequency Communication Requirements for IPng*, RFC-1677, NRL, August 1994.

Bellovin, S., *On Many Addresses per Host*, RFC-1681, AT&T Bell Laboratories, August 1994.

Bellovin, S., *Security Concerns for IPng*, RFC-1675, AT&T Bell Laboratories, August 1994.

Bound, J., *IPng BSD Host Implementation Analysis*, RFC-1682, Digital Equipment Corporation, August 1994.

Brazdziunas, C., *IPng Support for ATM Services*, RFC-1680, Bellcore, August 1994.

Britton, E., and J. Tavs, *IPng Requirements of Large Corporate Networks*, RFC-1678, IBM, August 1994.

Brownlee, J., *Accounting Requirements for IPng*, RFC-1672, University of Auckland, August 1994.

Carpenter, B., *IPng White Paper on Transition and Other Considerations*, RFC-1671, CERN, August 1994.

Chiappa, N., *IPng Technical Requirements of the Nimrod Routing and Addressing Architecture*, RFC-1753, December 1994.

Clark, R., M. Ammar, and K. Calvert, *Multiprotocol Interoperability in IPng*, RFC-1683, Georgia Institute of Technology, August 1994.

Curran, J., *Market Viability as an IPng Criteria*, RFC-1669, BBN, August 1994.

Estrin, D., T. Li, and Y. Rekhter, *Unified Routing Requirements for IPng*, RFC-1668, USC, Cisco Systems, IBM, August 1994.

Fleischman, E., *A Large Corporate User's View of IPng*, RFC-1687, Boeing Computer Services, August 1994.

Green, D., P. Irey, D. Marlow, and K. O'Donoghue, *HPN Working Group Input to the IPng Requirements Solicitation*, RFC-1679, Naval Surface Warfare Center-Dahlgren Division, August 1994.

Ghiselli, A., D. Salomoni, and C. Vistoli, *INFN Requirements for an IPng*, RFC-1676, INFN/CNAF, August 1994.

Heagerty, D., *Input to IPng Engineering Considerations*, RFC-1670, CERN, August 1994.

Simpson, W. *IPng Mobility Considerations*, RFC-1688, Daydreamer, August 1994.

Skelton, R., *Electric Power Research Institute Comments on IPng*, RFC-1673, EPRI, August 1994.

Symington, S., D. Wood, and J. Pullen, *Modeling and Simulation Requirements for IPng*, RFC-1667, MITRE, George Mason University, August 1994.

Taylor, M., *A Cellular Industry View of IPng*, RFC-1674, CDPD Consortium, August 1994.

Vecchi, M., *IPng Requirements: A Cable Television Industry Viewpoint*, RFC-1686, Time Warner Cable, August 1994.

References

Part I: The Need for IPng

1. Callon, R., *A Proposal for a Next Generation Internet Protocol*, Proposal to X3S3, December 1987.

2. Vecchi, M., *IPng Requirements: A Cable Television Industry Viewpoint*, RFC-1686, Time Warner Cable, August 1994.

3. Taylor, M., *A Cellular Industry View of IPng*, RFC-1674, CDPD Consortium, August 1994.

4. Huitema, C., *The H Ratio for Address Assignment Efficiency*, RFC-1715, INRIA, October 1994.

Part II: Defining the IPng Process

1. Gross, P., and P. Almquist, *IESG Deliberations on Routing and Addressing*, RFC-1380, ANS, Stanford University, November 1992.

2. Fuller, V., T. Li, J. Yu, and K. Varadhan, *Classless Inter-Domain Routing (CIDR): An Address Assignment and Aggregation Strategy*, RFC-1519, BARRNet, Cisco Systems, MERIT, OARnet, September 1993.

3. Carpenter, B., and T. Dixon, *Minutes of the IPng Decision Process BOF (IPDECIDE)*, /ietf/93jul/ipdecide-minutes-93jul.txt, August 1993.

4. Bradner, S., and A. Mankin, *IP: Next Generation (IPng) White Paper Solicitation*, RFC-1550, Harvard University, NRL, December 1993.

Part III: How Long Do We Have?

1. Chaddham, R.L., and S.S. Chitgopekar, *A "Generalization" of the Logistic Curves and Long-range Forecasts (1966-1991) of Residence Telephones*, Bell J. Eco. Manage. Sci., 2 (Autumn 1971).

2. Gurbaxani, V., *Diffusion in Computing Networks: The Case of BITNET*, Communications of the ACM, December 1990.

3. Fuller, V., T. Li, J. Yu, and K. Varadhan, *Classless Inter-Domain Routing (CIDR): An Address Assignment and Aggregation Strategy*, RFC-1519, BARRNet, Cisco Systems, MERIT, OARnet, September 1993.

4. Rekhter, Y., R. Moskowitz, D. Karrenberg, and G. de Groot, *Address Allocation for Private Internets*, RFC-1597, IBM, Chrysler Corp., RIPE NCC, RIPE NCC, March 1994.

5. Lear, E., E. Fair, D. Crocker, and T. Kessler, *Network 10 Considered Harmful (Some Practices Shouldn't be Codified)*, RFC-1627, Silicon Graphics, Inc., Apple Computer, Inc., Silicon Graphics, Inc., Sun Microsystems, Inc., July 1994.

6. I. Assigned Numbers Authority, (IANA), *Class A Subnet Experiment*, RFC-1797, April 1995.

Part IV: The Role of IPng in Communications Technology

1. Bradner, S., and A. Mankin, *IP: Next Generation (IPng) White Paper Solicitation*, RFC-1550, Harvard University, NRL, December 1993.

2. *Ibid.*

3. Braden, R., D. Clark, and S. Shenker, *Integrated Services in the Internet Architecture: An Overview*, RFC-1633, June 1994.

4. Clark, D., *The Design Philosophy of the DARPA Internet Protocols*, Proceedings of the SIGCOMM '88 Symposium, Computer Communications Review, Vol. 18, No. 4, pp. 106-114, August 1988.

5. *ATM User-Network Interface Specification, Version 3.0*, ATM Forum, 10 September 1993.

6. *Ibid.*

7. *Ibid.*

8. Braden, R., D. Clark, and S. Shenker, *Integrated Services in the Internet Architecture: An Overview*, RFC-1633, June 1994.

9. Clark, D., *The Design Philosophy of the DARPA Internet Protocols*, Proceedings of the SIGCOMM '88 Symposium, Computer Communications Review, Vol. 18, No. 4, pp. 106-114, August 1988.

10. *Asynchronous Transfer Mode (ATM) and ATM Adaptation Layer (AAL) Protocols Generic Requirements*, Bellcore Technical Advisory TA-NWT-001113, Issue 1, June 1993.

11. Droms, R., *Dynamic Host Configuration Protocol*, RFC-1541, 27 October 1993.

12. Rekhter, Y., and T. Li, *An Architecture for IP Address Allocation with CIDR*, RFC-1518, 24 September 1993.

13. Clark, D., *The Design Philosophy of the DARPA Internet Protocols*, Proceedings of the SIGCOMM '88 Symposium, Computer Communications Review, Vol. 18, No. 4, pp. 106-114, August 1988.

14. HPN Planning Group, *Concepts and Guidance for High Performance Network (HPN)*, Work in Progress, 17 May 1993.

15. Rivkin, S., *Positioning the Electric Utility to Build Information Infrastructure*, U.S. Department of Energy.

16. Cass, D., and M. Rose, *ISO Transport Services on Top of the TCP: Version: 3*, RFC-1006, May 1987.

17. *Communication Architecture for Distributed Interactive Simulation (CADIS)*, Institute for Simulation and Training, Orlando, Florida, 28 June 1993.

18. Miller, D., *Distributed Interactive Simulation Networking Issues*, Briefing presented to the ST/IP Peer Review Panel, Massachusetts Institute for Technology, Lincoln Laboratory, 15 December 1993.

19. Braden, B., L. Zhang, D. Estrin, S. Herzog, and S. Jamin, *Resource ReSerVation Protocol (RSVP)—Version 1 Functional Specification*, Work in Progress, January 1996.

20. United States Television Census, 30 September 1993.

Part V: Features, Technologies, and Issues for IPng

1. Laubach, M., *Classical IP and ARP over ATM*, RFC-1577, January 1994.

2. Tsuchiya, P., *The "P" Internet Protocol*, Work in Progress, November 1992.

3. Estrin, D., Y. Rekhter, and S. Hotz, *A Unified Approach to Inter-Domain Routing*, RFC-1322, USC/Information Sciences Institute, May 1992.

4. Estrin, D., Y. Rekhter, and S. Hotz, *Scalable Inter-Domain Routing Architecture*, ACM SigComm '92, Baltimore, MD, August 1992.

5. Breslau, L., and D. Estrin, *Design and Evaluation of Inter-Domain Policy Routing Protocols*, Journal of Internetworking Research and Experience, 1991.

6. Rekhter, Y., *Inter-Domain Routing Protocol*, Internetworking: Research and Experience, Vol. 4, pp. 61-80, 1993.

7. Rekhter, Y., and T. Li, *A Border Gateway Protocol 4 (BGP-4)*, RFC-1771, SRI Network Information Center, March 1995.

8. Estrin, D., T. Li, Y. Rekhter, K. Varadhan, and D. Zappala, *Source Demand Routing: Packet Format and Forwarding Specification*, Internet-Draft, September 1993.

9. Kleinrock, L., and F. K. Kamoun, *Hierarchical Routing for Large Networks*, Computer Networks 1, North-Holland Publishing Company, 1977.

10. Jacobson, V., *Compressing TCP/IP headers for low-speed serial links*, RFC-1144, February 1990.

Part VI: Technical Criteria for IPng

1. Bradner, S., and A. Mankin, *IP: Next Generation (IPng) White Paper Solicitation*, RFC-1550, Harvard University, NRL, December 1993.

2. Internet Architecture Board, *IP Version 7*, Work in Progress, July 1992.

3. Gross, P., and P. Almquist, *IESG Deliberations on Routing and Addressing*, RFC-1380, ANS, Stanford University, November 1992.

4. Clark, D., Chapin, L., Cerf, V., Braden, R., and R. Hobby, *Towards the Future Internet Architecture*, RFC-1287, MIT, BBN, CNRI, USC/Information Sciences Institute, UC Davis, December 1991.

5. Clark, D., *The Design Philosophy of the DARPA Internet Protocols*, Proceedings of the SIGCOMM '88 Symposium, Computer Communications Review, Vol. 18, No. 4, pp. 106-114, August 1988.

6. Clark, D. D., et al., *Realizing the Information Future*, National Academy of Sciences, August 1994.

7. Private electronic mail from Tony Li to IPng Directorate Mailing List, 18 April 1994.

8. Mockapetris, P., *Domain Names—Implementation and Specification*, RFC-1035, November 1987.

9. Internet Architecture Board, *Report of the IAB Workshop on Security in the Internet Architecture*, RFC-1636, June 1994.

10. *Ibid.*

11. Saltzer, J., *On the Naming and Binding of Network Destinations*, RFC-1498, August 1993.

12. I. Architecture Board, I. Engineering Steering Group, C. Huitema, and P. Gross, *The Internet Standards Process—Revision 2*, RFC-1602, March 1994.

Part VII: IETF IPng Proposals

1. Gross, P., and P. Almquist, *IESG Deliberations on Routing and Addressing*, RFC-1380, ANS, Stanford University, November 1992.

2. Bradner, S., and A. Mankin, *IP: Next Generation (IPng) White Paper Solicitation*, RFC-1550, Harvard University, NRL, December 1993.

3. McGovern, M., R. Ullmann, *CATNIP: Common Architecture for the Internet*, RFC-1707, November 1994.

4. Hinden, R., *Simple Internet Protocol Plus White Paper*, RFC-1710, Sun Microsystems, October 1994.

5. Ford, P., and M. Knopper, *TUBA as IPng: A White Paper*, Work in Progress, October 1994.

6. Deering, S., and P. Francis, Message to sipp mailing list, 31 May 1994.

7. Deering, S., *Simple Internet Protocol Plus (SIPP) Spec. (128-bit ver.)*, Work in Progress, July 1994.

8. Mankin, A., and S. Bradner, Message to Big-Internet, tuba, sipp, catnip and ietf mailing lists, 7 July 1994.

9. Fuller, V., T. Li, J. Yu, and K. Varadhan, *Classless Inter-Domain Routing (CIDR): An Address Assignment and Aggregation Strategy*, RFC-1519, BARRNet, Cisco Systems, MERIT, OARnet, September 1993.

10. Deering, S., *Simple Internet Protocol Plus (SIPP) Spec. (128-bit ver.)*, Work in Progress, July 1994.

Part VIII: IPv6

1. Bradner, S., and A. Mankin, *The Recommendation for the IP Next Generation Protocol*, RFC-1752, January 1995.

2. J. Postel, *Assigned Numbers*, RFC-1700, October 1994.

3. R. Hinden, Editor, *IP Version 6 Addressing Architecture*, Work in Progress, April 1995.

4. Y. Rekhter, and T. Li, *An Architecture for IPv6 Unicast Address Allocation*, Work in Progress, March 1995.

5. Y. Rekhter, and P. Lothberg, *An IPv6 Global Unicast Address Format*, Work in Progress, March 1995.

6. Gilligan, R. E., S. Thomson, and J. Bound, *IPv6 Program Interfaces for BSD Systems*, Work in Progress, July 1995.

Part IX: Security Considerations

1. National Research Council, *Realizing the Information Future: The Internet and Beyond*, National Academy Press, 1994.

2. Internet Architecture Board, *Report of the IAB Workshop on Security in the Internet Architecture*, RFC-1636, June 1994.

3. Atkinson, R., *Security Architecture for the Internet Protocol*, RFC-1825, August 1995.

4. Atkinson, R., *IP Authentication Header*, RFC-1826, August 1995.

5. Metzger, P., and W. A. Simpson, *IP Authentication Using Keyed MD5*, RFC-1827, August 1995.

6. Atkinson, R., *IP Encapsulating Security Payload (ESP)*, RFC-1828, August 1995.

7. Metzger, P., P. Karn, and W. A. Simpson, *The ESP DES-CBC Transform*, RFC-1829, August 1995.

8. Bradner, S., and A. Mankin, *The Recommendation for the IP Next Generation Protocol*, RFC-1752, January 1995.

Part X: The Ongoing Process

1. Berkowitz, H., *IPng and Related Plug-and-Play Issues and Requirements*, Work in Progress, September 1994.

2. Gilligan, B., *IPng Transition (ngtrans)*, Work in Progress.

3. Huston, G., and A. Bansal, draft charter for the Transition and Coexistence Including Testing (TACIT) Working Group, June 1994.

4. Carpenter, B, and J. Bound, *Recommendations for OSI NSAP Usage in IPv6*, Work in Progress.

5. Postel, J., Editor, *Internet Official Protocol Standards*, RFC-1720, USC/Information Sciences Institute, November 1994.

6. Mills, D. *Exterior Gateway Protocol Formal Specification*, RFC-904, UDEL, April 1984.

7. Provan, D., *Transmitting IP Traffic over ARCNET Networks*, RFC-1051, Novell, February 1991.

8. Piscitello, D., *FTP Operation Over Big Address Records (FOOBAR)*, RFC-1639, Core Competence, June 1994.

9. Mogul, J., and S. Deering, *Path MTU Discovery*, RFC-1191, DECWRL, Stanford University, November 1990.

Glossary

AAAA term used to refer to IPv6 addresses in DNS databases.

AAL ATM Adaptation Layer, ATM protocol for repackaging data into cells.

ACK abbreviation for acknowledgment.

ACM Association of Computing Machinery.

address autoconfiguration A process of assigning protocol addresses to a device on a network without pre-configuration or human intervention.

ALE IETF Address Lifetime Expectation working group, chartered to track the assignment of addresses in the Internet and make projections of the remaining useful lifetime for these addresses.

ANSI American National Standards Institute.

anycast address A host transmits a datagram to an anycast address and the internetwork is responsible for providing best effort delivery of the datagram to at least one, and preferably only one, of the servers or routers that accept datagrams for the anycast address. (See *RFC-1546.*)

API Application Program Interface, a defined set of subroutine calls to access a specific function.

AppleTalk an internetworking protocol defined by Apple Computer, Inc.

ARCNET Attached Resources Computing Network, a 2 Mbps LAN technology.

ARP Address Resolution Protocol, used to obtain link-layer addresses for a node given that node's IP address. (See *RFC-826.*)

ARPA Advanced Research Projects Agency, a U.S. DOD agency which provides funds for basic research.

ARPANET an early international packet-switching data network, sponsored by ARPA.

ATM Asynchronous Transfer Mode, a network technology which transports data in small, fixed-length packets called cells.

ATM Forum a group which develops specifications related to the use of ATM, generally accepted as the definitive ATM standards organization.

BOF Birds of a Feather, a session at an IETF meeting used to explore a specific topic or guage the interest in forming a working group on some topic.

BGP Border Gateway Protocol, an IP inter-organizational routing protocol; the current version is BGP-4.

Big-Internet mailing list an Internet mailing list which was set up to facilitate discussion of the issues surrounding the growth of the Internet. (Send email to Big-Internet-request@munnari.OZ.AU to join.)

BOOTP bootstrap protocol, used to autoconfigure nodes with IP addresses.

cache handle the field in the item to be cached which is used to find the item in the cache, if it is present.

CCITT Comite Consultatif Internationale de Telegraphique et Telephonique, now ITU-T.

CDPD Cellular Digital Packet Data.

CIDR Classless Interdomain Routing, an address assignment and routing information aggregation strategy. (See *RFC-1519.*)

circuit-switched a network in which a connection is established for the duration of a session.

CLNP Connectionless Network Protocol. (See *RFC-1162.*)

CLNS Connectionless Network Service.

CLTP Connectionless Transport Protocol.

CMIP Common Management Information Protocol.

congestion a situation in which there is too much traffic for the available network resources.

COTS commercial off-the-shelf.

CSNI NATO Communication System Network Interoperability project.

CSS Navy Communication Support System.

DARPA alternate name for ARPA.

datagram a block of user data along with a header. A datagram is the basic unit of data transfer in an internetwork.

DCE OSF1 Distributed Computing Environment.

DECnet An internetworking protocol developed by Digital Equipment Corporation.

DECnet/OSI A successor to Digital Equipment Corporation's DECnet, based on the OSI protocol suite.

DES Data Encryption Standard, the U.S. government's currently recommended encryption protocol.

DES-CBC Data Encryption Standard (DES)—Cipher Block Chaining (CBC) mode.

DHCP Dynamic Host Configuration Protocol, used to autoconfigure nodes with IP addresses and other information.

DHCPng A revision of DHCP to work with IPv6.

DME OFS's Distributed Management Environment.

DNS Domain Name System, a distributed database used to convert human-readable names for computers into IP addresses. (See *RFC-882*.)

DOD U.S. Department of Defense.

DS3 Digital Service - Level 3, a digital transmission service run at 44.736 Mbps.

ECM electronic counter measures.

EPRI Electric Power Research Institute.

ESP Encapsulating Security Payload, the protocol used to exchange encrypted data over an IPv4 or IPv6 network.

Ethernet a 10 Mbps LAN technology.

E.164 a CCITT-administered address used on ISDN networks, comprised of up to 15 decimal digits.

FDDI Fiber Distributed Data Interface, a 100 Mbps LAN technology.

firewall a gateway computer positioned between a vulnerable part of a network and the rest of the network, from which, it is assumed, attacks could originate. The computer is programmed to control who can transit the firewall and with what applications.

FIRP the Federal Internetworking Requirements Panel was established by the National Institute of Standards and Technology (NIST) to reassess federal requirements for open systems networks and to recommend policy on the U.S. government's use of networking standards.

flow a sequence of packets that shares all the attributes that the internetworking layer cares about, which includes but is not limited to: source/destination, path, resource allocation, etc.

FNC Federal Networking Council, a U.S. government panel charged with coordinating the federal use of data networks.

fragmentation the process by which an IP datagram is divided into a series of smaller datagrams so it can be transmitted along a path with an MTU smaller than the original datagram.

FTP File Transfer Protocol, an Internet application protocol that is used to transfer files from one computer to another over a TCP/IP network. (See *RFC-172*.)

gigabit a billion (thousand million) bits per second.

header the first part of a packet containing information needed to get the entire datagram through the network; this may include the entire destination address, or just a circuit identifier, depending on the kind of network in use.

HiPPI High Performance Parallel Interface

hybrid fiber/coax a cable TV design which would expand the capacity of local cable distribution systems.

IAB Internet Architecture Board, part of the IETF.

IANA Internet Assigned Number Authority, responsible for the assignment of protocol-related numbers for TCP/IP.

ICMP Internet Control Message Protocol, used to exchange error and control messages in an TCP/IP network. (See *RFC-792*.)

IEEE Institute of Electrical and Electronic Engineers.

IESG Internet Engineering Steering Group, which manages the work of the IETF.

IETF Internet Engineering Task Force, responsible for developing the TCP/IP related standards.

Internet the worldwide network of networks which use the TCP/IP protocol suite.

Internet-Draft documents proposed for discussion in the IETF are first posted as Internet-Drafts. These draft documents are stored in a number of repositories around the world for anonymous FTP access. One U.S. repository is on ds.internic.net in the subdirectory internet-drafts.

IP Internet Protocol, the protocol used to forward datagrams between nodes on an internet.

IPv4 the current version of the Internet Protocol, version 4.

IPv6 the new version of the Internet Protocol, version 6.

IPX Internet Packet eXchange, an internetworking protocol used by

Novell NetWare. IPX is also used to refer to the whole Novell protocol suite.

IPng Internet Protocol next generation, the process used to select a replacement for IP version 4.

ISO International Standards Organization, which has working groups that specify standards in many areas including data networking.

IS-IS Intermediate System to Intermediate System Protocol, an ISO routing protocol.

layer 2 a reference in the ISO 7 layer networking model to the Data Link layer—the layer which deals with link-local addressing and frame delivery.

layer 3 a reference in the ISO 7 layer networking model to the Network layer—the layer that deals with internetwork addressing and routing.

M&S Modeling and Simulation.

mask a pattern of bits used to select what part of an IP address should be seen as selecting a specific host and what part should be seen as selecting the subnetwork to which the host is connected.

media the basic physical connection used by a network. Media types include coax cable, twisted pair cable, fiber-optic strands, microwave radio, laser light, etc.

media independent the ability to make use of a variety of underlying transport media.

MD5 Message Digest - 5, an algorithm used to produce a 128-bit "fingerprint" or "message digest" of a data file. It is conjectured that it is computationally infeasible to produce two messages having the same message digest, or to produce any message having a given prespecified target message digest. (See *RFC-1321.*)

MTU Maximum Transmission Unit, the largest packet that may be transported over a particular media type or data link.

multicasting a process by which copies of a single source packet may be delivered to more than one recipient.

network provider a vendor of Internet connectivity.

NFS Network File System, a distributed file system specification developed by Sun Microsystems.

NIC Network Information Center.

NIMROD Nimrod is a project which aims, in part, to produce a next-generation routing architecture for the Internet; but also, more generally, to try and produce a basic design for routing in a single global-scale communication substrate. (See *Nimrod IPng Technical Requirements.*)

NSAP Network Service Access Point, normally used to refer to the types of addresses used in the ISO protocol suites.

NTP Network Time Protocol, a protocol which can be used to synchronize the clocks in a number of computers on a network. (See *RFC-1305.*)

OC-3 Optical carrier level3, a Sonet standard with a data rate of 155.52 Mbps.

OSPF Open Shortest Path First, the IETF-recommended interior gateway routing protocol. The current version is OSPFv2. (See *RFC-1583.*)

packet (See datagram.)

path MTU discovery a technique for dynamically discovering the maximum transmission unit (MTU) of an arbitrary internet path. (See *RFC- 1191.*)

protocol a standard procedure or set of rules for defining and regulating data transmission between computers.

PPP Point-to-Point Protocol for the Transmission of Multi-protocol Datagrams over Point-to-Point Links. (See *RFC-1661.*)

QoS Quality of Service.

RFC Request for Comments, the Internet standard and documentation series.

RIP Routing Information Protocol, a distance-vector routing protocol first implemented for TCP/IP networks in the Berkeley 4BSD UNIX distribution.

router an internetwork device that forwards data packets based on the protocol destination addresses contained in those packets.

routing the determination of a path through a data network that a packet can follow to get to a specific destination. Most often this is done one hop at a time, rather than by figuring out the full path from source to destination.

RSVP Resource ReserVation Protocol.

set-top box the term used to refer to a device attached to the cable TV network in order to provide a variety of services to a residential user.

SDRP Source Demand Routing Protocol, a working group in the routing area of the IETF.

SMTP Simple Mail Transfer Protocol, a protocol used to exchange electronic mail messages between computers. (See *RFC-821.*)

SNMP Simple Network Management Protocol, a protocol used to monitor and manage TCP/IP networks. Now extended to support many other protocols. (See *RFC-1157.*)

SNMPv2 a proposed update to SNMP.

source-routing a procedure by which the source of a packet can insert a series of IP addresses into the packet to define the path which the packet should follow.

SPX Sequenced Packet eXchange, part of the Novell IPX protocol suite.

ST2 Experimental Internet Stream Protocol, Version 2. (See *RFC-1190.*)

subnet The part of a network that is partitioned using a router from other parts of the network (also known as "LAN").

TCP Transmission Control Protocol, used to provide reliable transport of data between networked computers. (See *RFC-793.*)

Telnet the Internet remote terminal protocol. (See *RFC-854.*)

TP4 ISO Transport Protocol class 4. TP4 includes error detection and recovery.

transport-layer (see *Layer 3.*)

TTL Time To Live, a field in the IP packet header decremented by each router that the packet passes through, used to limit packet looping in the case of faulty routing information.

tunneling the process of encapsulating packets from one protocol within packets of another protocol. In some cases the protocols can be the same (e.g., encapsulate IPv4 packets in IPv4 packets).

T1 a digital transmission line running at 1.544 Mbps.

UDP User Datagram Protocol used to transfer packets between application programs. UDP does not assure reliable data delivery. (See *RFC-768.*)

unicast an address which specifies a single recipient.

uucp UNIX to UNIX Copy, a protocol used to transfer files between UNIX computers, originally via dial-up connections, currently often run over TCP/IP networks.

WAN Wide Area Network, nominally a network spread over a wide geographic area.

WWW World Wide Web.

X.121 a CCITT-administered address used on X.25 networks, comprised of up to 14 decimal digits.

X.400 the CCITT electronic mail protocol specification.

Index

A

Accounting
  billing issues and, 120-21
  needs, 191
  transition and, 141-42
  usage-sensitive, 127
Adamson, R. Brian, xxiii, 27
Address/addressing
  architecture issues, 211-12
  assignment efficiency, 207-9
  autoconfiguration, 233-36, 269-70
  in dual IP-layer networks, 241
  mobility and need for unique
      global home, 160-61
Address-based authentication, 126-27
Addresses, IPv6
  anycast, 221, 225-26
  assignment and routing, 221-22
  multicast, 221, 226-27
  unicast, 221, 223-26
Addresses per host, advantages of multiple
  accounting and billing issues, 120-21
  determining number of addresses
      needed, 122-23
  encoding services and, 119-20
  IP address per user, 121-22
  low-grade mobility and, 122
  merging of subnets and, 122
Address Lifetime Expectations (ALE)
      Working Group, 15, 21, 23
Address lifetime expectations, IPv4
  background of, 17
  CIDR introduced, 19-20
  debate over which model to use to
      estimate Internet growth, 21-22
  delegation of address space to
      regional service providers, 20, 22

delegation of Class A address space
    to regional service providers, 22
heavy demand of Class B network
    numbers, effects of, 18, 19
problem with routers, 18-19, 23
recycling of addresses, 22-23
32-bit IP address limitations, 17-18
Address mapping, transition and, 139-40
Address size and format
  address assignment efficiency,
      207-9
  hierarchical and topological
      significance, 203-6
  issues regarding, 201-2
Advanced Research Projects Agency
    (ARPA), 63
Algorithms, extensibility of, 186
Allard, J., 13
ANSI, 89
Anycast addresses, IPv6, 221, 225-26
AppleTalk, 92, 189, 236, 243, 271
Application program interfaces
    (APIs), 273-74
Archie, 120
ARPANET, 192
Asynchronous Transfer Mode (ATM), 77
  addressing parameters, 40
  characteristics of, 38-39
  connection management, 41
  connection quality-of-service
      (QoS) parameters, 40-41
  mapping IPng to, 39-42
  transition and, 141
  user-network interface (UNI), 39
  virtual circuit identifiers, 41-42
  virtual circuits, 37-38
Authentication
  address-based, 126-27

K

L

M

Usage-sensitive accounting, 127
User state, 51-52
Utility Communications Architecture
        (UCA), 90-91
UUNET, 121

V

Vecchi, Mario P., xxx, 105
Vistoli, Cristina, xxxi, 85

W

WAN, 37, 45
Williams, David, xxi
Wood, David C., xxxi, 95
World Wide Web (WWW),
        63, 65, 120, 142

X

X.25, 38, 141
X.121, 92

Y

Yu, Jessica, 23

Z

Zhang, Lixia, 13